THE BRITISH AUXILIARY LEGION
IN THE FIRST CARLIST WAR IN SPAIN, 1835–1838

The British Auxiliary Legion in the First Carlist War in Spain, 1835–1838

A forgotten army

EDWARD M. BRETT

FOUR COURTS PRESS

Typeset in 11 pt on 13 pt Ehrhardt by
FOUR COURTS PRESS LTD
7 Malpas Street, Dublin 8, Ireland
e-mail: info@four-courts-press.ie
http://www.four-courts-press.ie
and in North America
FOUR COURTS PRESS
c/o ISBS, 920 N.E. 58th Avenue, Suite 300, Portland, OR 97213.

A catalogue record for this title is available
from the British Library.

ISBN 1–85182–915–6

Printed in England
by MPG Books, Bodmin, Cornwall.

Contents

ACKNOWLEDGMENTS   vii

LIST OF ILLUSTRATIONS   ix

GENEALOGY   xi

INTRODUCTION   1

1 The background to the war   5

2 The outbreak of war   15

3 Britain's involvement: the birth of the Legion   25

4 Finding cannon fodder   31

5 Journey and arrival in Spain: military discipline and first engagement   48

6 The march to Vitoria   57

7 The city of death   61

8 The battle of Arlaban   74

9 Return to the coast and into battle; a costly victory, 5 May 1836   79

10 Further fighting   91

11 The Legion repulses a massive Carlist attack, 1 October 1836   101

12 Rest and recreation: a quiet Sunday in San Sebastian   108

13 Relief of Bilbao: a second winter at war   113

14 Oriamendi   119

15 The taking of Hernani, Astigarraga, Irun and Fuenterrabia   139

16 Disbandment and repatriation of the old Legion: a cold reception   150

17 The new Legion   160

18 The end in sight 172

19 Women and children last 183

20 The aftermath of the war 189

21 Spain's later history 204

Appendices

I Further careers of General Evans and others 211

II Some notes on the uniforms, weapons and medals of the British Legion 226

BIBLIOGRAPHY & REFERENCES 229

INDEX 233

Acknowledgments

My thanks are due to the staff of many libraries in Britain and Ireland, where most of the relevant publications in English may, with patience and persistence, be found, and also to the staff of the National Army Museum, London, for much help.

The staff of the Museo Zumalacárregui in Ormaiztegui, Guipuzcoa, former home of the great Carlist general, welcomed me to their historical collection, much of which was previously in the museum of San Telmo in San Sebastian, and to their enviably extensive library, in English, Spanish and Euskeria, despite my being on the 'wrong side' in the conflict, and we had interesting discussions in English, French and pidgin Spanish. My sincere thanks to them.

The late Mr R. John Corbett of Co. Wicklow kindly allowed me to see the typescript he had prepared of the diary kept by Colonel Gilbert Hogg, an ancestor of his late wife, during his service in the British Legion and in the previous Portuguese war of succession. I am grateful to him and to his son and daughter-in-law, who welcomed me in Wicklow to read the diary. Sadly I was not able to meet Mr Corbett himself before his death, but I am grateful for his positive response to my short article in the *Irish Sword*.

Richard Holmes, Professor of Military and Security Studies at Cranfield University and the Royal Military College of Science, whose book, *Redcoat: The British Soldier in the Age of Horse and Musket*, is a source of much useful information, kindly allowed me to borrow a series of 145 pension certificates relating to men of the Legion, giving medical and social details of great interest. I thank Ian Robertson, an historian of the Peninsular War, and familiar with sources on the first Carlist War, for his help and advice, and Christopher Hibbert for his encouragement.

My thanks, too, to Anna Daventry, who has typed the manuscript in several versions, not only for her painstaking work, but also for much advice which her familiarity with the idiosyncrasies of publishers has enabled her to give me.

I thank Michael Adams and his colleagues at Four Courts Press for their help and advice.

In memory
of those who fought and died
on both sides in the first Carlist war

Illustrations

COLOUR PLATES *appearing between pages 114 and 115*

1 Portrait of Assistant-Surgeon Morgan O'Connell, 10th Munster Light Infantry
2 The Legion in Vitoria, 1836 – a caricature
3 The French Foreign Legion in action against the Carlists
4 Beggars in scarlet. From a drawing by Edwyn Gill (1810)
5 View of San Sebastian
6 The former convent of San Telmo as it is today
7 View of San Sebastian in 1835
8 Vitoria – with Legionaries in the foreground
9 Hernani – with lancers and infantry of the Legion in the foreground
10 The siege of Irun, May 1837
11 Fuenterrabia
12 The Town House of Irun
13 Monument to British war dead
14 Gravestone of Col. Ebsworth
15 Plaque in honour of British soldiers who died
16 Tombstone of Col. William Tupper
17 Church at Andoain
18 Medal for the action of 5 May 1836
19 Medal for the action of March 1837

BLACK AND WHITE FIGURES *appearing between pages 146 and 147*

1 Contemporary cartoon representing Spanish patriotism
2 Queen Cristina of Spain
3 Ferdinand VII, king of Spain
4 Isabella II, aged 13, on assuming powers
5 Don Carlos, brother of Ferdinand
6 Entry of Cristina into Madrid, in December 1829
7 Lieut. General George de Lacy Evans, Commander-in-Chief of the British Legion
8 The British Legion and their allies in action at Arlaban
9 Capture of Irun by Generals Evans and Espartero, May 1837
10 Pension certificate of Private Patrick Finegan
11 Pension certificate of Private John Galvin

12 Citation for award of the Order of San Fernando to Dr Morgan O'Connell
13 Burial place of British officers, San Sebastian
14 Title page of Dr Alcock's *Notes*
15 Memorial to Col. Sir Duncan MacDougall
16 Emblem of the British Auxiliary Legion

MAPS

1 Map of the Basque Provinces and Navarre, showing the route of the Legion on the march from the coast to Vitoria
2 Map showing the Cristino and Carlist lines during the siege of San Sebastian

CREDITS

Colour plates   1, 4, 18, 19: author's collection; 5, 6, 12–17: photographs taken by the author; 2, 3: from a print by J.W. Giles, *c*.1836; 7, 8–11: lithographs by Thomas Shotter Boys (based on sketches by Staff-Surgeon Henry Wilkinson), published in 1838.

Black and white figures   1: from a portrait by Lopez; 3: from a lithograph by J.J. Martinez, Madrid; 4: from a portrait in the Facultad de Medicina, Madrid; 7: from an unattributed portrait in A. Somerville, *History of the British Legion* (1839); 10, 11: reproduced by kind permission of Professor Richard Holmes; 12: author's collection; 13: from a coloured lithograph based on a sketch by Staff-Surgeon Henry Wilkinson published in 1838.

The maps were prepared by Duncan MacInnes, map 2 being based on a map in Evans, *Memoranda* (1840).

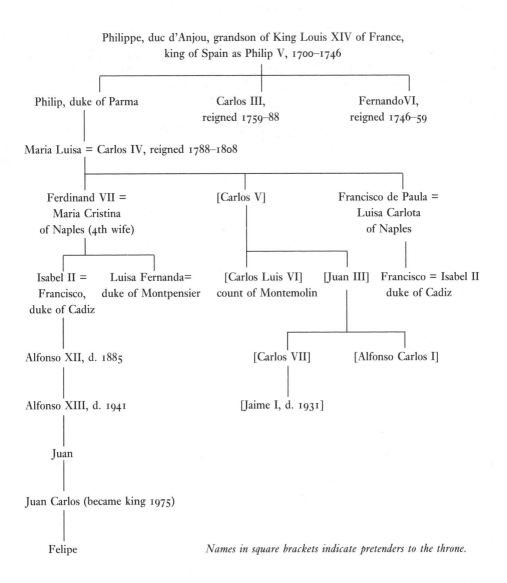

Philippe, duc d'Anjou, grandson of King Louis XIV of France,
king of Spain as Philip V, 1700–1746

Philip, duke of Parma

Carlos III,
reigned 1759–88

FernandoVI,
reigned 1746–59

Maria Luisa = Carlos IV, reigned 1788–1808

Ferdinand VII =
Maria Cristina
of Naples (4th wife)

[Carlos V]

Francisco de Paula =
Luisa Carlota
of Naples

Isabel II =
Francisco,
duke of Cadiz

Luisa Fernanda=
duke of Montpensier

[Carlos Luis VI]
count of Montemolin

[Juan III]

Francisco = Isabel II
duke of Cadiz

Alfonso XII, d. 1885

[Carlos VII]

[Alfonso Carlos I]

Alfonso XIII, d. 1941

[Jaime I, d. 1931]

Juan

Juan Carlos (became king 1975)

Felipe

Names in square brackets indicate pretenders to the throne.

Abbreviated genealogy of the Spanish royal family

MARCH OF THE
BRITISH LEGION FROM
BILBAO TO VITORIA,
November–December 1835

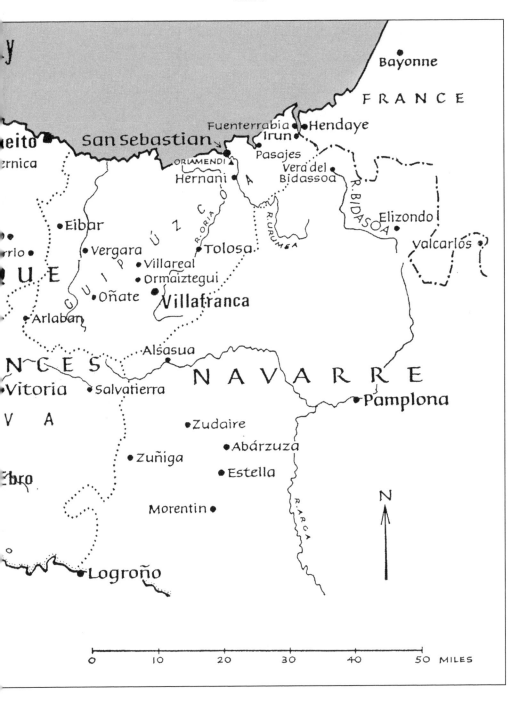

Map of the Basque Provinces and Navarre

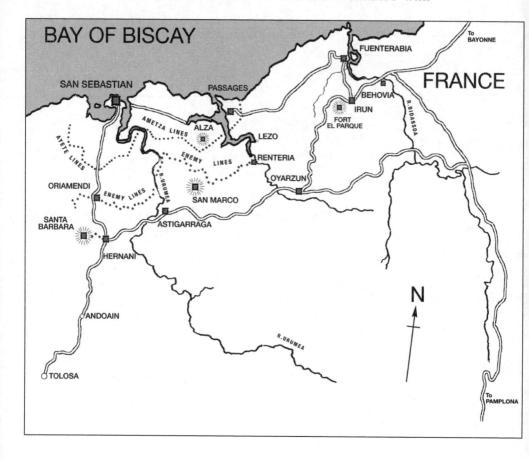

Map showing the Cristino and Carlist lines during the siege of
San Sebastian

Introduction

'History is a series of tricks which we play on the past.'

Voltaire

'Time hath, my lord, a wallet at his back,
Wherein he puts alms for oblivion,
A great-sized monster of ingratitudes:
Those scraps are good deeds past, which are devoured
As fast as they are made, forgot as soon as done.'

Shakespeare, Troilus and Cressida

The phrase 'a forgotten war' is applied to many conflicts, but is particularly appropriate to the two Carlist wars in the nineteenth century. Both wars were the result of the fourth marriage of King Ferdinand VII of Spain, a union which represented the triumph of hope of an heir over the experience of three childless marriages. The birth of a daughter sparked the disputed succession.

The first Carlist war, as H. Butler-Clarke wrote in 1906, was a confused struggle, carried on generally in guerrilla fashion by small bodies of men. It was characterised by much heroism and much brutal ferocity. Small, local and even personal jealousies often overshadowed the great principles to which appeal was ostensibly made. Only at great length can the incoherent military movement, the small and indecisive actions, the petty rivalries and often treacherous intrigues which make up the history of the contest be intelligibly described. From this tangle it is difficult to pick out main threads. To follow them without attention to minor threads is to receive a false impression.

For the rest of the world, the little-remembered Carlist wars probably had only two lasting consequences: the invention of the political term 'liberal' and the popularising of the beret. The involvement of the ill-fated British Legion in the first Carlist war is seldom remembered today in Britain, though the war still remains fresh in the minds of many Spaniards, for some of whom the Carlist cause, closely allied to that of Basque separatism, is a living issue which continues to cost lives in Spain in the twenty-first century.

In Britain, mention of the first Carlist war usually evokes a blank stare, a reference to the Spanish Civil War one hundred years later, or sometimes a confusion with the Peninsular War waged some twenty years earlier by Wellington's victorious troops, in part of the same arena in northern Spain.

The Legion's involvement in the war at Lord Palmerston's instigation was a more than minor thread in the tangled tapestry, yet it receives scant or no mention in most histories of the period or in biographies of the bellicose British foreign secretary. The war split political opinion in Britain into two irreconcilable camps, the Tories mainly supporting the pretender, Don Carlos, and the Liberals Queen Isabella II and her mother, the queen-regent. Politicians and journalists of the time castigated their opponents robustly with pens dipped in venom. The publications in book, letter or pamphlet form, written by those who served in the Legion, are often coloured by personal prejudice or jealousy towards General Evans, its commander-in-chief, while the Tory politicians' criticisms of him were often excuses for attacking their parliamentary enemies. It was forty years before a more impartial account, *The English in Spain*, appeared from the pen of Major Francis Duncan and 130 years before a professional historian focussed on the Legion and its contribution in the war.

My own interest in the Legion was sparked by the involvement of an ancestor, a young Irish surgeon who served in the 10th Munster Light Infantry and survived the war. His portrait in uniform, his medals and a citation, with the oral family tradition but sadly no personal written record, provided the starting point. The search for information, though fascinating, was often a frustrating challenge. Edgar Holt's *The Carlist Wars in Spain* (1967) gave the most helpful relatively recent in-depth account by an historian, with a detailed bibliography. Holt in his introduction excuses himself to any readers in Spain who might think he had given too much prominence to the Legion's exploits, believing that a British writer has an inescapable prejudice in favour of his own countrymen, but it seems to me that any such apology was, and is, unnecessary.

Among contemporary accounts the writings of Alexander Somerville stand out for their detail and uncommon psychological insights. Contemporary newspapers, Foreign Office records, the *Annual Register*, the *United Service Journal* and the writings of men who served in the war, from Evans downwards, provide information on the Legion's activities from many different viewpoints. During the 1830s *The Times* published a twice-weekly column with detailed descriptions of military and political events in Spain, which were quoted extensively in the provincial press throughout Britain and Ireland.

The Order Book of the Legion, kept at its headquarters in San Sebastian, or as much of it as is available (from June 1836 to January 1837), brings to life the day-to-day experiences of its officers and men, with its details of battles, casualties, sickness, promotions, honours awarded, desertions, mutinies and the many 'housekeeping' minutiae of an army in hostile territory, as well as giving an insight into the mind of the commander-in-chief as he strove to maintain the highest standards of the British army in a mercenary force operating in unfavourable conditions, with at best half-hearted support from the governments of Britain and Spain.

Evans' own *Memoranda* are remarkably laconic and far from the apologia which might have been written by a man so often maligned and vilified.

The contribution of Irishmen, quite apart from their commander-in-chief, to the Legion is very striking, both in terms of their numbers and of their resilience and fortitude. With over ten thousand men serving in the Legion there must be some of their descendants who have knowledge of their ancestors' involvement. I was encouraged to receive a response to my short article in the *Irish Sword* from the late Mr R.J. Corbett regarding Colonel Gilbert Hogg, a gallant officer who was always in the forefront of battle with his regiment, the 8th Highlanders. It is my hope to hear from any readers who have recollections or records of their own forebears' experiences in this forgotten war.

The Army List of the British Auxiliary Legion, published at varying intervals between August 1835 and 1 April 1837, gives details of the officers in the various regiments, with their dates of commission, casualties, promotions and decorations. Although it omits the names of a few officers known from newspaper reports and other sources to have served in the Legion, it remains the most comprehensive source of information on the commissioned personnel. Sadly, similar data on non-commissioned officers and private soldiers seem not to be available. Press reports, Foreign Office documents, pension certificates and the publications of the amateur historians who served in the Legion give a limited amount of selected information on the rank and file.

The medical aspects of the campaign – of particular interest to me – are dealt with in detail by Dr Rutherford Alcock who, with his medical officers, emerged from the war with almost universal credit. A volume of pension certificates relating to non-commissioned men of the Legion, to which I was given access by Professor Richard Holmes, provided me with a wealth of medical and social information to flesh out the bare bones of the historical records.

At least two fictional accounts of the Legion have been published. Sixty years after the war its story attracted the prolific G.A. Henty, author of so many 'rattling good yarns' of brave young Britons fighting for their queen and country in the colonial wars of Victoria's reign, as well as tales set in earlier periods of British history. The subject of the Legion is a rich seam for the writer of historical fiction to mine. Henty, as usual, had done his homework, read much of the available material and included many of the most dramatic incidents in his book, *With the British Legion: A Story of the Carlist Wars*, published in 1903.

A similar book by the less known Herbert Hayens, published at about the same time, has its young British hero, about to be burned at the stake by his cruel Carlist captors, released on the orders of the Spanish beauty whom he has previously rescued. The sufferings of the Legion's women and children receive some attention, but less sympathy than they would be accorded today, and both books are clearly targeted at the adventurous young male reader.

I would like to think that I have succeeded to some extent in confounding the tricks which have been played on the past, in bringing back from near-oblivion the story of the ten thousand, and in passing a more just and generous judgment on their efforts and achievements than the disparagement which history has often accorded them. For this reason I have included in the Index the names of officers and men who appear in the written records on one or few occasions only, often with no mention of their Christian names, in the hope that they might jog memories or stimulate curiosity in those in whose families some faint tradition may yet linger of an ancestor who served in the Legion.

CHAPTER ONE

The background to the war

'The princes orgulous, their high blood chafed ...'

Shakespeare, *Troilus and Cressida*

In May 1836 Charles Fitzgerald, a 50-year-old colonel in the Irish Brigade of the British Auxiliary Legion, was leading his men against withering enemy fire south of San Sebastian in northern Spain. All his fellow officers in the brigade had been hit. With ribald cries, Fitzgerald encouraged his devoted men to follow him, inspiring them to go on to victory. On another part of the field, the Scottish Colonel William Tupper, charging the enemy with his 6th Scotch Regiment, was shot through the arm but, hiding his wound under his cloak, fought on until two hours later he was shot through the head. In the following year a young Irishman, recently promoted colonel, was surrounded by enemy cavalry and killed, being lifted bodily off his horse, in one account, by a dozen Carlist lances.

What brought these men, with ten thousand more, many with their wives and children, to these foreign fields where almost half of them died, by bullet or disease, to be buried, often in unconsecrated ground, while many more were maimed?

The issue of whether a female may inherit her father's crown has been a cause of civil and international wars from early times. This was the origin of the two Carlist wars in nineteenth-century Spain. The first of these, from 1833 to 1839, is estimated to have cost 270,000 lives. Most of these were Spanish, but the war embroiled many other European powers, and the involvement of Britain through the British Auxiliary Legion led to the loss of many British lives in Northern Spain, the scene of some of Wellington's greatest victories in the Peninsular War of Liberation, some twenty years earlier.

The roots of the dispute lie in the thirteenth century, when Alfonso X, king of Castile and Leon, 1252–84, had recognised the right of female succession in the *Siete Partidas* (Seven Laws). This remained the law until 1713, when the first Bourbon king of Spain, Philip V, grandson of Louis XIV of France, introduced the so-called Salic law, which originated in

5

France and provided that no female might succeed to the French throne. Since France and Spain had the same law, Philip's decision prevented any possible Franco–Spanish union through the marriage of a king of one country to a reigning queen of the other. For the next seventy-six years this remained the position, but in 1789 Philip's successor, Carlos IV, the father of King Ferdinand VII, abolished the Salic law, obtaining without difficulty the agreement of the Cortes, the Spanish Parliament, which had little power, to restore the earlier law which upheld a daughter's right to succeed to the Spanish throne should the king have no sons. Carlos' reasons for taking this step are unclear, as he already had sons. The decision, known as the Pragmatic Sanction, was not made public, the Cortes being pledged to keep it secret. Indeed so secret was it that even Carlos' second son, the Infante Don Carlos (fig. 5), claimed never to have heard of it until his brother Ferdinand VII published it forty years later. Had Ferdinand had a son, the Salic law and the Pragmatic Sanction would have been irrelevant. It was only his fourth marriage, to Maria Cristina (fig. 2), daughter of the king of Naples, which produced a child. This was the Infanta, the future Queen Isabella II (fig. 4), whose accession on her father's death would have been ruled out by the Salic law, but was permitted and legalised by the Pragmatic Sanction. Since the latter was so little known, the situation was contentious, and ultimately a cause of war.

The victorious troops of the Emperor Napoleon in 1808 had occupied a large part of Spain and Portugal, from which they were eventually evicted in 1813 by the duke of Wellington. The Spanish king, Carlos IV, had abdicated in favour of his son Ferdinand (fig. 3), but when the entire Spanish royal family went to France to meet Napoleon, both Carlos and Ferdinand were persuaded at Bayonne to renounce all claims to the throne, which was given instead to Napoleon's brother, Joseph Bonaparte. Ferdinand's younger brother, the Infante Carlos, however, who naturally regarded himself as next in succession to the then childless Ferdinand, refused to surrender his birthright, saying that he would rather die than live without honour. He was to stick to his principles through all the years to come, so that civil war became almost inevitable.

Resistance to the occupying French, seen as godless and oppressive enemies of their country and their Catholic faith, had sprung up in Spain; guerrilla warfare, for which the country is ideally suited, kept much of the French army tied down and constantly on guard against the sudden sallies of irregular forces, which easily eluded pursuit in the mountains. It was a savage campaign, with atrocities against the Spanish civilian population, as graphically depicted in Goya's 'Horrors of War'. The difficult task of Wellington in the Peninsular War was eased by the help of the Spanish guerrillas. Throughout these years the young Ferdinand, though an exile in France, was a beacon of hope for Spanish independence, and became known as *Fernando el Deseado,* Ferdinand the Desired, a name which his later behaviour, when he seized the reins of power, would make sadly inappropriate (fig. 1).

In 1810 the wartime Cortes had met in Cadiz in the unoccupied part of Spain to consider a Constitution. It consisted of deputies from town and country, as well as from the South American Spanish colonies, many of which were struggling for independence from Spain. Representation of the more cosmopolitan and radical coastal towns was stronger than that of the rural, more conservative and traditional regions, so that the Cortes of 1810 had a revolutionary majority unrepresentative of the country as a whole. The Constitution of 1812 which it produced was intended to replace the Spanish tradition of absolute monarchy by democratic parliamentary government with the king as head of the executive. It abolished the Inquisition, but accepted the Catholic Church as the sole religion of Spain. It greatly reduced the power of the clergy and the aristocracy, thus ensuring that these two groups would oppose it. At first opposition to absolute rule was the main feature of Spanish liberalism, but later it turned against the Church, and has been described as eventually meaning little more than anti-clericalism and the repeal of whatever the previous government had done.

When Wellington finally drove the French from Spain, Napoleon allowed Ferdinand to end his exile. The Cortes, anxious that their reforms should be recognised, returned to Madrid and sent instructions to Ferdinand to take the oath to the new Constitution and then to go at once to the capital. Unsurprisingly, Ferdinand refused to do this. Arriving in Spain in March 1814 with his brother Don Carlos, he arranged to 'test the waters' by travelling through Catalonia and Aragon to assess the feelings of the people. His welcome was as warm as his popular title implied, and it was clear that there was little love for the Constitution. Though he declared himself ready to swear to it if his refusal would lead to bloodshed, Ferdinand found the army and the people were on his side. The fall of Napoleon and restoration of the French monarchy with Louis XVIII strengthened his hand, and with it his resolve to assume absolute power. He issued a decree on 4 May abolishing the Constitution and dissolving the Cortes, but giving pledges of a new Cortes, freedom of the press and personal liberty and security, which were never honoured. Instead he embarked on a path of reaction, with the arrest of the liberal deputies who had drawn up the Constitution. Now aged twenty-nine, he showed himself cruel and merciless to his opponents, to the disgust of English Liberals, who felt that British soldiers had freed Spain from one tyrant only to open the door to another. Eventually the army temporarily deserted Ferdinand, and in 1820 Colonel Rafael del Riego and another senior officer staged a succesful rising in Cadiz aimed at restoring the 1812 Constitution. Ferdinand was now forced to take the oath he had refused in 1814 and pretended to be converted to the liberal position. The newly-elected Cortes, more balanced than its predecessor, included some so-called 'moderate' members, but the three years of supposedly more democratic rule which followed were marked by anarchy and lawlessness, with the growth of anti-clericalism and murderous reprisals against priests and army officers for their repression during the period of absolute rule. The wealth of the Church was plundered and bishops and archbishops were exiled. Royalist risings occurred repeatedly, especially in Navarre, where a fighting priest, the Curé Merino, led a successful guerrilla campaign. Two other prominent royalist soldiers were Tomás Zumalacárregui and Miguel Gomez, the first of whom later became Don Carlos' most successful general. The royalists of this anarchic period have been described as 'pre-Carlists'.

The pendulum swung again in Ferdinand's favour in 1823, when help came from France with an army of '100,000 sons of St Louis' sent by Louis XVIII to evict the constitutional government and restore the king to absolute rule. English supporters of Riego's government had offered to raise a foreign legion before the French intervention, but the dilatory response of the Cortes meant that it was too late to provide effective help. A small expeditionary force was raised and went to Spain with General Sir Robert Wilson, but does not appear to have seen action;* this was twelve years before the British Auxiliary Legion sailed to Spain to support the claim of the infant queen, Isabella.

The next phase in 'this cannibal war' was, predictably, more savage than before, with brutal persecution of the liberals. In a reign of terror Riego and his followers were executed, thousands killed and many more imprisoned or exiled. The extreme reactionaries, known as the Apostolic Party, dissatisfied

---

* Wilson himself was imprisoned twice, once in Corunna and again in Braga in Portugal.

with the rigour of Ferdinand's repression, looked for help to his brother Carlos, who was still heir-presumptive, and was pious, devoted to the Church, honourable and more jealous of the royal rights than Ferdinand. It was at this time that a Carlist party began to take shape. Carlos himself was in no hurry; he had always been loyal to his brother, who had now had three childless marriages (to Maria Antonia of Naples, Isabella of Braganza and Maria Amelia of Saxony),* and it seemed very likely that he would die without a son. Carlos was generally expected to be the next king of Spain. Some of his supporters were too impatient to wait to put him on the throne. In 1824 a conspiracy was suppressed at Saragossa. In 1827 a manifesto was distributed throughout Spain calling for Don Carlos' immediate accession, and an insurrection started in Catalonia, which was actually the first Carlist revolt, though Carlos himself had no part in it. This was put down with the utmost brutality; the ringleaders, who had surrendered believing their lives would be spared, were executed.

The political spectrum now ranged from the extreme position of Don Carlos, backed by the apostolic or ultra-absolutist party, through the dominant absolutist party of Ferdinand's own supporters, particularly Francisco Calomarde, his minister of justice, prepared when necessary to compromise with the liberals, the liberals themselves and other constitutionalists, still reeling from their recent persecution, to the Neapolitan Party, led by the Infanta Luisa Carlota of Naples, the wife of Ferdinand's youngest brother, the Infante Francisco de Paula.

Carlota's energetic interventions were to have a profound effect on Spanish history. She has been described as the Cinderella of the Spanish court since her husband was believed to be the illegitimate son of Godoy, the minister who was the lover of Carlos IV's wife, Maria Luisa, and not the son of Carlos, for which reason Francisco had been excluded from the succession. Carlota saw her chance as a marriage-broker to Ferdinand. She was one of the dozen daughters by the second marriage of King Francis I of Naples, who was understandably anxious to procure suitable matches for the girls. The second of these, Maria Cristina, was still single at twenty-three. Ferdinand's third wife, Maria Amelia, had been increasingly ill for some time. Soon after her death, the Neapolitan ambassador showed Ferdinand a portrait of Cristina, which impressed him so favourably that

---

† The first two of these were, respectively, his niece and his cousin. It is as well, perhaps, that neither marriage produced a child.

preparations for his fourth marriage began at once. The situation had some analogies with that of Henry VIII and Anne of Cleves, but Cristina was no Flanders Mare. She was captivatingly beautiful and coquettish, too, and it was said before her marriage 'that more than one young noble had been advised to travel for his health, because detected in looking too often towards the pretty Christine'. When she entered Madrid in state in December 1829, having been met at the frontier and escorted to the capital by her future enemy, Don Carlos, she fascinated the citizens (fig. 6).

The marriage was a major setback to the supporters of Carlos. Should Cristina have a child, the succession (it seemed at that time) would depend on its sex; a boy would inherit the crown, while a girl would be excluded under the Salic law. Early in 1830 it became known that the queen was pregnant. Cristina and Carlota were among the few who knew of the Pragmatic Sanction, which had re-established the right of female succession, but had never been made public. Cristina persuaded Ferdinand to publish it before the birth of her child, and in May a formal proclamation was made that the Salic law was abrogated, and the old law of succession restored in accordance with the petition of 1789 to the Cortes. Controversy surrounds Ferdinand's decision to make this proclamation without summoning a new Cortes and seeking its approval. Arguments could be made, and were, on both sides. Carlos' claim to the throne depended on this question. One argument among others in favour of Carlos was that, since he was born in 1788, the Pragmatic Sanction, dating from 1789, could not act retrospectively to the prejudice of those who were living *before* that date. Hence he could argue that he was born with an inalienable right under the Salic law to succeed to the throne if his elder brother had no male heir. This right, he claimed, could not be taken away from him by later pronouncements.

On 10 October 1830 Cristina was safely delivered of a girl. Custom demanded that the child be presented to the king on a silver salver. To Ferdinand's question 'What is it?' the attendant replied 'A robust Infanta, Your Majesty.' Don Carlos' supporters felt there was still some hope of his inheriting the crown. The child was christened Isabella, a reference to her illustrious ancestors, Ferdinand of Aragon and Isabella of Castile, who had united the warring kingdoms of Spain under one crown, and seen the new world opened up by Columbus.

A second girl was born to Cristina in January 1832, the Infanta Luisa Fernanda. Cristina's reproductive capacity was far from being exhausted, as she showed later by her unofficial liaison. Should she produce a son, the succession would be clear, but Ferdinand's failing health at forty-seven made this seem unlikely. He further strengthened Isabella's claim by making a will leaving the throne to her. Despite this, Carlos insisted on his right to succeed. Though he would not intrigue against the king, the Apostolic Party, through Calomarde, tried hard to persuade Ferdinand to revoke the Pragmatic Sanction. It was now a contest between Calomarde and Cristina, who was determined that her child would be a reigning queen. The sisters Cristina and Carlota together controlled the king.

Increasing ill health in September 1832 confined Ferdinand to bed in the palace of San Ildefonso, the royal summer residence at La Granja, fifty miles northwest of Madrid. Calomarde advised Cristina that, in order to avert civil war on Ferdinand's death, she must propitiate Carlos, and ask Ferdinand to sign a decree making his wife regent and Carlos her first adviser during his illness. Though Ferdinand agreed to this, Carlos refused, unwilling to accept a position subordinate to Cristina.

As the king's condition worsened, great pressure was put on him by the Carlists. It was suggested that the only way to avoid civil war on Ferdinand's death was for the Pragmatic Sanction to be cancelled, and Carlos' right to succeed restored. To this Cristina after long argument agreed. The next day the king seemed near to death. He sent for Calomarde to ask his advice and was told that he must revoke the Pragmatic Sanction. Cristina and Ferdinand both agreed to this, but he insisted that news of the revocation must not be published until he was dead. The decree was signed and given for safe keeping to the president of the Council of Castile, who was ordered not to break the seal until the king had died. Ferdinand now seemed at death's door, and it was assumed that he would not long survive.

The order to keep the revocation secret was now flouted, since the Carlists wanted their victory to be publicised throughout Spain. Far away in Cadiz (Luisa) Carlota heard the news, and with her husband returned post-haste to La Granja, covering the four hundred miles in forty hours.

Ferdinand, however, was still alive, so that the decree was not yet operative. Arriving at the palace, Carlota acted aggressively and effectively to save the situation. She summoned the president of the Council of Castile and, taking the king's decree from him, tore it to pieces. She berated Cristina for giving way to her enemies and surrendering her daughter's rights. Calomarde she dealt with vigorously, upbraiding him and finally soundly boxing his ears. His diplomatic response evoked admiration. He politely said, *'Las manos blancas no ofenden'* ('White hands do not offend'), quoting the title of a play by the seventeenth-century Spanish dramatist, Calderón de la Barca.

Remarkably, Ferdinand now recovered from his state of torpor, and was persuaded that he had been tricked into revoking the Pragmatic Sanction. On 6 October Cristina became sole regent for the remainder of the king's illness, and Calomarde was dismissed. Returning in a closed coach to Madrid, the king, still very ill, voiced to Cristina his concern over the obstinacy and strength of the Carlists. 'Spain,' he repeated, 'is a bottle of beer, and I am the cork; as soon as that comes out all the liquid inside will pour out, God knows in what direction.'

On the last day of 1832, Ferdinand issued a public statement finally re-establishing the right of female succession. Four days later he resumed his powers, thus ending Cristina's first regency. During this time she had alleviated the repressive treatment of the liberals, re-opened the universities, which had been closed, and declared a general amnesty, allowing some ten thousand who had been in exile since 1823 and 1824 to return home. Cristina endeared herself to the people with her tolerance, vivacity and interest and support of music and the arts.

These liberalising measures were much resented by the Carlists. The bishop of León, one of the most fanatical adherents to the cause of Don Carlos, left the court in disgust, a signal that the Carlist leaders were preparing for action. Carlos himself made no move, but his supporters began to intrigue in his favour. Conspiracies were discovered in Toledo, Leon and Madrid, and Ferdinand decided it would be safer if his brother were out of the country. Carlos was told that he was 'authorised' to go to Portugal with the younger sister of Cristina and Carlota, another of the twelve Neapolitan princesses. He obediently left Madrid for Portugal on 16 March 1832 and did not return to Spain for more than a year.

Ferdinand now arranged for the three-year-old Isabella to be given the title 'Princess of the Asturias' borne by the heirs to the Spanish throne. On 20 June the Cortes met in the church of San Geronimo, and took the oath of allegiance to the infant princess. Those who had attended the ceremony and pledged allegiance were now clearly separated from those who had not, chief of whom was the child's uncle, Don Carlos. Ferdinand had written to him in Portugal to ask if he would take the oath of allegiance, but Carlos had replied that neither his conscience nor his honour would allow it. He wrote that only God could take his rights away from him 'by granting you a son, which I much desire, possibly even more than you'.

Believing that Portugal was too close to home, and that Carlos should be further removed, Ferdinand ordered him to go to the Papal States in central Italy, where the Pope reigned as a temporal monarch as well as the spiritual leader of the Church, of which Carlos was a devoted son. Carlos made no haste to leave Portugal and was still there when Ferdinand died suddenly on 29 September 1833.

Cristina immediately implemented Ferdinand's will, by which Isabella became queen of Spain and she herself the child's guardian and regent until she should come of age. She announced her intention to introduce administrative reforms and appointed a ministry of moderates, the more right-wing liberals, but she failed to satisfy either the Carlist Apostolics or the liberals.

The nations of Europe had followed events in Spain with close interest and concern. The Whig government in England with Earl Grey as prime minister and Viscount Palmerston as foreign secretary welcomed the new situation. They had no problem with Isabella's accession; the young Princess Victoria was heir-presumptive in England and was to ascend the throne within a few years on the death of her uncle William IV. The king himself favoured Don Carlos, as did most of the English Tories. France under King Louis-Philippe recognised Isabella and offered support to Cristina. Spain's neighbour Portugal was embroiled in a civil war of succession, with a very similar situation of uncle against niece; the Pretender, Dom Miguel, sympathised with Don Carlos, his brother-in-law, but the young Queen Maria II, whose claim was to be upheld with the military help of English volunteers, supported Isabella. The axis of England, France and Portugal was balanced by the absolutist autocratic monarchs of Austria, Prussia, Russia and Sardinia, the so-called Holy Alliance, who would have preferred to see Carlos in power to check the dangers they saw in liberalising tendencies in Europe. The Pope for the time being would not recognise either Isabella or Cristina.

When he heard the news of his brother's death from General Córdova, the Spanish minister in Portugal, and was urged to undertake his journey to Italy, Carlos refused, and immediately assumed the title of Carlos V, king of Spain, by which he was now known to his supporters. A visit to the Spanish border in the hope of finding Spanish troops who would flock to his standard was unsuccessful. Cristina's General Rodil was there with orders to capture Carlos. General Pedro Sarsfield, a well-known soldier of Irish ancestry, though an old friend of Carlos, remained faithful to the queen's cause, and his large army was denied to the Carlists. Sarsfield was one of many prominent soldiers who had fought in Spain in the War of Independence and who were to fight on either side in the coming civil war, who were of Irish origin, many of them descendants of the 'wild geese' who had accompanied an earlier Patrick Sarsfield to Europe after the defeat of James II in Ireland and the disastrous Treaty of Limerick in 1691.

Carlos issued a proclamation on October 15 to his 'beloved subjects', though his finances were at such a low ebb that his wife Dona Francisca and her sister are said to have set the type for the document with their own hands. He still hoped to receive enough support from the people of Spain to win the throne without bloodshed. Although hostilities had already opened, he himself did not declare war until November 1833, when hope of a peaceful outcome seemed vain.

CHAPTER TWO

The outbreak of war

'Cry "Havock!" and let slip the dogs of war'

Shakespeare, *Julius Caesar*

With Ferdinand dead, the cork was finally out of the bottle and the dogs of war were soon let loose as he had prophesied. The war proper started in Talavera in Castile where the Carlist postmaster, Gonzales, shortly after Ferdinand's death, called out the royal volunteers, deposed the civil authorities and proclaimed Carlos as the lawful king of Spain. The rising was quickly put down by regular government troops, and Gonzales and many of his followers were executed. Elsewhere similar small uprisings occurred, especially in the north. In early October the Basque provinces of Biscay, Alava and Guipuzcoa declared their support for Don Carlos. Revolts followed in Navarre and the Rioja. The strength of Carlism in the Basque region, especially marked in the rural areas, derived from the determination of these fiercely independent people, distinct from other Spaniards in their character and their own unique language, Euskera, whose origin is uncertain, to retain their historic local privileges, or *fueros*. Dating back to the Middle Ages, these allowed the Basques their own Parliament, law courts and mint. They could also raise their own militia, and enjoyed financial advantages, paying no customs duties on imports from abroad and contributing a fixed sum to the Spanish treasury instead of regular taxation. To the Basques, whose *fueros* Ferdinand and Isabella had sworn to preserve at Guernica in 1476, the king was known as Lord of Biscay. The 'liberal' government in Madrid with its centralising tendencies and the threat which this represented to the Catholic Church, of which most Basques were loyal adherents, encouraged them in their support for Carlos, whom they saw as defender of both their faith and their rights. To what extent they supported Carlos' claim to the throne, regardless of their own ancient rights, is debatable. One Englishman, Captain C.F. Henningsen, who described his twelve-month campaign as a cavalry officer with the Carlist forces under his hero, General Zumalacárregui, wrote that the Basque Carlists, when asked what they were fighting for, made their royalist feelings very evident in their replies, 'For Carlos V' or 'For the King'. In the countryside Carlos had a potential army of countless devoted followers. In the towns and cities, especially the more cosmopolitan ports such as Bilbao, the situation was different; there the citizens included many liberals and supporters of Isabella. Town and country were in opposition. This was to be a handicap for Carlos, who (like his grandson, the second Don Carlos forty years later in the second Carlist war) always suffered from his failure to capture or control any important city. Bilbao was to survive three separate sieges by the Carlist armies.

In the early days of the war the best-known and most successful Carlist leader was a Castilian, the *cura*, or priest, Jerónimo Merino. His military experience was extensive, gained in the War of Liberation against Napoleon's occupying troops, and also in the struggle against Riego's government in the 1820s. Though aged sixty-four at the start of the Carlist War, his hunting pursuits had kept him physically fit and his bravery and charisma attracted thousands of volunteers to the Carlist cause. Merino fared much better than his fellow Carlist leader, Field-Marshal Ladron de Guevara, who, on advancing in Navarre, had been defeated in his first contact with the Cristino forces, captured and shot in the citadel of Pamplona. The custom of killing prisoners was already well established in the recent clashes, and was to continue throughout the war on both sides, despite attempts by Lord Eliot and other Englishmen to mitigate the savagery with which the war was prosecuted. Merino's success had made it clear that the Cristino generals would not have an easy victory; his unexpected advance with eleven thousand men towards Madrid greatly alarmed the Madrilenos, whose relief was intense when he withdrew to the north.

Don Carlos was still in Portugal. Few would have predicted that the hostilities would continue for a full seven years. English observers of the Spanish political scene made their predictions. The duke of Wellington, whose experience of warfare in Spain was unrivalled, was wildly wrong in his forecast: 'Leave them alone; they will not do each other much harm,' while the foreign secretary, Viscount Palmerston, expressed the confident opinion that the Cristinos, the supporters of Maria Cristina, would carry the day. Such optimism was understandable at that stage of the war, but the situation was to change with the declaration to the Carlist cause of Tomás Zumalacárregui, who was to be their most successful general. This 45-year-old retired colonel, who had also fought in the War of Independence, was invited to rejoin the queen regent's army with the rank of brigadier-general, but refused the offer, being a fervent supporter of absolute monarchy, and in October 1833 escaped from his home in Pamplona and offered his services to the Carlists in Navarre. The jealousy between the generals on both sides in the war was exemplified at this early stage by the attempt of the local military chief, Ituralde, to have him arrested. Instead, Ituralde was himself arrested, and Zumalacárregui was appointed commanding general in Navarre, choosing Ituralde as his second in command, with the aim of placating his rival and unifying the Carlist leadership. The three Basque provinces of Biscay (Vizcaya), Alava and Guipuzcoa were then brought under his command. The loyalty he inspired in the Carlist volunteers caused them to call him 'Uncle Tomás' or simply 'Uncle'. His organisational skills had enabled him, starting with 800 poorly armed infantry, to build up an effective army of 35,000 volunteers within a year, trained and disciplined. Guerrilla tactics were developed in the mountainous north of Spain, with the army divided into battalions, each commanded by a colonel, and operating as independent units which would unite for major engagements. The inhabitants of the Basque region and Navarre were mostly Carlist sympathisers, so that intelligence regarding Cristino plans and movements was readily available from local peasants, priests or pedlars, and food supplies were easily obtained. For the Cristino forces and supporters in towns and villages life was difficult. While Zumalacárregui was besieging a Cristino garrison, any attempt to supply food to the defenders was dangerous, with death the fate of men and whipping that of women. Tomás' successes grew with more ambitious engagements. The best of the Cristino generals were successively worsted over a period of eighteen months, during which the Carlist star rose. In May 1834 General Quesada, under whom Zumalacárregui had served in the War of Independence, was heavily defeated at Alsasua, and only saved from rout by another of Tomas' former chiefs, the Cristino General Jauregui, known as *El Pastor* (The Shepherd). Quesada lost many men killed or wounded, and one hundred prisoners were taken by the Carlists. The pattern of shooting prisoners as rebels against what each side considered to be legitimate authority was now established practice. The private soldiers could often save their lives by agreeing to serve in the victor's army, but officers would seldom take this escape route; the dishonour involved in such a course, especially for a senior officer, in a culture in which honour was jealously guarded, was unthinkable. Zumalacárregui had all the Cristino oficers captured at Alsasua shot. They included Colonel José O'Donnell, a member of a famous family of Irish extraction, whose father had fought in the War of Independence. Other members of the O'Donnell clan fought and died on either side in the years that followed.

The defeated Quesada was replaced by General Rodil, who had failed to capture Don Carlos near the Spanish–Portuguese border. When Carlos entered Spain soon after Rodil's appointment, the latter again pursued the Pretender, but with no more success than before. The Carlists' control of most of the Basque country and part of Navarre was gradually strengthened, and Carlos set up his first headquarters in the ancient town of Oñate, where he held court with his supporters and advisers.

The situation in the Cristino party became more complicated in the winter of 1833–4, not long after her husband's death in September, when Cristina herself, whose reputation for romantic affairs was well known, fell in love with Fernando Muñoz, a handsome corporal in the royal bodyguard. The affair progressed rapidly, and in December 1833 the devoted Muñoz was admitted to the royal bed. The pair were secretly married on returning to Madrid with the help of the Papal Nuncio, Muñoz was appointed groom of the royal bedchamber, given his own room in the palace, and became Cristina's constant escort and companion. In November 1834 she bore their first child, who would not be the last. Cristina's regency, already difficult, was made yet more troubled by the liaison. The secrecy of her marriage exposed her to the accusations of an extramarital affair, providing the Carlists and other enemies with another stick with which to beat her. The insults of 'whore' and 'royal prostitute' hurled at her at home and abroad, though undeserved, made good propaganda. Cristina's periodic retreats from Madrid to bear her children in secret must have sapped her energies, and at times diverted her attention from the arduous task of balancing conflicting interests as regent for her daughter. Further, her elder sister, Carlota, to whom she owed her position as queen and then queen regent, was so outraged by Cristina's liaison with Muñoz that she tried to make her abandon it, and even attempted, without success, to have the regency transferred to herself and her husband.

Cristina's problems were also increased by the intervention of two of her generals, who complained of the slow progress of the war, claiming that the only way to defeat Carlos was to appoint a more liberal ministry and summon a popularly elected Cortes. She was forced to act, and Martinez de la Rosa replaced Bermudez as chief minister. The reforms he introduced satisfied no one. The royal statute of 1834 attempted a compromise between the radical Constitution of 1812 and the maintenance of an absolute monarchy, leaving final power in the hands of the crown – for the time being of the regent – and re-establishing the Cortes, with a lower house elected by a restricted number of voters and an upper chamber of members of the privileged clases with their seats held by heredity or by royal appointment.

The limited measure of parliamentary 'democracy' in this statute allowed Cristina to appear 'liberal' in the eyes of England and France, and enabled Palmerston to support her against Carlos, which he saw as being in the interests of Britain and of resolving the chaotic situation in the Peninsula. He opened negotiations early in 1834 with France, Spain and Portugal. At that date both the Portuguese pretender Dom Miguel and Don Carlos were still in Portugal. Miguel's attempt on the Portuguese throne was near its last throes, but Carlos remained a very real danger. By this plan also Palmerston hoped to anticipate any unilateral effort of France in favour of either Cristina or Carlos; as members of an official alliance France could be prevented from acting on her own. Palmerston quickly presented his plan to the cabinet, giving no time for objections to be raised. The Quadruple Alliance was signed in London on 22 April 1834 by the French and Spanish ambassadors, the Portuguese envoy and Palmerston himself. The alliance provided that all four countries should unite to expel Dom Miguel and Don Carlos from Portugal, that France should give moral support, and Britain assist with her navy, but no mention was made of evicting Don Carlos from Spain should he raise rebellion there. Palmerston had skilfully forced the hand of France; King Louis-Philippe's support was lukewarm; despite having recognised Isabella, he would have preferred the triumph of absolutism under Don Carlos to the success of a liberal government in Madrid. Had he not joined the alliance France would have been the odd man out between a western triple alliance and the axis of Austria, Russia and Prussia. Palmerston was delighted with the alliance and congratulated himself on its success, for which he deserves credit, but when he wrote to his brother soon afterwards, 'Nothing ever did so well as the Quadruple Treaty. It has ended a war which might otherwise have lasted several months,' he was being as over-optimistic as Wellington had been in his forecast of the war.

In Palmerston's view the safest place for Don Carlos to reside was England, and the British government was happy to convey him there by sea. In June 1834 Carlos sailed from Portugal in the naval vessel *Donegal* with a modest retinue including Colonel Carlos Luis O'Donnell, another member of the clan, many of whom fought for the Pretender.

The correspondent of *The Times* reported the arrival of Carlos at Portsmouth on 18 June, the anniversary of the battle of Waterloo, commenting that few officers of distinction received him. The admiral had not called to pay his respects, and it was said that an indisposition had prevented him. One officer who did call on Carlos was Sir Frederick Maitland, who had received Napoleon on board the *Bellerophon* in the Basque Roads on his way to exile. It was hoped that Carlos would give up his claim to the throne in return for a generous pension and, on his arrival at Spithead, John Backhouse, a Foreign Office under-secretary, was sent to start negotiations. A pension of £30,000 a year was offered by the Spanish government on condition that Carlos should never return to Spain or Portugal, nor assist in any way in disturbing their tranquillity. Backhouse also appealed to him to surrender his claim on the grounds of humanity, in order to avoid further bloodshed in Spain. There followed the threat that King William IV would withhold the marks of respect usually given to European royalty if he refused the terms. All was in vain. Carlos was adamant, as he had been in the face of Napoleon and later of Ferdinand, that he would never cease to assert his title to the crown. He then moved to London, to Gloucester Lodge, Brompton. For a week or more he saw the sights, visited the Tower of London and the Blackwall Tunnel. He was visited by the duke of Wellington who advised him to remain in England and warned him to be careful about what he said, since his conversation would quickly be reported in Downing Street. Carlos laughed at the warning. He had planned his journey to England only as a stage on his return to Spain, and he now put his plans into action in a near-farcical way. It was given out that he was ill and a friend took his place in his supposed sick-bed, while Carlos escaped to the house of a French sympathiser. Disguised, with his moustache shaven off, which must have cost him many pangs, and his hair dyed black by his wife, he left London for Brighton at midnight of 1 July, crossed the channel to Dieppe, and travelled on to Paris and Bayonne under a Mexican name and with a Mexican passport. Bayonne, in the Basque region of France, was a hotbed of Carlism from which it was easy to re-enter Spain. He crossed the border after little more than a year's absence from Spain, and would remain there for over five years.

Carlos reached Elizondo, a training centre for Carlist volunteers, in July 1834, to an enthusiastic welcome. The Navarrese volunteers whom Zumalacárregui had inspired, trained and organised were an impressive and encouraging sight for the man who hoped to become their king.

During the next year the Carlist cause prospered, so that many saw Carlos as the eventual victor. The success and effectiveness of Zumalacárregui and the unifying and stimulating presence of the prince whom they regarded as their king created optimism in the hearts and minds of Carlos' followers. Both factions needed money and arms. The Carlists could raise forced levies of money in Spain and fines imposed on Cristino villages. This paid the charges of the many willing smugglers who imported food, horses and material for making weapons across the French border. Factories were set up for manufacturing muskets, swords and gunpowder. Success in battle gave the Carlists access to weapons captured from the Cristinos, so that muskets bearing the marks of the Tower of London or French factories, supplied to the queen under the terms of the alliance, changed hands.

The Constitutionalist government, meanwhile, remained as unstable as ever. The British ambassador in Madrid, Sir George Villiers (the future Lord Clarendon), was very pessimistic about the situation, critical of the confusion in the capital, the 'imbecility' of the new government of Martinez de la Rosa, and concerned about the harm which Cristina's association with Muñoz had done to her cause. An outbreak of cholera, spread from Portugal, was blamed by the mob in Madrid on friars having poisoned the water; riots broke out, monasteries were attacked and many monks slaughtered before the government moved to restore order, the ringleaders of the riots going unpunished.

A new, young Carlist general, Ramon Cabrera, was waging guerrilla warfare with great success. The Cristino troops were dispirited, poorly clothed and fed, while morale in the victorious Carlist army, whose material needs Uncle Tomás ensured were met, was excellent. Don Carlos' army, though short of cavalry, artillery and competent surgeons (as Zumalacárregui was to discover to his own cost) was nonetheless an efficient fighting force and a credit to its training. Cristina's government reacted to the army's failure by dismissing General Rodil and appointing General Mina, a liberal and another veteran of the War of Independence, to take command in the north.

The war was waged with great ferocity on both sides, and the routine slaughter of prisoners horrified many citizens of the northern European nations, especially the British, to whom it seemed a return to the mores of the Middle Ages (or worse, since in the Age of Chivalry the lives at least of the nobles captured in battle were a marketable commodity in terms of ransom money). In March 1835 General Mina punished a Carlist village by burning it to the ground and shooting one in five of its male inhabitants.

Although the Whigs in Britain were temporarily out of office between December 1834 and April 1835, and Palmerston had been replaced as foreign secretary by Wellington, Britain's policy towards Spain was unchanged. Martinez de la Rosa appointed General Miguel de Alava as Spanish ambassador to London. A veteran of the Peninsular campaigns, Alava was said to have been the only man who was present both at Trafalgar* and Waterloo, and his relations with Wellington were excellent. The appointment was to have a profound effect on the Anglo-Spanish accord. Alava's plea to Wellington to try to alleviate the suffering caused by the needless savagery on both sides met a ready response. Wellington arranged for two envoys to go to Spain to urge a more civilised conduct of the war on the combatants. These were Lord Eliot, a former MP who had served in the British embassies in Lisbon and Madrid, and Colonel Gurwood, another veteran of the Peninsular War, and editor of Wellington's despatches. Lord Eliot was also given secret instructions to tell Don Carlos that Britain could not recognise his claim to the throne, that he would get no effective help from the absolutist powers, Austria, Prussia and Russia, and that he would be well advised to give up the hopeless struggle. Eliot was also to contact Villiers in Madrid and discuss the possibility of Cristina's government coming to terms with Carlos. Wasting no time after receiving Wellington's orders on 20 March, Eliot reached Bayonne by 4 April, corresponding there with Villiers about the secret part of his mission. The ambassador believed that there was no hope of any compromise between the two parties, so that Eliot and Gurwood left Bayonne on 16 April for Spain to open negotiations with the Carlists.

Captain Henningsen wrote in detail in his account about Lord Eliot's mission, having been involved in meeting and escorting Eliot and Gurwood. Eliot was hospitably received by Don Carlos at Segura, but the Pretender was unshakeable in his resolve to maintain his claim to the throne. Henningsen was ordered to meet the two emissaries, after they had left Carlos, at Asorta, Zumalacárregui's headquarters. There too they met a friendly reception and both created an excellent impression, being fluent in Spanish and French and well acquainted with Spain. Gurwood made a particularly good impression on the Carlist chief. Lord Eliot presented him with a gift from Wellington, a telescope used by the duke in several of his actions. Henningsen wrote that the general set great store by this and

* At Trafalgar Nelson had defeated the combined French and Spanish fleets.

always carried it around with him (Zumalacárregui carried the same telescope when at the siege of Bilbao only a few months later he received the
wound of which he died). The attempts to humanise the war seemed likely
to succeed. The casual attitude of the Carlists towards human life shocked
Eliot, who later described how at the very moment he reached Asorta sixteen prisoners were being led out to be shot, and he at once asked for their
lives to be spared. His request 'was granted with the same indifference as
if he asked for a pinch of snuff.' Henningsen wrote of twenty-seven
Cristino prisoners who were spared at Eliot's request, and threw themselves at his feet to thank him for his intercession. Zumalacárregui also
told Eliot that, had he arrived the previous evening, he might have spared
twenty-two more from being shot.

General Valdes, the new Cristino commander-in-chief, and the Carlist
general willingly signed the agreement, which became known as the Eliot
Convention. The provisions of this were: that the lives of prisoners taken
on either side should be spared; that prisoners should be exchanged two
or three times a month; that no person should be sentenced to death on
political grounds without trial; and that sick and wounded found in hospitals, houses and villages should be humanely treated.

Eliot was deservedly congratulated by Villiers on his achievement.
Captain Henningsen, a witness to the birth of the agreement, estimated
that it saved five thousand lives. He dedicated his book to Lord Eliot as
'one of the very few who have in any way, in the civil strife now devastating Spain, whose name will not be a curse to her people, but on whom
the blessings of all ranks of Spaniards will be showered, for the manner in
which you discharged one of the noblest offices of humanity, and of its
effect in saving the lives of thousands.' Later events were to show the
Convention to be rather less beneficial than Henningsen's eulogy suggested.

The Convention applied only to the Basque provinces and Navarre,
but it was hoped that it would also operate in other regions to which the
war might spread. As time passed it became clear that commanders in other
provinces would refuse to honour an agreement in which they had not been
involved. Exchanges of prisoners did take place between the two armies,
though their treatment while in captivity was often extremely inhumane;
a witness described seeing the arrival of a batch of Carlist prisoners released
by the Cristinos in a terrible condition of near-starvation.

Nonetheless the Eliot Convention had the effect of reassuring, at least
temporarily, the British government and public that the war in Spain would

be less savage than before, thus smoothing the way to a closer degree of British support for the cause of the queen. In June 1835, however, when Palmerston's plans for fuller British involvement were proceeding, Don Carlos' decision, published in the so-called Durango Decree, that on mature reflection he had concluded that the Convention did not apply to *foreign* troops, who were therefore beyond its pale, greatly increased concern for the safety of any Britons who might become involved in the war.

CHAPTER THREE

Britain's involvement:
the birth of the Legion

General Alava, the Spanish ambassador in London, a devoted supporter of Queen Isabella and the queen regent and a fierce opponent of Carlism, was anxious to obtain permission to enlist a force of ten thousand volunteers for service against the Carlists in Spain.

As matters stood, the Foreign Enlistment Act prevented British subjects, including at that time all inhabitants of Ireland, from legally entering the service of a foreign power without King William IV's permission. On 5 June Alava wrote to Palmerston requesting that the government of His Britannic Majesty be pleased to authorise him to raise in the United Kingdom a body of ten thousand troops, giving the king's permission to British subjects, particularly such officers as desire it, to enlist in the same for the service of Queen Isabella. Alava was confident of his response, and on 8 June Palmerston replied positively.

Palmerston, whose tendency to abrasiveness has caused some to speak of him as 'Lord Pumicestone' and others to suggest that ships of war were a part of his concept of diplomacy, persuaded the king to grant this permission. This is surprising in view of William's distrust of foreigners in general, and of Spain in particular. The sailor king's opinion of all Spanish governments was such that he could see little point in becoming involved in their affairs; he believed that even the most limited intervention in Spain represented a futile exercise in knight errantry. Palmerston, however, had his way, and by an order in council at the Court of St James on 10 June 1835, the Foreign Enlistment Act was suspended. Enlistment of British subjects in the military and naval service of Isabella was now permitted: 'It shall be lawful for every person whomsoever to enter into the military or naval service of Her Majesty, as a commissioned or non-commissioned officer, or as a private soldier, sailor or marine, and to serve Her Said Majesty, in any military, war-like or other operations, either by land or by sea, and for that purpose to go to any place or places beyond the seas, and to accept any commission, warrant, or other appointment from or under Her Said Majesty, and to enlist and enter himself in such service, and to accept any money, pay or reward for the same.' This was to be in force only for the term of two years from 10 June, unless this period should be further extended by order in council. The *London Gazette* for 10 June gave exact details of the composition of the army of ten thousand men – 8,448 infantry, 552 rifles, 700 cavalry and 300 artillery.

The Bill went through with unusual speed. One of the Tory newspapers of the time, violently opposed to the plan, wrote 'It is quite clear that some meanness, some paltry evasion is about to be practised: but unless the Bill by which it is to be effected, be carried through both Houses at a Rail-road pace, we think it not impossible that Don Carlos will be quietly settled at Madrid before it can be acted upon.' The *Standard* argued that if men were to be raised by an order in council, the parliamentary control of the army would be removed and the precedent could authorise a levy of one hundred thousand Repealers 'in the name of the Queen of Spain or the Pope of Rome'.

Alava and Palmerston can be considered joint midwives at the birth of what became known as the British Legion, Legio Britannica, or British Auxiliary Legion (fig. 16). The Tory press was outraged at the thought of a British mercenary force fighting against Don Carlos, while the Whigs generally supported the development. The arguments raged in both Houses of Parliament and continued throughout the coming years. The politics involved affected the choice of the commander of the Legion, restricting it to those who supported Isabella and the queen regent – the Cristinos or Constitutionalists. Alava offered the command to Colonel George de Lacy Evans, an Irishman aged forty-eight, who sat as the Radical MP for Westminster (fig. 7). In the Peninsular War the two men had been close colleagues, Evans as an officer on Wellington's staff and Alava as the duke's ADC. Evans had also served in India and, in 1812, in the war against the United States, when he occupied Washington with a small force of light infantry and burned the White House. At Waterloo, Evans had had two horses shot from under him. In 1818 he had gone on half-pay as a lieu-tenant-colonel and in 1830 entered Parliament as MP for Rye, losing his seat there but winning another at Westminster by 152 votes.

Evans accepted the command, but must have had some reservations as he did so. It was many years since his days of active soldiering; he was well aware of the hostility he would attract from his political enemies, and had some idea of the difficulties he would meet in his unusual, and largely unoffical position as servant of a foreign monarchy, with little guarantee of support from his own government. This military adventure was to be very different from his earlier campaigns, and there cannot have been many competitors for this poisoned chalice. Palmerston's wife Emily, however, was not impressed by Alava's choice. In a letter to her friend the Princess Lieven, wife of the Russian ambassador, Lady Palmerston wrote that Alava could have chosen a better general, and that 'everyone was so anxious to be appointed that he would have had no difficulty in finding a better person'. In thinking this she was overlooking the problems facing any general appointed to the Legion.

One major obstacle was the opposition of the Tories in general, and of Wellington in particular, who still exercised immense influence. He set his mind against the appointment of regular British officers to commissions in the Legion, thus denying it the services of many of the best candidates, at a time when there were few officers with recent active military experience. The knowledge that 'certain high military personages were decidedly averse to the measure' deterred many officers, whose services Evans had hoped to secure, from engaging in the corps, as he wrote later. Wellington's jaundiced comment was that 'Evans will find a mighty difference between holding forth to a set of constituents in a Westminster pot-house, and commanding an army in a poor country without a commissariat and with little or no money.' This Olympian opinion reflected a widespread view that it would all end in tears. Evans' politics provided a useful stick with which to beat him at this stage and throughout the war. The Tory journalists were sharpening pens for a long campaign of vilification. Some idea of Evans' mixed feelings about his position is given by the vigorous debate that raged in the House of Commons on the rights and wrongs of the formation of the Legion. Lord Mahon strongly supported Wellington, doubting whether 'a half-pay lieutenant-colonel was altogether a fit individual to be commander of ten thousand men'. Evans himself replied that he had not sought the appointment and was willing to resign it to any general or field-marshal who was ready 'to take such steps as were necessary for putting down Don Carlos'. Needless to say no alternative commander offered his services.

Despite his difficulties Evans was able to find some senior field officers to serve in the Legion among his personal friends. These included Charles Chichester, half-pay unattached, who was appointed brigadier-general, and William Reid. *The Times* for 30 July 1835 carried a report on the Anglo-Spanish expedition with a 'List of Officers of the British Army and of the East India Company's service, who had entered into the Auxiliary Corps raising for the Service of the Queen of Spain'. The list is probably not complete.

Apart from those from the British Army, there were six officers from the Madras Army, and a seventh listed as 'late Madras Army'. One of these was Evans' own brother, R.L. Evans CB, who was appointed brigadier-general, and became known to his men as Old Mumble Chops, and resigned in February 1836 to return to India. Another example of the family rallying round the flag was Evans' brother-in-law, Lieutenant J. O'Leary, who was appointed second major in the 10th Regiment (Munster Light Infantry) and joined in Cork. He is said to have served in the army upwards of twenty-two years and was the first lieutenant on Lord Hill's list for a company, according to the *Tipperary Free Press* of 15 August 1835. Another of Evans' brothers-in-law to serve was Colonel Alexander Arbuthnot, who commanded the depot at Santander, and distinguished himself at the storming of Irun.

Two other officers had served in the Bengal Engineers and the East India Company Service. Lieutenant William A. Clarke was listed as 'late Newfoundland Veterans', and Lieutenant Maurice Charles O'Connell as '73rd Regiment', which his father, Sir Maurice Charles O'Connell, had commanded. He was appointed lieutenant colonel. Both were to serve in the reorganised legion, after Evans' retirement at the end of his two years service. Another lieutenant was listed as 'Late Marine Artillery'. The previous ranks of the 54 officers listed comprised three lieutenant colonels, three majors, 24 captains and 24 lieutenants. Almost all were promoted to higher rank in the Legion, at least to the next level, with some captains and even some lieutenants promoted to lieutenant colonel, as was O'Connell. For half-pay British officers the prospect of regular pay must have been attractive, since the half-pay emoluments were not generous. After Waterloo the daily half-pay for infantry lieutenants was 2s. 4d., for captains 5s. and for lieutenant colonels 8s. 6d.

Despite the ruling by Lord Hill, commander-in-chief of the British army, that he would in no circumstances give leave of absence to half-pay officers to join the Legion, and that all those granted long leave must pledge not to go the Peninsula, many officers risked breaching the rule. Some decided quite late in the day, and others had second thoughts. Newspaper reports of July and August refer to officers selling out to join the Legion. In August, Lieutenant Malcolm Ross of the 23rd Fusiliers and Captain Keogh of the 29th sold out to join the 8th and 9th Regiments respectively. At the same time the Hon. Captain Clements, son of the earl of Leitrim, and Captain Burgess were reported to have joined, although neither name appears in the

Army List of the Legion. An important exception to the veto was made for Captain J.N. Colquhoun, Royal Artillery, in charge of a field battery at Clonmel, who was placed on half-pay and joined the Legion on 1 August. The contribution of this skilled gunner officer to the Cristino cause was to prove invaluable. The importance of the artillery was recognised by a circular from Sir Hussey Vivian, major-general of ordnance, to commanding officers of all British artillery regiments, to let a certain number of NCOs and privates enter the Legion's corps of artillery, with guaranteed reinstatement in their original ranks at the end of hostilities.

For the rest of his experienced officer strength Evans was dependent on a number of veterans of the recent wars in Greece and Colombia and, importantly, of the campaign in Portugal in support of the young Queen Maria II in her dynastic struggle against her uncle, Dom Miguel, in a situation similar to that of Isabella and Don Carlos. The conditions of warfare in Portugal resembled those in northern Spain, though geographical and climatic features may have been less hostile to a foreign army than proved to be the case in the Carlist conflict. Among 'Portuguese' or 'Pedroite' officers were Lieutenant Charles Shaw, half-pay 52nd Regiment, and his friend Bruce Mitchell. Shaw's *Personal Memoirs and Correspondence*, a narrative of the War for Constitutional Liberty in Portugal and Spain from 1831 from 1837, is a valuable source of information about the two campaigns. A man of strong views and very touchy as to his honour, Shaw wrote in July 1835 to Mitchell commenting that it had been fixed by the ruling powers in London 'that Portuguese officers' (as they were known) 'were only to have the rank they had in Portugal, it being quite impossible that, after four years of active service in that country, you or any of them can be supposed to know so much of war as the young gentlemen of the British service who have had such glorious opportunities of studying that profession in the garrisons of England!' After this sour comment Shaw advised Mitchell to hurry to enlist, 'since I can promise you a majority in one of the Scotch regiments.' Shaw was appointed colonel and involved in recruiting for the Legion in Scotland, but was greatly upset since he believed he had been promised a higher rank, which he eventually achieved when promoted to brigadier-general. Another Pedroite officer was Gilbert Hogg of Gilstown, Co. Roscommon, who, with Shaw, was involved in recruiting for the Scottish regiments.

The Legion had an indirect link with the poet John Keats. Fanny Brawne, with whom John Keats had an unhappy love affair, married Louis Lindo in 1832, twelve years after Keats' death. After the birth of his first son, Lindo joined the Legion as captain and paymaster in the 2nd Lancers, serving in Spain until 1838. The allure of Mars seems to have been stronger than that of Venus, for the young husband and father could have returned home with most of his comrades in June 1837.

Forty or fifty British Army sergeants were commissioned in the Legion, many of whom proved a great asset through their experience of warfare and discipline. The Irishman, Edward Costello, who had fought in the Rifle Brigade in the Peninsula as a sergeant, was appointed lieutenant in the 7th Irish Regiment by General Evans, and charged with raising a rifle regiment for the Legion. In this he was very successful, recruiting five hundred men in two months, with one sergeant and one corporal, mainly old soldiers, for every fifteen rank and file. Costello commented that in his own regiment there were three different classes of officers. The first were those who had formerly held commissions in the British Army, the second those who, through interest, obtained commissions from General Evans, and the third and by far the largest group, Pedroites, 'self-taught heroes brought up in neither military nor civil life who had passed a little Quixotic tour under Don Pedro'. He regretted that every regiment was full of Pedroites, and it is clear that relations between these and the ex-British Army officers were bad.

Many of the Legion's four hundred officers had no previous military experience and, like their men, were accepted without careful assessment of their characters or abilities as 'officer material'. They thus had to learn their trade 'on the job' in the hard school of experience. That some should fail abysmally is not surprising; the worst were dubbed by their colleagues the QHB – the Queen's Hard Bargains. Many of these left the Legion or had to be repatriated during its early months in Spain. General orders of the Legion would from time to time refer to officers 'dismissed this service', no details being given; these were presumably individuals who fell short of the desired standards in one way or another. Over-indulgence in severe flogging and other punishments for military offences ordered by certain unsuitable officers was a criticism levelled at the Legion, which gave it a bad name among the British public. The comments of some private soldiers, such as Alexander Somerville, the self-educated, intelligent and reformist Scot, throw light on this problem, with his account of one very unpopular martinet eventually falling foul of his men. It was also suggested that some officers killed in some of the earlier actions were shot by their own men; later known as 'fragging', this practice was not unknown in the British army.

CHAPTER FOUR

Finding cannon fodder

RECRUITING SOLDIERS FOR THE LEGION

It proved easier to find recruits for the ranks than officers, and recruitment proceeded rapidly after the formation of the Legion was sanctioned on 10 June. Within four or five weeks the first detachment reached the port of San Sebastian in northern Spain.

Poor social conditions have always been a stimulus to military recruitment, with the 'compulsion of destitution' a major spur. Unemployment, low wages, poor diet, the fear of famine, the desire to escape from the law or oppressive employment, combined with the wish to better themselves or seek their fortune, have all driven men into the arms of the recruiting sergeant. In Britain in the 1830s the enclosure movement had greatly increased the landholdings of the upper and wealthy classes. The more enterprising small freeholders became large farmers, while the weaker and the poor sank to the status of labourers at a time when, due to the increase in the rural population, there was already a steady drift of the labouring class to the towns. In the towns themselves the introduction of machinery had led to misery for countless workers and their families. As Woodward put it, 'the fate of the thousands of handloom weavers, and of others whose humble skills had lost their economic value, was harsh beyond tears. For those who had been disinherited of their skill by the new machines life was a long and losing fight against starvation.'

The situation generally was worse in Ireland, where abject poverty had for long been the lot of the rural poor. The wars of the seventeenth century had established English hegemony and an alien religion in that unhappy land. The flight of the 'Wild Geese' to Europe after the Treaty of Limerick in 1691 marked the end of the old Ireland. Thereafter, as Elizabeth Bowen wrote, 'the complete subjugation and the exploitation of Ireland became the object of the English burgess class. The Sword of the Lord was drawn for the rentier. Ireland, already dense with her own sorrows, reflected English changes as a cloud reflected distant changing light.'

The nineteenth century brought recurrent famines with failures of the vital potato crop; the worst of these still lay some ten years ahead, but none could tell when hunger and starvation would strike again. A population of eight million was maintained with great difficulty; it was soon to be pruned drastically by starvation, disease and emigration. The 'Age of Reform' had brought some benefits to the largely Catholic population with Catholic Emancipation in 1829* and the Reform Bills giving the vote to some of the previously disenfranchised in 1834, but these had done little to alleviate the lot of the poorest.

Ireland had long been a recruiting ground for the British – and other – armies. Irishmen had formed a large proportion of Wellington's armies, and though the Duke referred to his men as ' the scum of the earth' these men had defeated Napoleon and saved Europe from French domination. The proportion of Irishmen among the rank and file of the British army had risen from 16 per cent during the American War of Independence to 42 per cent in 1830, while that of the Scots had fallen. It is not surprising therefore that Ireland should have contributed about one-third of the strength of the Legion. As in the British Army, Irish soldiers served, not only in the regiments with specifically Irish affiliations, but also in the English and Scottish regiments.

The Legion originally consisted of two regiments of lancers, ten of infantry, a rifle corps, staff corps, artillery, engineers, medical staff and commissariat. The 2nd and 5th Regiments suffered so severely from typhus in the winter of 1835–6 that they were broken up. By 1836 the regiments were:

1st Reina Isabella Lancers	7th Irish Light Infantry
2nd Queen's Own Irish Lancers	8th Highlanders
1st Regiment of Infantry	9th Irish Regiment
3rd Regiment or Westminster Grenadiers	10th Munster Light Infantry
4th Regiment, Queen's Own Fusiliers	Rifle Corps
6th Scotch Grenadiers	

---

* The Catholic Emancipation Bill was passed in Parliament following the victory of the Catholic Association leader, Daniel O'Connell, known to his supporters as the Liberator, at an election in County Clare. There had been fierce opposition to the Bill from the Establishment. A cartoon of the period shows O'Connell being asked by a peasant, 'I say, Dan, will Mancipation make the praties grow?' to which Dan answers, 'Yes'.

as well as the medical staff and commissariat. There were thus four Irish regiments, while many Irishmen served in other units.

The unusual political background to the raising of the Legion imposed exceptional restrictions on its formation and training. The terms of the agreement involved in the order in council prevented any training in Great Britain. Palmerston had pointed out to Alava that 'it will be necessary that the men, as fast as they are raised in this country, should be sent off to a Spanish port, there to be armed, equipped and organised'. It was inconsistent with the laws and the constitution of England to allow within the kingdom a body of armed men, neither under the authority of the king nor subject to the Mutiny Act, unless Parliament had specially consented to their presence. The training of these inexperienced civilians in military discipline and the arts of war could only begin on a foreign shore, a situation seldom if ever seen with British soldiers sent abroad to fight.

RECRUITMENT IN IRELAND

The recruiting of the legionaries seems mainly to have been conducted by the officers of the Legion.

In Ireland they joined in Dublin and Cork, though recruiting parties also sought men further west. Much information comes from the contemporary press in Ireland and in England. Although Macaulay believed that the history of a country is best studied through its newspapers, the formation and activities of the Legion were viewed in very different lights by members of different political parties, so that very conflicting pictures are painted in the contemporary press. The unionist Irish papers in general tended to denigrate Evans and all those involved in the enterprise, their venomous pens swift in character assassination and prophesying doom. The voices of the Catholic O'Connellite pro-Repeal and Whig papers, and *The Times* of London and *The Spectator* were less strident and less critical. Evans himself was the repeated and most popular target of the Tory newspapers; he was described as a mercenary, which to some extent he was, and a *condottiere*. *Old England* reported in June that measures for the Legion were going ahead with extraordinary rapidity and recruiting going on with vigour, while the 'Radical papers are all chanting "See the conquering hero comes," in chorus.' They predicted that all would end in disappointment.

In June 1835 the *Cork Evening Herald* amused itself at the expense of Feargus O'Connor, a fiery barrister who had recently been dispossessed of his parliamentary seat for County Cork, suggesting that he was to fight in Spain with the Legion. 'Mr Feargus O'Connor is about to hie him to the Spanish wars! Fact indubitable – Colonel Feargus proposes to raise an Irish regiment – I hope of his Electors. The ex-Knight of the Shire, the learned and gallant Feargus, has turned Colonel!'* After Don Carlos, in the Durango Decree, declared that the Eliot Convention did not apply to foreign troops such as the Legion, who were therefore to be shot when captured, the *Clonmel Herald* on 27 June wrote that the courage of many of the volunteers had wonderfully cooled. 'It is understood that even the late Knight of the Shire for the County of Cork, instead of "seeking the bubble reputation in the cannon's mouth" remains quietly in England.'

Great anxiety prevailed at this time about Carlos' Durango Decree. During the debate in the House of Lords on 3 July Lord Melbourne considered it was a forgery, but referred to the 'revengeful nature of the Spaniard', of which those going to Spain might well be ignorant. In the House on 12 June Lord Strangford had asked whether His Majesty's Government would contemplate making any provision for the widows and orphans of the British subjects who might enter the service of the queen of Spain, and perish in the conflict, and for those wounded or disabled. Melbourne's pragmatic reply was that they must look to the government

---

* Feargus O'Connor had been unseated in June due to his lack of the necessary £600 property qualification. Although no mention of his military ambitions is made by his biographers (Read & Glasgow, 1961), other more impartial journals confirmed that he did indeed toy with the idea. The *Globe* reported rumours that O'Connor intended raising a body of men in Ireland for the service of the young queen, while the *Dublin Mercantile Advertiser* wrote that he had resolved to lead an Irish Brigade, that in Spain his principles of liberty would have 'a clear stage and fair fighting' and that he was the man, above all others, whom they would recommend. After his political setback, however, O'Connor focussed his attention on the problems of the workers of England in the new era of the Industrial Revolution, and became a key figure in the developing Chartist movement, being elected as MP for Nottingham in 1847. His eventful career included a period of eighteen months' imprisonment in York Castle for seditious libels, and from the moment of release he was engaged in a series of bitter quarrels with almost every important man in the Chartist movement. The *Dictionary of National Biography* recorded that 'O'Connor was insanely jealous and egotistical, and that no one succeeded in working with him for long.' In 1854 he was pronounced insane and placed in an asylum in Chiswick. It seems fortunate that he did not pursue a military career, since the unhappy story of the British Legion might have been yet more wretched.

they meant to serve for all the consequences to arise from that service. They would enter it with their eyes open to what they were doing, and must take all the chances with the service in which they were engaged, and should these chances prove unfavourable to them, they would have no claim, either for compensation or otherwise, on the British Government. We are told that the marquis of Londonderry looked on the matter as of the highest importance, and 'the conversation then dropped'. These exchanges in retrospect seem quite inadequate to the gravity of the situation, with the inevitable harvest of death and disability resulting from any war, and with crippled and limbless 'beggars in scarlet', veterans of the Napoleonic Wars, roaming the streets of Britain's cities as reminders of the horrors which war brings, its effects rippling out far beyond the deaths of men in battle.

Such thoughts, however, were probably far from the minds of the men and boys who thronged to the recruiting offices in Cork and Dublin, to many of whom it would have seemed a great adventure. Most were farm workers, peasants with minimal holdings, or unemployed. Some would have been tradesmen down on their luck, others men desperate to escape the law or some intolerable domestic situation. More positive motivation would have provided by the sense of adventure, the fighting tradition and the desire for glory, pay and plunder. Few would have had any idea about Spain, its civil war or the rights and wrongs of the conflict. Very few would have been driven by political motives, as was their commander, Evans, and the situation was quite different from that of the Spanish Civil War a century later, in which men from many nations would hasten to fight on either side with intense political commitment.

The simile of lambs going to the slaughter was perhaps more appropriate to these simple volunteers than to most military recruits. Despite Melbourne's lordly comments, they did not go into it with their eyes open to what they were doing and the chances they would encounter; even their officers can have had only a limited idea of the future, and Evans himself could not have predicted what difficulties would face him and his men.

On 31 August the *Cork Evening Herald* recorded that

> some 40 idle young fellows belonging to Fermoy enlisted last week, and on Friday marched to Cork, under the care of a NCO, but 'tis understood several of them straggled on the way, and are already missing. One fellow who went by the name of Kippeen, should know who he was going to fight against, and on being told 'Don

Carlos', he exclaimed 'blur an onns man is not that Mr Cussen's Jack Ass! Bang me if I go to fight against Donkies [*sic*]': so saying Kippeen left the ranks and marched back to fight as usual in the square of Fermoy.

While allowances should be made for journalistic licence and political axe-grinding, the scene is one which can readily be imagined. In similar vein, the *Clonmel Herald* on 5 September reported that twenty idle young fellows belonging to Cashel enlisted for the Spanish auxiliary service, and a few days later marched to Cork. The emphasis on 'idle' in both these reports exemplifies the critical attitude of the writer and probably his readers, not only to the venture itself but also to the men; idle they probably were, but they would have had very few opportunities, if any, for employment.

Their officers, many of whom had little military experience themselves, had to make the most of the human material; comments about silk purses and sows' ears come to mind. The *Cork Chronicle* in September reported that 'the spirit with which the young men in this city and county have entered into the Spanish service did not seem to abate.' They still pressed on, anxious to enlist under the orders of their favourite officers.

> On Saturday a draft of those aspirants for military fame and honour, consisting of 85 lads, went down to the steamers awaiting their embarkation – and this morning another 66 followed, making a complement of nearly 800 men who have engaged here for the expedition.

The *Limerick Chronicle* was more sympathetic in its coverage of recruiting for the 10th Regiment, suggesting on 25 July that the agents of the queen of Spain might easily find a thousand young fellows willing to enlist, and that some chagrin was felt at Evans' overlooking Limerick. In late August the regiment had only half of the thousand men required and Surgeon Maybury went with Captain M. Franks* to Kerry to find 180 more. Their results exceeded expectations at Tralee, where 30 'fine young fellows' joined, who marched to Killarney under Maybury en route to the depôt at Spike Island, Cork. At Killarney they raised more than 30 recruits, and at Iveragh 50 more, making a total of over 120.

---

* Franks, late of the 11th Light Dragoons, was the son of Sir John Franks, supreme judge of Calcutta, and was to die of fever at Vitoria.

Some of these were the men of the 10th Munster Light Infantry, who sailed on the *Earl Roden* for Santander in northern Spain on 2 September, under the command of Captain Charles H. Gallwey. The *Cork Herald* had printed comments critical of his men and their behaviour on the march, and Gallwey wrote on 1 September to the editor from shipboard to defend their record in having marched unaccompanied by any officer, and embarked at the appointed hour and place. He hoped that in the service of the queen of Spain they would 'maintain that character of loyalty and intrepidity for which Irish soldiers are remarkable'.

The officers of the 10th Regiment (Munster Light Infantry) were mainly Munstermen. Their medical officers included Dr Morgan David O'Connell of Kilmallock, who was appointed an assistant surgeon; he was to survive the war and later the horrific conditions of the Famine, in charge of the Infirmary and Workhouse in his native town. Others were Thomas Maybury, a fellow Dublin graduate and later MO to the Kerry Militia, and Dr M. Grove of Cork. The *Limerick Chronicle* in June reported that several 'old subalterns' doing duty with regiments in Ireland had applied for the unattached rank to enter the Spanish service, and some officers from the Limerick garrison had forwarded their papers with this intention. Hugh Joseph O'Donnell of Swinford, Mayo, joined in August as an ensign. Another officer was Ensign Alexander Ball, a Scot, who sailed from the Cove of Cork on 1 September on the *Fingal*, and who later wrote a detailed account of the Legion's actions, not only in the first two years, but also in its reorganised form until his resignation in 1838. Ensign H. Meller, who joined at Cork, was an Englishman attracted by the romance of fighting in support of 'a young Queen in a land the most celebrated and picturesque in the world'. He later wrote, in his recollections, of the chaotic conditions in the former Waterloo glass factory in Patrick Street where the levies were lodged, the desertions and the rioting when the families of the recruits tried to rescue them.

In Dublin men were recruited from the city and its neighbourhood, and from remoter counties for which Dublin was more convenient than Cork. Some came from as far north as Belfast and Omagh, and as far west as Galway. The 7th Regiment or Irish Light Infantry, under the command of Lieutenant Colonel Lothian Dixon, formerly of the 25th Regiment, British Army, was recruited by Major Polden. In the *Cork Evening Herald* on 27 July he exhorted his officers to be 'temperate with the soldiers, who were their fellow men'. This suggests that the experience of many of the young officers made him doubt their skills in 'man management'. The first group of the 7th sailed with Colonel Dixon on 30 July for Santander, from which they sailed later to San Sebastian. A further contingent of the 7th followed in August.

The 9th Irish Regiment was also raised in Dublin. Five hundred and thirty-four of its men sailed for Spain under the command of Major Talbot on the *Earl Roden*, arriving safely at Santander on 2 September. Talbot wrote enthusiastically on arrival that the 9th was the finest regiment in the British Legion, and that many had applied to be allowed to exchange into it. This was the third trip of the *Earl Roden* to Spain with Irish troops, and she had now disembarked 1,500 men. A further 240 men of the 9th were to follow under the command of Major Harley (who was wrongly reported as being shot as a prisoner by the Carlists on 9 December).

An attitude of hostility and criticism towards the troops is evident in much of the local press comment. A Dublin paper of July recorded that six hundred recruits raised in Dublin would shortly leave for San Sebastian under Colonel Alexander Cruise, late 12th Regiment, accompanied by one or two surgeons with full diplomas. The writer expressed the view that the queen of Spain deserved a bonus for their 'asportation' (*sic*). Later, the unruly conduct of four hundred recruits who had been for some weeks at Monkstown was indignantly condemned in the columns of the *Cork Constitutional* of 19 September, which reported their departure on the *Earl Roden*; no regiment is named but these may have been a further draft of the 9th. The account certainly suggests that life for those weeks had been uncomfortable for the peace-loving citizens of Monkstown, who had sometimes needed police protection.

DESERTERS FROM THE BRITISH ARMY IN THE LEGION

The recruiting campaign for the Legion created problems for the authorities of the British Army, since a number of regular soldiers serving in Ireland deserted in order to enlist for the Spanish service. One episode in particular verging on farce attracted much attention at the time. War Office documents of December 1835 refer in anxious detail to the actions of a Lieutenant Pearce* and two NCOs of the Legion who had enticed

---

* Somerville in his Nominal Roll of the Legion's officers devoted generous space to W.G.

soldiers in the 14th Foot to desert, and had hidden them on board the steamer *Royal Tar* at Cove, taking them to Spain. When their comrades discovered them in their hiding places they were forcibly prevented from taking them ashore.

Staff Surgeon Henry Wilkinson was later told by a friend in Cork how 'crimps' had induced some of the British 60th Rifles to desert to the Legion. The most notorious of the Legion's young recruits was a Sergeant Sweenie, 'whose shillelagh was at work in all riots'. Some of the deserters were concealed about Cove, and others on board the *Royal Tar*. When the garrison commander Colonel Ellis asked permission of Colonel Jacks of the Legion to examine his recruits, a small party of soldiers boarded the ship, but were attacked by Sweenie and his party, who threw their muskets into the sea. A stronger party was then sent to take possession of the ship but the deserters had by then been sent ashore. Sweenie was arrested, tried, found guilty and condemned to six months on the treadmill. Though Colonel Ellis now ordered the *Royal Tar* to be detained, Colonel Jacks had slipped anchor and sailed for the north coast of Spain with his Lancers and his illicit recruits.

Two civilians were press-ganged by the zealous staff of the Legion on the *Royal Tar*, along with the riflemen. Mr Coleman, the master-tailor of the 3rd Light Dragoons, and Mr Rigley, shoemaker, had boarded the ship in search of payment for equipping the troops, and were forcibly carried off to sea. Rigley was later put ashore near Kinsale. Eleven women, who went on board to take leave of their friends, were also carried off. The *Limerick Chronicle* (4 November 1835) in relating 'this monstrous invasion of the privileges of British subjects,' does not record whether these ladies were also landed at Kinsale.

Palmerston, when he heard of these problems, suggested that all transports carrying the Legion should be carefully searched immediately before departure. It was also proposed that recruiting should be moved from Cork to Kinsale, but the obvious disadvantages of such a change, with the better military and naval facilities at Cork, clearly ruled it out. General Evans

Pearce, for whom he clearly felt sympathy, and who was almost certainly the man who had seduced the soldiers. Pearce, he reported, was appointed cornet in the 2nd Lancers in July 1835, by virtue of recruiting for that regiment in Cork, but was refused his commission on landing in Spain from some capricious, unexplained motive of Colonel Jacks, in command of the Lancers. He ultimately got a commission in May 1836, as Ensign in the 4th Regiment, and was later promoted lieutenant and captain.

was informed of the outrage, and in April 1836 at his headquarters at Vitoria held a court of enquiry. Its outcome is not known, but at that stage in the history of the Legion he must have had many more pressing problems. Similar cases of deserters attempting to stow away on transports of the Legion were reported from Portsmouth, involving privates of the 73rd, 87th and 97th Regiments who, stupefied by drink, were inveigled on board. At a court-martial several of the deserters were condemned to transportation. Those who evaded recapture and reached Spain may well have deeply regretted their actions and may even have deserted to the Carlists, as many of the Legion were to do.

RECRUITING IN SCOTLAND

On recruiting of the Scottish regiments we have detailed information from the letters and memoirs of two men who were deeply involved, one a senior officer and the other a private soldier. Colonel Charles Shaw, late of the Portuguese service, published his *Memoirs and Correspondence* of the war in Portugal and Spain in 1837. Although he resigned halfway through the two-year life of the Legion, his account covers the whole period.

He had left Scotland in 1829 and in July 1835 was back in Britain, writing from Falmouth to his brother in Glasgow, commenting on the problems he had had with the Portuguese government over unfulfilled contracts with the British brigade in their war of succession, and his optimism as to his own usefulness in the formation of the Auxiliary Legion for Spain. Unfortunately, there was confusion or misunderstanding about the length of the engagement of the men of the Scottish regiments. Whereas this was clearly known to be two years for private soldiers and NCOs for the other elements of the Legion, an impression was created that the Scots were to serve for only one year. This was to be the cause of major problems in June 1836, when many were unwilling to serve a further year. The men were assured by Colonel Shaw that the campaign would last only three or four months, or six at the very most. This bullish approach led to a very light-hearted attitude in many potential recruits. Many young men, Somerville wrote, went 'for a three-months spree or a lark', believing that they would never see a shot fired, since the Carlists would give up as soon as they saw Evans land. He wrote later in his history of the Legion, when looking back with regret after the death from typhus in Vitoria of a Scottish legionary, remembering how the young giant had been persuaded by his friends to join them, 'as it would be fine sport', and had leapt impulsively into the boat taking them out to the ship on the Clyde.

Writing to General Evans in London in August, Shaw related that he had just commenced 'a system which will bring numbers of recruits, in spite of the harvest and plenty of work'. Shaw gives some statistics of the numbers of women and children, dependants of the three Scottish regiments: the 2,104 men and 69 officers who embarked in Scotland for Spain were accompanied by 43 women and five children. Those already embarked, he wrote, were a good body of men. Colonel Tupper, with 317 men of the 6th Scotch Regiment, which had called at Falmouth to take on water, had written to him with high praise for the conduct of the men, whom he was proud to command. In view of the need for officers used to working with men, Shaw was keen to obtain those on half-pay, and he also sought Evans' sanction to 'get many respectable, active young fellows to go out as volunteers to fight for their commissions', a plan which was implemented.* Recruiting went well, and further drafts of Scottish soldiers sailed for Spain in August. Problems of bounty money paid to the men on enlistment were a frequent cause of concern, since if large sums of money were taken abroad with them by soldiers who had never before seen such wealth, they were likely to be dissipated on drink, to the prejudice of good order and military discipline. Shaw had sent to London a receipt for £812, the bounty paid to men who had sailed on board the *Cumberland*. He had hoped to sail himself on that ship, but had delayed in order to settle his arrangements for recruiting. These were finally left with his colleague, Colonel Swan. Shaw eventually sailed with four hundred raw recruits from Greenock in early September.

He wrote home to describe the extraordinarily quick passage they had from Glasgow until within forty miles of the Spanish coast, when part of the machinery gave way, and their luck in getting to Santander before the onset of rough weather. The men on board were generally remarkably well

---

* The status of the gentleman volunteer in the British Army in the Peninsula is reviewed by Holmes (2001). These volunteers, anxious to be recommended for commissioned rank without the expensive outlay involved in purchase, were noted for their recklessness in battle in the hope that their conspicuous gallantry would lead to their commission as ensign, the lowest commissioned rank. The death rate among them was high. In the Legion many volunteers were promoted to ensign as death thinned the ranks of its officers, but the financial motivation was less powerful than in the regular army.

behaved 'although there is little doubt that four or five fell overboard the first night; but who they were no one knew and I fear no one cared'. Shaw referred also to a man named Somerville, who was on board with the 8th Highlanders and who had earlier, as a trooper in the Scots Greys, been at the centre of a *cause célèbre* when he was punished for comments he had made in connection with involvement of the military in the control of civil insurrection. The presence and motives of what he saw as a potential barrack-room lawyer alarmed Shaw, although his anxieties proved groundless.

The accounts which Somerville himself wrote in his *Narrative* (1838) and *History of the British Legion* (1839) and in his later *Autobiography of a Working Man* (1848) give the most detailed and personal accounts of the experience of a soldier involved in the first Carlist war, and indeed of any private soldier written up to that date. John Keegan, in *The Face of Battle* (1976), wrote that it was only with the First World War that we hear the voice of the common man, but Somerville's account is an exception to this generalisation. It supports the view that battles should be and are best described through the words of participants. He had the intelligence, powers of observation and the ability to reflect on his experiences, together with a desire to help, as far as possible, other sufferers in horrendous predicaments, which rarely combine in one man from any background.

Alexander Somerville was born in 1811 in the Scottish lowlands, the eleventh and last child of humble parents of strictly religious, dissenting persuasion, and he 'came into the family at a time when I could have been very well spared'. He learned to read at home and did not go to school until his eighth year, partly for want of clothes, wearing rags since the cost of clothes was beyond his father's purse. Periodic farming work kept him from school at intervals, and agricultural work continued to occupy him when his formal schooling was ended, until he enlisted in the Scots Greys in Edinburgh in 1831. The slow progress of the Reform Bill through the two Houses of Parliament was attended by hot debate among the public, which had spread to involve the army. Civil unrest in Birmingham, where the regiment was based, had led to discussion among the men when it seemed likely that they would be used to put down a march on London by the Birmingham Political Union, precursors of the Trade Unions. Inevitably, political opinions had been uttered by some soldiers. This was denied by the duke of Wellington, who claimed that the rumours were fabrications by some of the pro-Reform newspapers. Somerville had been present at the discussions, and wrote to the Press to corroborate the report.

Part of his letter was published, a hunt ensued for its author, and his dis-
covery led to a court-martial and a court of enquiry, and to his punishment by a severe flogging. The public reaction to this strengthened the
already strong movement for the abolition of flogging in the army.
Somerville became a hero to many, especially those of reformist or radical
views. He purchased his discharge in 1832 for the sum of £30, and his
next and last military involvement was in the British Legion, in which he
enlisted in 1835.

In his autobiography he wrote that it was less from a desire to *fight* for
the Spanish 'liberal cause' that he went to Spain, than for a desire to travel,
write a book of travels and have an original subject to write about. There
was a free passage to Spain and, filled with ambition to be an author, he
thought that a book about Spain would introduce him as a writer to the
public. There is an honesty in his admitting his motives, but also a naïvety
about his apparent ignorance of the horrors which the war might bring, a
naïvety shared by most of those involved. He went on to confess that, when
he gave the war a trial, he felt he would rather have been a thousand miles
away, but 'being in it I resolved that nobody should know that I did not
love lead and steel'.

Somerville enlisted in the 8th Highland Regiment, and he gives a
detailed analysis, social and moral as well as physical, of his fellow soldiers.
Despite the name, most of the 'Highlanders' had never seen the Highlands,
and about a quarter of them were recruited in Belfast and the north of
England. Large numbers hailed from Edinburgh and Glasgow. Most of the
Edinburgh men were bakers and printers, while weavers and cotton-spin-
ners predominated among the Glaswegians. About 130 had been in regular
or militia regiments of the British Army, and about 20 were deserters. Ninety
were runaway apprentices – deserters from their servitude and, as such, liable
to be apprehended. Another 90 were 'known law transgressors by profess-
sion'; no details are given, but a multitude of sins may be imagined; some
would have been debtors. Twenty-three men had wives or women with
them, while 120 had left wives at home, most, we are told, having quarrelled
with them. Children are not mentioned but Shaw referred to 43 women and
five child dependants with two Scottish regiments, as we saw.

Somerville had time and means to observe his mates in detail since he
also gives information on their stature and their ages, though the figures
seem incomplete. The majority, 300 men, were over 5 ft 6 in. in height,
55 were over 5 ft 10 in. and 61 under 5 ft 3 in. In age, the largest group

of about 500 were between twenty-five and thirty-five, a suitable military age, while 50 were under seventeen and 23 over forty-five.

The troops spent seven days aboard a vessel on the Clyde while awaiting a steamer to take them to Spain. These days were not uneventful. Somerville describes how sheriff-officers would come and take away debtors and apprentices. Boats hovered around the ship with wives, sisters, fathers and brothers determined to rescue their menfolk, who had regretted their engagement, and they would often succeed in getting, besides their own quarry, 'one or two more, who, leaping overboard and swimming, were taken up by them'. Sometimes boats from the ship were sent in pursuit of the fugitives, when a desperate fight would take place with oars, cudgels and pieces of coal.

The Scottish regiments of the Legion had their critics and detractors as much as the Irish and English, and this is understandable in view of the detailed social inventory above given by Somerville. Shaw was addressed by a Scottish banker, as one of the Scots detachments embarked for Spain, 'Well, Colonel Shaw, we are much obliged to you in Glasgow for taking so many blackguards away.'

On 5 September the Bristol steamer *Killarney* came alongside the ship and the troops were transferred. Each man was issued with 'a slop dress and a worsted rag'. Colonels Shaw and Godfrey, a half-pay British officer, and some others came on board to pay the men their bounty of two pounds. At seven in the evening, 'the *Killarney* got up steam and dashed away with 600 of us'. This was two hundred less than the eight hundred men with whom Somerville started his narrative, suggesting that the sheriff's men and the would-be rescuers had often achieved their objective. The *Killarney* reached Santander without mishap, unlike the ship which conveyed Shaw soon afterwards.

RECRUITING OF THE ENGLISH REGIMENTS

The five English regiments of the Legion were recruited in London and the south of England. The 4th Regiment, or Queen's Own Fusiliers, was recruited in the west country. Captain Augustus Losack wrote that 'the officers were distributed to different places to recruit – for we had not a man! I chose Exeter, and a damn bad place it was for men, though remarkably productive of women!' Nonetheless three hundred men had been raised by

September 1835. The 1st Regiment of infantry was the first detachment to reach Spain, landing at San Sebastian on 10 July 1835, just over a month after the formation of the Legion. The four or five hundred men of the 1st Regiment sailed in the *Royal Tar*, a steamship that later carried many of the Legion, including the deserters who stowed away at Cove. The *Royal Tar* belonged to the City of Dublin Steam Packet Company, whose London agents were the firm of Willcox & Anderson, which had supplied transports in the recent Portuguese conflict. The Spanish government now chartered the ship for the transport of the Legion. It was later renamed the *Reyna Gobernadora* (Queen Regent) in honour of Queen Cristina. Later the firm of Willcox & Anderson was invited to provide a regular steamship service from London and Falmouth to Spain. This eventually developed into the prestigious Peninsular and Oriental Steam Navigation Company (P&O Line) whose house flag, with its white and blue, red and yellow, still commemorates its services to the royal houses of Portugal and Spain.

A veteran who spent three months in the 3rd Regiment, or Westminster Grenadiers, sometimes known as 'the Isle of Dogians', later wrote of the motley crew enrolled in July at the Isle of Dogs. More than forty men fell out and deserted, many re-enlisting at another depôt to claim another bounty. The recruits spent forty-eight hours on board a hulk off Deptford before being transferred to the *Lord Lynedoch*. Their seventeen-day voyage to Spain was dogged by misfortunes; the captain died suddenly off Deal, the ship ran aground off the French coast, and the men mutinied over their rations, so that fifty of the most refractory were sent back to England in a steamer. On their arrival in early August in Santander, Saturnalia began, most of the men being beastly drunk or fighting, having been paid their bounty of two sovereigns just before disembarking. Only on the third day was discipline sufficiently restored for drilling to begin.

A recruiting depôt for Marines for the Spanish service was set up in July near the Tower of London, and another for the Rifle Brigade at Union Street in the Borough, while the Legion's Artillery recruited at Blackheath. There was a shortage of suitable recruits for the Artillery, so that special concessions were made. Two gunners of the Royal Artillery, who had been drummed out of the corps at Woolwich as irreclaimable thieves, immediately enlisted in the Legion, and some artillery pensioners in the north of Ireland were induced to enlist (*Limerick Chronicle*, 14 October 1835). In September a circular from Sir Hussey Vivian, major-general of ordnance, to the commanding officers of all British regiments of artillery, ordered them to allow a certain number of NCOs and privates to enter the Legion's artillery and to be reinstated in their previous ranks at the end of hostilities. The Artillery was among the last of the Legion's regiments to embark for Spain, but would be one of its most effective arms in the war.

The First Reyna Isabel Lancers were recruited at their headquarters at Kingston-on-Thames, where many Poles and Germans joined, proving to be 'capital and ready-made soldiers'. The Queen's Own Irish Lancers recruited mainly in Cork.

THE INVOLVEMENT OF THE FRENCH FOREIGN LEGION

Britain's support of Isabella and her cause by the expedient of the British Legion obliged Louis-Philippe, king of the French, to follow her example by supporting the Quadruple Alliance with men and arms. Unlike Palmerston, who had to raise a force in haste, he had one ready-made and conveniently to hand in the shape of the French Foreign Legion. This 'légion composée d'étrangers', or Algerine Legion, had been formed in 1831 as a special unit of the French army. The king had recently taken the throne from his hated predecessor, Charles X, at a time when political upheavals over much of Europe had led to an influx of refugees into France from Poland, Germany, Belgium, Italy, Spain and Portugal. Such men were potentially dangerous as penniless and desperate civilians but, incorporated into a legion of foreign soldiers, could be neutralised and used to advantage when trained and shipped to Algeria to fight in the French campaign of colonisation against France's Arab enemies.

Louis-Philippe lost no time in implementing his design. In August 1835 three battalions of the Legion sailed from Algiers to Tarragona in southern Spain, disembarking only a few weeks after the first elements of the British Legion reached the north of Spain. The French marched northwards to the theatre of war in Navarre and Alava, led by their commander, Colonel Joseph-Nicolas Bernelle, mounted on his horse and followed by his wife astride a mule and, behind her, by Madame Bernelle's maid.

The French Legion was well trained and disciplined compared with its British allies, but confronted a more organised and better equipped enemy in the Carlists than the North African tribesmen whom they had previously faced. The French were ill-equipped, their main firearm being an antiquated muzzle-loading musket, and their bright blue and red uniforms made them easy targets (pl. 3).

Despite their difficulties, akin to those of the British, the French Legion fought bravely, often to the last man. Disease took the same heavy toll of both forces. Though the billets of the French were better than those of the British in Vitoria (see Chapter 7) their casualties from typhus, dysentery, typhoid, pneumonia and starvation were similar.

Of the 9,000 men who came to Spain from Algeria over 3,600 were either killed in battle or died of their wounds, with 150 of their officers. Over 4,000 were 'missing', many of them deserting, either escaping into France or going over to the enemy, so that the Carlists were able to form a foreign legion of their own. In 1838, at the battle of Barbastro, the French Foreign Legion came face to face with the foreign legion of Don Carlos, and in a furious exchange the two forces almost annihilated one another. Of the Carlist legion, only 160 men remained out of 875, with all their officers dead or wounded, and the casualties of the French Foreign Legion were comparable. In January 1839 the remnants of the Foreign Legion crossed the border into France, numbering 63 officers, 159 men and 75 mules.

Despite their heavy losses, the French Foreign Legion lives on, with battle honours won in wars waged on three continents.

CHAPTER FIVE

Journey and arrival in Spain: military discipline and first engagement

CHARLES THOMPSON'S LETTERS

One of those who sailed with the 1st Regiment was a 19-year-old Englishman, Charles Thompson, the son of General Thomas Thompson, whose letters to his parents in London formed the basis of his account, *Twelve months in the British Legion*, written under the pseudonym 'An officer of the Ninth Regiment'. (He later transferred from the 1st to the 9th in the re-organisation of 1836.) These and other letters, with those of Colonel Shaw and the more detailed accounts of Somerville, give some of the best descriptions of life in the Legion and the battles in which it fought. Thompson's letters convey the enthusiasm of a young man for the exotic surroundings in which he found himself and the immediacy of the excitement of battle. He urged his parents to keep his letters so that he could use them if he decided later to write a 'Xenophenetic history of the ten thousand'.

His first letter was written to his father on Sunday, 5 July 1836, from on board the *Royal Tar* in Plymouth harbour. The day had been eventful, with a mutiny at 5 a.m., soon after leaving harbour, by some of the men resentful at not having received their bounty money. This outbreak was put down quite easily by the officers. While the men were being paid later that morning the cry of 'Fire' was raised and smoke was seen rising from the main hatchway. The heat of the boiler had ignited the beams and planks nearby. All hands were put to the pumps and the ship returned to harbour for refitting. This was not a lengthy process, since the *Royal Tar* reached Spain on 10 July.

Thompson's first glimpse of Spain early in the morning was of the steep mountains of Navarre, which he mistook at first for dark masses of clouds. Gradually the castle of San Sebastian, its houses and lighthouse came into view, and half an hour later the ship entered the harbour, welcomed by a salute from the castle and the ringing of church bells (pls. 5, 7). A fleet of boats and other small craft came out to greet them loaded with men, women and children, and circled round and round the ship. The dark-eyed women with their mantillas, which he thought the most lovely of all headgear, impressed the young man: 'We were all delighted each with the other.' He would have sprung into the deep blue water and swum to the lovely *señoras* as they rowed slowly round the vessel, 'as if to inspect us on all sides'. Once ashore Thompson was appointed to act as an interpreter, since he was one of only three who confessed to any knowledge of Spanish. (The more mature Somerville, on his arrival in Santander in September, was much less impressed by the Spanish beauties, whom he described as short, dumpy, dun wenches, with a long plaited tail of hair hanging down their backs.)

A detachment of the 3rd Regiment or Westminster Grenadiers left the Isle of Dogs for Spain on 14 July. Some of the most critical comments were directed at these men, perhaps because of their association with Evans' parliamentary constituency. They were reviewed and addressed by Evans and General Alava, the Spanish ambassador, with advice regarding their behaviour in a strange country. A reporter for the Irish papers described them as a sorry looking set, 'with whom Jack Falstaff might have been ashamed to march through Coventry', whereas writers in the Radical press were more complimentary. The arrival in Santander of a further contingent of the 3rd Regiment under Colonel De Lancey, with a troop of Lancers under Captain Wingfield, was reported in August. They were conveyed by the East Indiaman, the *Lord Lynedoch*, which had a very tedious passage of fifteen days from London and narrowly escaped shipwreck on a cluster of rocks in thick fog.

The welcome that the Legion received in Spain, at least officially, was enthusiastic, though time would cool the relationship. Immediately after the first arrivals at San Sebastian, the correspondent of *The Times* reported the greatest harmony and fraternal feeling between the English and the Spaniards, who were walking around arm in arm. On 20 July a grand dinner was given in the Legion's honour in San Sebastian. The seat of honour was occupied by Brigadier-General Charles Chichester, the most senior of the Legion's officers in Spain at that time, and many Spanish Cristino officers, with some French naval officers and civilians in attendance. Portraits of the queen and queen regent decorated a throne of crimson damask, along with military trophies and Spanish banners. Spanish military bands played throughout the meal, which was punctuated by frequent toasts – 'To the Quadruple Alliance', 'To the King of the England',

'To the Queen of Spain', 'To the King of the French', 'To the Queen of Portugal', 'To the English and French Legions', 'To the Spanish Army', 'To the Urban Militia', 'To the Spanish, French and English Navies', 'To the Constitutional Nations of Western Europe', 'To the destruction of the Liberticide Faction' and 'To the progress of liberty and civilisation all over the world'. In a lighter vein a British officer gallantly proposed a toast 'to the dark-eyed beauties of romantic Spain'. Many who attended the dinner, with its celebration of Anglo-Spanish entente, must have looked back on it later with mixed feelings.

General Evans himself did not reach Spain until 17 August on the steamer *Queen Isabella* from Portsmouth. He had recently met his West-minster constituents at the Crown and Anchor in the Strand, London, to explain his views regarding his seat in Parliament, and could now devote himself entirely to his military command. He was accompanied to Spain by General Alava and some staff officers, Colonels Le Marchant, the adjutant-general, De Lancey, Considine (military secretary) and Captains Herman and Hall, as well as Mr Rutherford Alcock, staff-surgeon, and others. Evans' first sight of the Legion *en masse* was soon afterwards at Bilbao, where Somerville described the scene. Evans was the plainest dressed man among the gaudy staff officers who surrounded him. He looked more like a Spaniard than an Englishman, and closely resembled General Espartero, the Spanish commander, with whom collaboration was to prove so difficult. Comparison of portraits of the two men confirms their likeness.

Evans' arrival in Spain led to many unfavourable comments in the English press. The duke of Wellington, asked what he thought Evans would produce at San Sebastian, replied 'probably two volumes of octavo'. (Evans' actual written *oeuvre* only amounted to a single slim volume on the campaign.)

Many men of the Legion were quartered, both on arrival and later, in the disused convents from which the monks or nuns had been evicted. Thompson and most of those at San Sebastian were billeted in the convent of San Francisco, about half a mile outside the town. Though this struck him as very large, he was told by a Spaniard that it was one of the smallest in Spain. It was built as a square with cloisters around the interior, occupied by a garden now overgrown with weeds and briars. He reflected on the clam-our of the unruly and riotous soldiers in the stairs and passages where quiet monks had earlier walked 'with the missals and Acts of the Apostles'. The ornate chapel was locked to prevent the soldiers from entering. Thompson's main discomfort at this time was from the bites of fleas, which though smaller than English fleas, bit harder, so that he was bitten all over and looked as if he had the smallpox or measles. General Chichester was nonetheless pleased with the convent as quarters for his men since, with no taverns in its immediate vicinity, it was much easier to attend to their discipline and training.

In Santander the 10th Regiment were content with their quarters in the convent of Corban, which Alexander Ball believed could have contained the whole Legion in perfect comfort. A private from Limerick wrote that it was 'the first convent that Buonaparte ever robbed'; he found that food was plentiful and a pint of wine could be bought for threepence. Ensign Ball had been disconcerted to find that there were not half a dozen Protestants in the whole regiment besides himself, which is likely to have been an underestimate. The whole corps attended Mass on Sundays in the small chapel in the convent. Ball noted, with mixed feelings, the activities of a Spanish friar who blessed the men, saying that *los Irlandeses* were Christians even though enemies of Charles V.

The men made extraordinary progress in their drill, though discontent over pay was already leading to insubordination, which became much worse when the regiment had marched to Olaveaga and were inspected by General MacDougall. The cry of 'Pay, pay' from the ranks prompted the general to flog one man as an example, but when Colonel Maurice O'Connell explained that they had been three days without rations MacDougall relented, saying that he had never known men serve three days without rations before. He assured them he would take good care this should never happen again, threatening to 'hang the Quartermaster, shoot the Commissary and strangle the Contractors' for such neglect of duty. It seemed the rations had been sent in error to Portugalete. MacDougall was to continue to do all in his power to supply the needs of the Legion in the increasingly hard times to come.

Discipline was a major problem for the officers in the Legion. Already mutinous behaviour had broken out on board the *Royal Tar* and had been contained by firm action. Now, in a foreign country, with hostile forces nearby and with inexperienced men unused to military discipline, and with the need for the instant and unquestioning obedience to orders which obtains in all armies, it was imperative to instil these principles into what otherwise would be a rabble at the mercy of any enemy. Many of the soldiers had no idea of what they had undertaken, the concept Sir John Hackett later described as the 'unlimited liability' clause being unknown to them. They had to learn the hard way, and they did.

A special correspondent of *The Times* who had joined the first levies of the Legion at San Sebastian on 14 July complained that the men were being too well treated and was critical of their having been paid their bounty money, and of the effect of so much cash on those who had probably never had such wealth. He believed that this contributed to a mutinous spirit which had sprung up among them, leading them to abuse their officers, in particular an episode in which a man had assaulted his major, who had been forced in self-defence to cut him down. Despite this, 'the man had again rushed at the major, down some steps and coming against his sword, it entered his abdomen, and he fell to the ground apparently dead'. His wound, however, had not proved fatal. It was hoped he would recover. General Chichester, aware of the misrepresentations which might arise from the affair, at once set up a court of enquiry and put the major on trial, which led to his acquittal and had a salutary effect on the men.

Somerville, no stranger himself to strict military discipline, describes the punishment of a Highlander who, while drunk, struck and severely injured an officer. It was clear that, if such incidents were not dealt with vigorously, there would be no hope of discipline in the regiment, and Colonel Godfrey, a regular officer who was in command, acted forcefully. With the full panoply of martial law the offender was flogged at the triangle, receiving two hundred lashes, murmurs of complaint which rose from his comrades being stifled by Godfrey's threatening stance. The lesson was learnt and discipline thereafter was maintained with greater ease. Floggings were awarded from time to time, and perhaps overzealously by some junior officers, but Evans, though sometimes pilloried by his political opponents for his severity, was also often criticised by his own officers and men for being too lenient.

Drilling and training were the first priority of the Legion, and occupied all ranks for many hours each day. Thompson, in the garrison of San Sebastian, was drilled with all the other young officers of the 1st Regiment in the manoeuvres which in a more normal situation he and his men would have learned on the parade grounds of Britain. Each day the troops drilled for eight or nine hours in two sessions.

Social life also had its place, and Thompson wrote of the Grand Ball his regiment gave to the inhabitants of the city in return for their generous entertainment. Shortly afterwards Evans and his staff arrived in San Sebastian by sea from Santander. Travel by land was out of the question, since the intervening country was controlled by the Carlists, and the Tory press mocked Evans, the 'Sea-General', for his inability to subdue the Carlist forces who, outside the towns and cities, enjoyed all the advantages of lightly armed troops able to operate in difficult but familiar and friendly territory. In such conditions the Chapelgorris, the irregular Cristino troops, with their motto 'War even to the knife', highly mobile skirmishers capable of rapid movement in mountainous terrain, were more appropriate opponents to the Carlist soldiers. Thompson was impressed by the Chapelgorris, whose Basque name means 'red caps', referring to the distinctive headgear which marked them off from their Carlist enemies, the Chapelchurries, in their white caps.* Lightly armed, unencumbered by traditional heavy uniform such as the Legion wore, and shod in hemp-soled sandals or *alpargatas,* with a pouch slung round their waists instead of a heavy knapsack, they were far more fitted for irregular warfare than the Legionaries. Writing in late August, Thompson described the two sallies which his regiment had already made in the mountains; he concluded that all the 'field movements' they had learned would be 'as useless to us as if it were to have Taglioni and Perrot to teach us opera dances'. When carrying only their muskets and forty rounds of ammunition, the men were quite exhausted on their scramble among the hills that was designed as an exercise or field day. If the Carlists had been there, Thompson believed, they would all have been picked off like so many sparrows. How, he wondered, would they have managed with 60lbs, four times their present load, to carry?

The Legion had its first experience of war on 30 August, soon after these comments were written, when the 1st, 2nd and 3rd Regiments were in action, together with a body of Spanish Cristino troops, in an attack on the Venta hill, a Carlist strongpoint about four miles from San Sebastian, which was to be the target of later attacks and finally fell to the queen's forces in 1837. The 7th Regiment under Lieutenant-Colonel Dixon were also present, but not engaged. The exercise was intended as a reconnais-

---

* Contemporary British chroniclers of the war, such as Thompson and Somerville, refer to the Chapelgorris as Cristinos and the Chapelchurries as Carlist soldiers. However, coloured illustrations of the period depict Carlist irregulars in red hats and Cristinos in white. Two dictionaries of the late nineteenth and early twentieth century define both groups as irregular soldiers of Don Carlos (*Encyclopedia Universal Illustrada Europeo-Americano,* vol. 6 and Zerolo's *Dicionario Enciclopedico de la Lengua Castellana*) – but the latter adds that a body of Chapelgorris served in the army of Isabella. It seems appropriate to continue to use these opposing terms in the sense in which they were used by these English writers. Certainly any legionary who mistook a 'redcap' for a Cristino would have been in mortal danger.

sance to see what progress the enemy had made with their entrenchments, but the Carlists under General Gomez, by abandoning their positions, drew the Cristino force further on than was intended, and then turned and attacked them, driving them back.

Writing years later, in 1866, Cornet Henderson of the 1st Lancers was critical of Evans for sending untried men into action and sending them in pursuit of the fugitive Carlists. With a cavalryman's rather scornful attitude to the infantry, he wrote:

> Boldly the little Legion recruits trotted down the hill after the enemy, cheered on by their officers, all full of pluck. The Carlists retreated almost to the gates of Hernani, and then turned at bay, with a rattling volley of musketry, then fixed bayonets and charged the advancing Cristinos. Both the Spanish and English were seized with panic and a regular stampede ensued – a little Bull Run. The Carlists easily outran their less fleet opponents and slaughtered the poor Legion recruits without mercy.

The action became known as 'the Hernani races'. The British and Spanish troops only regained San Sebastian after sustaining heavy fire and some loss.

The *Cork Evening Herald* of 3 September reported the casualties. Four British officers were wounded including General Chichester, whose wound was slight; 21 men were wounded and four killed in battle while four were missing, captured by the Carlists and later shot in accordance with the Durango Decree, which was by now being almost universally put into practice by the enemy. Casualties of the Spanish Cristinos were much heavier, five officers and 88 men being killed and six men wounded. Among the severely wounded officers was Assistant-Surgeon Dade of the 1st Regiment, who was repatriated. An act of gallantry by Ensign Knight, Chichester's ADC, was noted. Staying on the hill when the rest of the Legion had retreated, he tried to carry off on his back a soldier with a broken leg. The Carlists fired several shots and he was forced to leave the injured man to his fate – to be butchered five minutes later. Knight was promoted to lieutenant on the field. This first experience of battle was not what the men of the Legion had expected. The drill and manoeuvres they had learned proved quite unhelpful in the face of such 'unsporting' behaviour.

Much comment in the British Tory press on this action was highly critical and satirical. It was hailed as a great Carlist victory and a shameful defeat for British arms. One report wrote that the people of the Isle of Dogs (the 3rd Regiment or Westminster Grenadiers) had made a sortie from San Sebastian with a view to possess themselves of the town of Hernani. 'It was thought that the quarters of San Sebastian were better suited to the constitutional combatants than those at Hernani, and, accordingly, they retraced their steps without giving the young recruits, as far as we can learn, the benefits of a practical lesson in "ordinary time".' It could be said, in their defence, that most of the Legion's men were indeed raw and inexperienced recruits, exposed for the first time to powder and shot. Their performance in later engagements was far more soldierly and creditable.

There had been great concern in the Legion about the Durango Decree, unallayed by anodyne comments in Parliament. Thompson and no doubt most others had soon realised that it was indeed being implemented and that prisoners were being shot. News of the shooting of the four British prisoners quickly spread. The Spaniards avenged their executed comrades by shooting a larger number of Carlist prisoners. The Eliot Convention now seemed a dead letter. There is no evidence that the Legion retaliated by shooting its prisoners, although in the heat of battle there may have been exceptions. The soldiers of the French Legion were officially instructed by order of General Bernelle, their commander, on three separate occasions, of their certain fate if captured, and of the consequent need to sell their lives dearly rather than surrender and so risk a thousand tortures before being put to death. Certainly many of the British Legion were later shot or more barbarously put to death when captured by the Carlists, and these atrocities could not fail to fuel the desire to avenge their murdered mates.

Colonel Shaw, who had recruited the three Scottish regiments of the Legion, the 5th, 6th and 8th, and believed he had been promised the rank of brigadier-general and commander of the brigade, found himself at Portugalete on the estuary north of Bilbao with command of the 8th Highlanders (Somerville's regiment) and the 9th Irish Regiment, following reorganisation of the Legion. He considered the Basque peasantry to be Carlists and inimical to a man, and lost five men while on the march, picked off while straggling.

Towards the end of September the Legion began to concentrate at Bilbao, where medical examination showed that at least one eighth of their total strength were unfit for military duties. Most of these were not sent home but stayed with the Legion, and were to suffer disproportionately high morbidity and mortality in the epidemic which attacked them in the coming winter in Vitoria. The stronger soldiers were fit and reasonably healthy, having benefited from their vigorous drills and exercises. In mid-September the agents of the queen of Spain received orders from General Evans to recruit three thousand more men for the Legion as soon as possible and forward them direct to Spain.

Thompson, now promoted to lieutenant, found Bilbao an attractive city, but so crowded that he had difficulty in finding even a modest billet. His personal camp bed saved him from exposure to the fleas in the straw beds that were all that was available to most. His social connections assured him *entrée* to higher military society and a place at Evans' dinner table.

The Carlists, after their failure in July with the death during the siege of Bilbao of General Zumalacárregui, seemed for the time being to have given up their attempts to capture Bilbao, though they would renew their attack later. Thompson wondered whether the Legion would winter in San Sebastian or in Vitoria, the capital of Alava province, and hoped it would be in the latter as he was keen to get further south. Had he known what the coming winter in Vitoria would bring, he might have changed his mind, but the choice of Vitoria had been made in order that the Legion could collaborate with General Córdova, the Cristino general in that region.

CHAPTER SIX

The march to Vitoria

Vitoria lies about thirty-five miles from Bilbao as the crow flies, but much further by the primitive roads of the time, through difficult mountainous country. General Córdova planned to assemble a force of 20,000 men at Vitoria. It would have been too dangerous for the Legion to march there directly through Carlist-held territory. Instead, it was planned that they should march westwards out of the Basque provinces via a circuitous route through Old Castile (see Map 1).

In late October and early November the bulk of the Legion moved out of Bilbao, the Artillery and the Lancers remaining at Santander for the time being. Lieutenant Edward Costello of the Rifle Corps described the regiments' march to Vitoria. Leaving the coast they followed a lengthy route of some sixty leagues (about 180 miles) at a cracking pace, often marching twenty miles a day, and spending three weeks at Briviesca, a small town on the plains of Old Castile, some forty-five miles south-west of Vitoria. The Rifles were drilled there, though Costello thought that light infantry manoeuvres would have been more useful, and persuaded his colonel to issue the men with blank cartridges and to exercise them in sham fighting. They left behind them in Briviesca two large hospitals full of sick men, since typhus and other diseases had already begun to claim many victims. Costello wrote with gallows humour of the spectre of very sick soldiers riding on donkeys and, later, in the pass of Pancorbo, was overcome by emotion in revisiting the scenes of the fighting twenty years earlier in the Peninsular War, in which he himself had taken part.

Major Gilbert Hogg of the 8th Scotch, who had fought in Portugal and had been involved in recruiting for the regiment in Glasgow, gave details in his diary of the route they followed, with an abortive start on 1 November and a return to base. They covered the distance to Vitoria in twelve stages including a stay in Briviesca where they, too, left many sick and some dead behind them. Accommodation for men and officers on the route was often primitive and provisions were short, while the weather conditions steadily worsened.

Both Alexander Somerville of the 8th, and Lieutenant Thompson of the 1st Regiment remained behind their units and only joined them some time later. Somerville had been promoted to sergeant in the Grenadier Company by Colonel Godfrey, his commanding officer, but having sustained a bayonet wound to an arm in a fracas between an unpopular NCO and some legionaries, he was sent to Santander with the baggage-train, only rejoining his regiment some months and many privations later. In Santander he found appalling conditions, with very poor accommodation and with sick men left for days without food or medical help, until relieved by boats from the British naval sloop *Ringdove*. Later he moved to Astelero, where over two hundred women and children, dependants mainly of the Irish regiments,* with over a thousand men crowded the village, most of them quartered in the convent of Corban. More men were arriving daily, deserters and stragglers, some with plunder and others who had been robbed. The situation was chaotic; baggage stores were pillaged by men of the Legion and sold to the Carlists, and discipline had almost broken down. New detachments of recruits from Britain joined the thousand or more housed in the convent. These were from various regiments and included the whole of the 2nd Lancers, newly arrived from Cork and still unmounted.

Some of the fitter men were put to work on roadworks and Somerville, in charge of working parties from various units, found that the Irish soldiers were the best for hard work and cheerfulness in adversity. He called on 'all the Pats, Barneys and Mikes' that he could get to fall in with him. Their positive approach to hard work, with a better standard of health, was a theme referred to later in the grim conditions in Vitoria by Dr Alcock, now Assistant Inspector of Hospitals, and other officers.

In early December orders came for the baggage-train with the artillery and about two hundred men to leave Santander for Vitoria. Somerville marched with them and described their difficulties. The train was robbed by the Spanish bullock-cart drivers and their accomplices so that all but nine of 250 shirts were stolen. Some Irishwomen and children accompanied the troop, and Somerville reported the deaths of an Irishwoman and her young child from sickness after being denied help by the colonel and medical officers. Bad as conditions were for the men, they must have been yet worse for the women and children.

---

* Despite strenuous efforts to prevent them, many wives with their children had insisted on following their menfolk.

On 16 December his detachment reached Briviesca, where earlier the main body of the Legion had spent three weeks. Here they had their first taste of the grim weather, with daily rain or snow, which would last for the next few months. With inadequate bedding, winter clothing and shelter, their miserable conditions were as bad as 'the worst hovels in Ireland' and Dr Alcock believed that the seeds were sown there of 'the disease so shortly destined to thin our ranks'. When the main body of the Legion left Briviesca about three hundred sick men remained behind.

Somerville himself now became ill and was forced to stay in Briviesca with twenty-five of his comrades. Fever had broken out with high mortality, and only fifty or sixty of the whole group survived to join their regiments. At first Somerville was nursed by a fellow Scot, a Highlander, who then fell ill himself and died. So hostile to the Legion were the townspeople that his burial was achieved only by a ruse, when the corpse of a Spaniard was dressed in the red coat of the dead legionary, leading to its removal from the grave and, eventually, to the provision of a burial ground for the English.

The so-called hospital was crowded with the sick, and most of the medical officers were themselves ill. Mr Greenwood, a surgeon of the 4th Regiment, did what he could for the patients, but had very limited medical supplies. The hostility of the pro-Carlist citizens was aggravated by the disgraceful conduct of three subalterns and a commissary of the Legion, whose quarrelling nearly led to a duel. Three of these officers were later marched as prisoners to Vitoria; one ensign was to die in the battle of 5 May 1836, and another was dismissed the service in February that year and later deserted to the Carlists.

To his great vexation the young Lieutenant Thompson, eager for action, was also ordered to stay behind in Santander 'with traps and wives of the soldiers', while his regiment marched away. He spent several unhappy weeks there and wrote from the convent of Corban on 24 November reporting a rumour that General Evans' baggage, which Thompson had brought from Portugalete, had been captured by the Carlists, together with a lieutenant and twenty men deputed to escort it to Vitoria. Happily the rumour proved false, like many circulating at that time of anxiety and uncertainty. Thompson was happy finally to leave Santander and to reach Vitoria on 7 December after a wearisome journey of thirteen days, and was overjoyed to rejoin his regiment, having become sick and tired of looking after the impedimenta and being bothered with the compaints of vociferous soldiers' wives. His journey took him and his men through high mountain passes and to Burgos and Briviesca, but his stay there was briefer than Somerville's and his health better, though he was attacked by 'a sort of cholera or dysentery' which forced him to travel by mule-cart.

CHAPTER SEVEN

The city of death

The advance guard of the Legion entered Vitoria on 3 December to an enthusiastic welcome arranged by General Córdova. Over the town gate on the Miranda road a globe was erected, decorated with the flags of Britain, France, Spain and Portugal, inscribed: 'The generous British who fight for the freedom of the nations'. Cristino troops lined the streets and their regimental bands played martial music as Evans rode into the city.

When Thompson reached Vitoria a little later with his smaller group, he was warmly welcomed by the officers and men of his regiment in view of his rumoured capture. Epidemic disease was drastically thinning the ranks of the Legion.

In January 1836 Vitoria was described as a city of death. 'For some time we have been burying 6 to 8 soldiers each day.' An anonymous account by a Legionary published in 1837 in Scarborough reported that 'the hospitals were soon full with sick English soldiers, and the scenes which occurred in the city were the last word in horror and warranted the descriptions usually reserved for the Great Plague in London. From morning till night the oxcarts bore load after load of corpses, which were piled naked, one on top of the other without any assistance of a ceremony.' The bodies were buried at first in the city's cemetery, but soon the authorities decreed that the dead should be buried in the gardens of the convents they had occupied.

By the time Somerville finally reached the city at the end of January the situation had deteriorated further. He was greeted as a ghost since he too had been reported dead at Santander. Colonel Godfrey hailed him, 'Why Somerville, you're dead! Go to Captain Shields and get something to eat, but by G-d, don't let the men eat you: damn you, if you are living now, you'll be dead tomorrow. Everyone's dying.' The state of the Legion in Vitoria was indeed dire; Somerville wrote that the misery he had seen among a few hundred in Briviesca was now extended among ten thousand men.

Death had reduced the Legion's numbers to well below the original ten thousand. Although *The Times* of 23 January stated that the number of effective men now in the field with Evans was 8,500, and that the army was reported to be in high spirits, this was quite untrue, as Godfrey's comments showed and many contemporary reports confirm. Vitoria had become a charnelhouse, the typhus first noted in Briviesca having become a raging epidemic, with high morbidity and mortality among officers and men. In February the Legion's effective strength had fallen to 7,784 and on 1 March the adjutant-general's return showed only 5,763 'total bayonets fit for service'. On 28 February *The Times* reported that 22 officers had died since 14 January, besides a great number of men. A letter of 27 February from Vitoria to the *Courier* recorded:

> The 'destroying angel' does his work fearfully fast, and many a gay and gallant officer has been cut down by his fell swoop ere well aware of his approach. His ravages in the medical department have been terrible; of 30 doctors 10 or 12 are already dead. Some lie dangerously ill, others are slowly recovering, and of the small number now performing duty the majority, I think, have had the fever. Of four doctors who came passengers with me from England, one (the Inspector-General)* has the Walcheren fever,† one has died of the fever which now rages, and the other two have been at death's door, and now cannot be said to be out of danger.

Four of the twelve medical officers in the three Irish regiments died of typhus. Assistant-Surgeon Morgan O'Connell of the 10th wrote to his brother of the death of his colleague Dr M. Grove after an illness of eleven days. Not less than 1,300 men had been affected and many were in hospital.

LIVING AND DYING CONDITIONS OF THE LEGION

The accommodation provided for the Legion, apart from the early days in San Sebastian, was far below the standard expected and needed for an army committed to a lengthy campaign. The disused convents in which they were generally quartered had not been adapted in any way for their new secular function. The supply of food was often inadequate and intermit-

---

* John Callender MD, whose wife and daughter died and were buried below the Castle at San Sebastian, where their tomb may still be seen (September 2001).
† This term probably described a form of malaria.

tent. The Legion's commissariat in its earlier months was woefully deficient, and Wellington's comments about the problems of supplying an army in a poor country proved well-founded. The first quartermaster-general was widely regarded as ineffectual – though he had a near-impossible task – and his replacement in February 1836 by Brigadier Duncan MacDougall was welcomed by all.

The detailed comments of Alexander Ball on the commissariat help to explain the reasons for its continuous deficiencies. Its formation had been, most unwisely, entrusted entirely to the Spanish government, he wrote, so that 'the important Department was almost necessarily in a most inefficient state'. The Spanish authorities in London had promised that on arrival in Spain the Legion would find ample stores and experienced field commissaries ready for their reception, so that they need only take from Britain a commissary staff for the account branch. As a result only seven officers and twenty clerks left England, and of these only three had any experience in their duties. On Ball's arrival in Bilbao not the slightest trace of stores or a commissariat could be found. The money intended for paying the troops had therefore to be spent on provisions, and the gentlemen intended for the account department were ordered to the field, most of them utterly unacquainted with their new duties, the country and its language. Worse still, in Ball's view, a Spaniard was put in charge of the commissary department. Under the British government the commissariat for a force such as the Legion would have consisted of at least 30 experienced officers and from 80 to 100 clerks.

Though an attractive town, Vitoria in 1836 (pls. 2, 8), with 15,500 inhabitants, was not suitable as winter quarters for a large army and could not cope with the influx of thousands of men in addition to the Cristino Spanish and French troops already in billets. The treatment of the Legion compared very unfavourably with that of the French or Algerine Legion under General Bernelle (which had marched all the way from the south of Spain), and the Spanish troops who were already billeted on the inhabitants of the city. Bernelle had insisted on proper accommodation for his men, threatening to march them back into France if their comforts were not attended to. Evans, by contrast, had no such bargaining power.

When the Legion entered Vitoria in the heavy rain typical of that season in northern Spain, arrangements for their quartering had not been completed. They were assigned to various empty convents and churches as their barracks, where the religious imagery and aura of ancient sanctity in no way compensated for the lack of basic necessities, and probably displeased the Protestant English and Scots. The provision of 'ablution' facilities and fresh water for so many men must have presented almost insuperable difficulties, as did the preparation and cooking of their food, the regular supply of which could not be relied on. Floorboards or flagstones formed their beds for most of the Legion. Blankets were few and their uniform, while suitable for the summer months, proved totally inappropriate for a winter of exceptionally heavy rain, snow and freezing temperatures. Foreign Office despatches of the period contain repeated pleas for the supply of blankets, tents, hospital stores and surgical instruments; little sense of urgency seems to have existed in London about meeting these requests. (Requests which poured in for the supply of armaments, gunpowder and clothing for the Cristino army seem to have been more sympathetically met; a request, however, for 100,000 muskets for the queen of Spain's army did elicit the sceptical query as to whether this number of muskets was really necessary.)

The three Scotch regiments, the 5th, 6th and 8th, of which Somerville had the most detailed knowledge, suffered very badly that winter, though less severely than the English regiments. The 5th Scotch, about six hundred strong, 'went to pieces and tumbled, by sections, into an inglorious grave, or was gnawed and eaten by rats and vermin, before its dead men could be buried'. Their home was a foul, damp convent, which had lain in ruins since Joseph Bonaparte was in Spain. The 6th Scotch suffered much less, but its men lost at Vitoria were numbered by the hundred, while two-thirds of the survivors were, for a time, prostrated by the epidemic. The 8th Highlanders, in which Somerville served, lost fewer men, 'but, out of 800, which it once numbered, we could not muster over 250 effective men in January 1836, the remainder being down with fever, dysentery, hunger, frost-bitten feet and – most horrible of all – eaten, until there were holes in their bodies, by vermin'. They occupied another old convent, as large as the Manchester Infirmary, nearly roofless, with no windows and no doors. They had only six beds for the whole company of eighty men, and gave these to the sick, as far as they would go. The men were largely condemned to sleeping in their wet clothing, with their greatcoats as cover. Fleas, lice and rats, those inevitable companions of large groups of people living in close proximity in unhygienic conditions, added to their discomfort and – more importantly – to the risk of disease.*

---

* Describing the conditions in Vitoria, an anonymous 'veteran' wrote in the *United Service*

MacDougall, the new quartermaster-general, was appalled by the conditions in which the men and officers of the Legion were living and dying. His memorandum of 4 March 1836, which with other papers was laid before Parliament in 1838, records their privations and progressive decline in health. From their arrival in Vitoria on 3 December, they were left entirely without blankets until the 16th, when three thousand were issued, enough for one man in four. On 6 January a few more were issued, but these had to be sent to the hospitals. MacDougall was highly critical of the Spanish authorities' failure to supply the bedding and blankets they had promised. He listed the steady increase in the numbers of sick and deaths from 3 December to 24 February, the sick rising from one hundred to a peak of 1,055 and deaths totalling 565. With all his thirty-two years' experience as a soldier, he wrote, he could not believe, had he not seen it himself, the state of the Legion, in respect to moral conduct and discipline, in men collected together within a few months from the plough and the workshop, and who were already nearly three months in arrears of pay.

In the midst of the miseries of Vitoria attempts were made to keep up some traditions of a more civilised nature. Plays were staged in the city's theatre, and many officers would ride out each night from Vitoria, when the performance ended, to rejoin their regiments at the outposts, risking attack by the Carlist cavalry. Among the pieces presented were a French work, *Des Circonstances*, and a play called *Charles II*, put on as a compliment to the English.

Christmas was celebrated by those well enough to enjoy the pleasures of the table with what food could be found. Major John Richardson of the 6th Regiment, who was appointed commandant in Vitoria, kept Christmas Day 1835 'with all the festivity peculiar to our ancestors, with wine and charity in abundance, to drink to a better feeling on the part of the Tories'. The spirits of the revellers were raised by the arrival that evening of a number of deserters from the enemy. Food was still available to those who could pay for it, as shown by Richardson's wry comments about the turkey

Journal in 1836 of the 'strenuous exertions made in England to fill up the chasm which sickness had made in the ranks. Receiving houses were opened in different parts of the country, placards posted, and men even liberated from the jails on condition of their entering the service.' He cites the case of a gang of resurrectionists (grave-robbers) committed to Newgate in Dublin for trial. 'These men were discharged from prison to join the British Auxiliaries of the Queen of Spain, their characters being too bad to be received into the English army!'

which should have formed the basis of his dinner. Aware of the English mania for turkey at Christmas, many of the local peasants had fattened up their birds and planned to take them to market in Vitoria. The Carlists, however, had decided to make their dinner off them instead, so that some substitute must have been found. Charles Shaw also dined on Christmas Day with thirty of his old Pedroite comrades-in-arms.

The dying did not stop for the Christmas festivities. On Christmas Eve, Major Robert Dundas of the 7th Regiment died of fever, and on New Year's Eve Captain J. Havelock of the 5th.

Richardson, who had secured palatial accommodation for himself for 'little more than one shilling and six pence English', with ten rooms, seven closets, beds for two servants and stabling for two horses, fell victim to typhus soon afterwards, and was unconscious for nine days. He referred on recovering to the long hiatus in his journal; 'thank God, it is not an eternal one'. He attributed his attack to mixing much with the convalescents in his capacity as commandant; his successor in the post died a few days later, though he had been in perfect health.

DESERTION FROM THE LEGION:
THE BAKER AND SUSPECTED POISONING

A further drain on the Legion's strength was caused by desertion to the enemy. In Vitoria that winter, with disease, inadequate food, arrears of pay and harsh housing and weather conditions, the grass outside the city walls must have appeared much greener. Don Carlos actively and successfully encouraged desertion by financial rewards, offering £10 to each deserter, and there were many takers. Sergeants were highly valued, especially if they brought men and weapons, and were usually given commissions. The Carlists were estimated to have formed two companies composed of ex-legionaries. Carlos also formed his own 'French Foreign Legion', four hundred strong, from deserters from the French Legion. It was suggested, and seems credible, that some men of the Legion may have committed suicide rather than continue their miserable existence.

With the increasing sickness after Christmas 1836 a rumour developed, firmly believed by many, that one of the city's bakers was poisoning their bread. This was linked with an episode involving would-be deserters whose escape from Vitoria was dramatically thwarted, as reported later in *The*

Times. A quartermaster sergeant of the 7th Irish Regiment named Richardson had gone over to the enemy in February 1836 and been commissioned. He wrote to his nephew, Sergeant Nangles of the same regiment, who was sick in hospital, to persuade him to follow his example, stressing the good treatment and food, and the regular pay he enjoyed in the Carlist army. He wrote that a baker named José de Elosegui would help him to desert. Nangles, however, felt more loyalty to the Legion than to his uncle, and showed the letter to the regiment's paymaster, Captain Byrne. Elosegui, who supplied the Legion's bread, was now incriminated in encouraging their desertion, and Byrne planned to trap him. Nangles approached the baker and showed him the letter, asking for his help to leave the city, and was offered a guide for that very night. On the pretext that he would bring with him a sergeant and six privates the following night, Nangles deferred the appointment. The baker promised to write letters of introduction to the Carlist general, which would ensure the deserters commissioned rank. General Evans was informed and a plan made to arrest Elosegui *in flagrante*. Byrne, disguised as a sergeant, accompanied Nangles to the baker's house the next night to meet the guide. Together they went to the city gates, where the pretended deserters arrested the guide. Two officers then went to the baker's house, arrested him and took him to General Córdova, who handed him over to be dealt with by a military tribunal. Córdova, like others, had suspected poisoning of the bread, and arranged for it to be analysed, also ordering the arrest of the contractors for meat and wine. The charge of poisoning was never proved and, despite the rumours that oxalic acid or white lead had been mixed with the bread, it seems that the suspicions were unfounded. Dr Alcock doubted that poisoning was involved. The bread was certainly of very poor quality, imperfectly kneaded and baked, forming a mass of black and heavy dough 'calculated to puzzle the digestion of an ostrich', and he thought this may have been enough to cause illness, though he also mentioned the gangrene which poisoned rye may induce (referring to ergotism) and wondered whether some harmful effect of bad corn might not produce a similar disease. Major Richardson, who had survived his attack of typhus after nine days of unconsciousness, did not believe that the epidemic was due to poisoning, but rather to 'honest, downright typhus', while Sergeant Somerville argued astutely that poison would have killed as many of the Irish troops as of the English.

Whether poisoners or not, Elosegui and his assistant were condemned to death for having helped deserters, and were executed by garrotting in the Plaza Vieja of Vitoria before a large and enthusiastic audience of citizens, Spanish soldiers and the Legion. A sum of 500,000 rials (£5,000 sterling) had been offered by his friends to spare his life, but the offer was refused. Two Legion officers commented approvingly that no women were present at the execution, which they thought would not have been the case in Britain.

Another baker was later publicly bastinadoed for issuing bread of 'a very deleterious composition' to the troops, who clearly retained their suspicions. These were strengthened when the number of deaths from illness in the Legion dropped to a trickle after the execution, but it is likely that this was a chance association and that the epidemic was declining spontaneously. The executions probably had a salutary effect on men tempted to desert.

On 2 January of the new year the Spanish Minister of War, Count Almodóvar, held a grand levée for those officers of the Legion well enough to attend. He told them that the queen regent had intended to visit them, but had been prevented by severe weather. Cristina's decision may have been prompted by fear of the epidemic raging in Vitoria. Had she come to the city and contracted typhus, the outcome of the war might have been different.

The efforts of MacDougall and Colonel Wylde, the senior English commissioner, to persuade the Spanish government to supply the arrears of pay due to the Legion and to provide regular supplies as promised were unsuccessful. Lack of funds tempted many men to sell their uniform, boots or trousers to the Spaniards for what small sums they could get, and to draw replacements from the quartermaster, the cost being debited against their future pay. Some soldiers cheated the Spanish shopkeepers by fashioning 'coins' from the buttons of their greatcoats.

The burial of the many dead of the Legion was hampered by the lack of wood for coffins, since this was in great demand as fuel for heating and cooking. At first military funerals were provided, with fife-and-drum bands playing the *Dead March in Saul*, but soon the overwhelming numbers prevented any attempt at ceremony and corpses were piled into carts to be taken to the burial grounds and tipped into a common grave. The frozen ground made it difficult to dig a deep enough grave and burial details were unpopular with the men. For the Spanish dead the situation was different; the funeral procession of an officer would include military bands and priests with lighted candles, where there seems to have been no official provision made for the religious needs of the Legion. Irish and other Catholic soldiers could have sought help from the Spanish clergy, but might have met problems of communication and perhaps of hostility towards the foreigners. It was only in October 1836 that a Spanish priest was appointed as chaplain to the Hospital but, as the Order Book specified, 'without the Pay and allowances attached to that rank'. Don Joaquín must have been kept very busy administering the last rites to the dying.

DR RUTHERFORD ALCOCK AND THE MEDICAL STAFF
OF THE LEGION; THE TYPHUS EPIDEMIC

The Legion was blessed in its senior medical officer, Rutherford Alcock, then Deputy Inspector-General of Hospitals, a position he had occupied in the earlier Portuguese war, where he had gained wide experience both of the typhus now raging in the ranks and of military surgery. He shared the concern of MacDougall, Colonel Wylde and others over the harsh conditions suffered by the army in Vitoria. His short book, published in 1838, on the medical history and statistics of the British Legion in Spain gives interesting details of the epidemic of typhus and the varying morbidity among different brigades. Nearly one-third of the English brigade, 'sickly Londoners, or men recruited in Liverpool and Bristol, accustomed to the enervating life of a large city', was swept into the hospitals with great rapidity – 'the Scotch next, about one-fifth* – and the Irish in a comparatively moderate proportion, probably not more than an eighth'.

Dr Alcock found the Irish undoubtedly physically and morally the best adapted for the service. Superior health among the Irish troops had been noted in the Peninsular War in Wellington's army.

Similar comments on the Irish were made by Colonel Shaw, who was loud in their praises when he assumed their command, and by Somerville, who found them resilient in the heart-breaking conditions of Vitoria. Alcock's statistics included the returns of the General Military Hospitals of the Legion over the 22 to 23 months of their service; 13,407 cases were admitted, with 1,588 deaths, giving a mortality of about one in 8.5 of the

---

* Somerville records that seven sergeants in his own Grenadier Company of the 8th Scotch Regiment died.

total treated, or, presuming the total force disembarked in Spain to be 9,600, a loss in hospital of one in six of the whole force.

Alcock also described the problems of providing medical cover to the Legion in Vitoria and elsewhere as the number of doctors dwindled with death and disease more rapidly than the combatant personnel. The many small hospitals needed more staff than would larger ones; Vitoria had several general hospitals, while every regiment had some sick men in its cantonments. Between January and April 1836 11 medical officers died and 17 lay seriously ill in Vitoria alone, leaving only 23 to service the whole Legion. Four of the 12 MOs in the Irish regiments died 'by fever'. Units based in outlying towns and villages such as Trevino had their quota of invalids housed in churches or other buildings, some of whom were brought into Vitoria. Captain Meller of the 10th was ordered to escort three wagon-loads of sick men and officers from the church of Trevino into the city.

Typhus, the cause of the widespread epidemic, was very familiar to Alcock and to most British and European doctors. Now recognised as due to an organism of the group Rickettsia, named after their discoverer, Howard Taylor Ricketts,* its cause was then unknown. It affects the small blood vessels, which are extensively damaged by Rickettsial invasion. Vessels of the brain and skin are especially liable to attack, explaining the prominent delirium and stupor, and the typical spotted rash. It is closely asssociated with the louse, which bites the infected patient, swallowing his blood containing the Rickettsiae, which then invade the cells lining the insect's gut. They multiply within these cells, which become swollen and ultimately burst, entering its gut and passing out with its faeces. If the louse migrates to another human host, as happens particularly when the first host has died, the cycle is continued as the Rickettsiae penetrate his skin, often being inoculated by scratching, which may also crush the louse on the skin of the new host, rupturing its intestinal cells with their teeming organisms.

Typhus was to be a scourge in the Irish famine some ten years later, and some of those who survived the epidemic in Spain and returned home probably fell victim to it in their native land. The disease was also endemic throughout Europe, with a penchant for killing medical men.

Alcock described the usual course of the disease in the objective style of most medical descriptions of disease. For some days the patient would

---

* Ricketts himself died of typhus contracted accidentally.

feel a sensation of lassitude, often with nausea or vomiting, with pain in the head and sometimes also down the spine. Diarrhoea was common. This preliminary stage, lasting on average two to five days, would render the victim incapable of work, when he would report sick. Delirium quickly ensued, often followed by rapid decline with death from the tenth to the twentieth day.

A modern textbook of tropical diseases (Schull, 1999) states that after the second week, those who have not died usually improve slowly. Today treatment is usually very effective if given early with antibiotics and supportive therapy. The sick in Vitoria had the benefit of neither, but nonetheless many did survive, like Major Richardson.

During the period of decline gangrene would often develop in the feet, sometimes spreading upwards to involve the whole of the legs, usually on both sides. This gangrene, so marked a feature of the disease in Spain, though not often referred to in accounts of typhus,* results from impaired blood supply caused by involvement of arterial blood vessels, perhaps with a contribution from the extreme cold experienced in unheated accommodation. Alcock believed he had seen three hundred cases of gangrened extremities, having asked all the medical officers to show him such cases. He had strong views on its treatment, favouring early amputation of the limb, believing that delay would result in the gangrene extending to a higher level. This surgery was performed under very unfavourable conditions on patients debilitated by fever and dysentery.†

Regarding his surgical results, Alcock could only speak of those who recovered and whom he saw later in July 1836 at the depôt in Santander. There he found twelve surviving after amputation of one or both legs or feet, but two of these died later. One Legion surgeon suggested that these twelve men were no more than a fifth of the total number of amputees. The results of amputations in civilian practice ten to twenty years later

---

* The 1919 edition of the Army handbook, *Memoranda on Medical Diseases in the Tropical and Sub-Tropical War Areas* states, in this connection, only 'that gangrene of the feet may be mentioned', while no mention of gangrene appears in the 1942 edition.

† Alexander Ball of the 10th Regiment was horrified by the gruesome scenes in the 'dead houses' where corpses awaited burial. In one he saw the bodies of seventeen men and one woman; one man had had both leges amputated, and these were placed neatly beside him. Ball thought he was seeing a pair of boots, since the gangrenous legs were quite black and shiny. Men were dying at the rate of twenty-five a day. Instead of asking each morning in the hospital 'Who is dead?' it became more appropriate to ask 'Who is alive?'

were somewhat better. In the far more favourable conditions of the London Hospital between 1852 and 1859, the mortality among amputees was 50 per cent, mainly in lower limb amputations.

It is difficult now to consider what influence the surgery may have had on the outcome of these very sick men, but it is easy to understand the reasons for a radical approach to a desperate situation. It is unlikely that other, less drastic forms of treatment then widely used, such as purging, emetics, bleeding or blistering, would have had any but a harmful effect. Bleeding was widely used in the treatment of battle wounds, aggravating the anaemia caused by blood loss.

Alcock himself refers to the plight of the medical officers during that winter in Vitoria in moving terms, which must resonate with medical men and women of today, when so much more effective treatment is available. Writing in a more emotional vein than in his clinical description, he allows his heart to speak, as well as his head, when referring to the trials calculated to paralyse all exertion from the conviction of its inefficiency to remedy evils which seem each day to increase and bring fresh sources of confusion and misery in their train:

> Even stout hearts seemed to quail, for many of our number were carried from the hospitals to their quarters to rave, in the sharp access of their delirium, of blackened feet rotting from the living flesh, of the screams of the dying still struggling among the dead, until they themselves were added to the list. Such scenes had they daily witnessed, and their painful picture and piercing shrieks, more than once, in spite of the stoicism of habit, made me start and shudder ... Strong motives and minds not easily unnerved, were necessary at such a period, and it is with pride and gratitude that I remember the courage and zeal with which the Inspector-General and myself were seconded and aided to the last by the medical officers of the Legion at head-quarters; so many of whom we had to regret, carried off in the midst of exertions, by which alone we could hope to prevent a still more serious loss of life.

This sad chapter in the Legion's history was covered by General Evans in his memoranda in one laconic sentence: 'It was at this interval that severe losses were sustained by the Auxiliaries in hospital.' The brevity of this comment should not be taken to indicate a lack of sympathy for the dead men and their families, since Evans fought hard, when the war was over, for the interests of the widows and orphans of the Legion.

Throughout this time the Carlists' efforts against the garrison of Vitoria were as nothing compared with the ravages of disease. Carlist cavalry would occasionally come up to the gates of the town, hoping to capture any odd man imprudent enough to venture outside. One morning Lieutenant Inman of the 1st (Queen Isabella's) Lancers and some of his men pursued a group of Carlist horsemen, killing all but one and riding back with the enemy's berets on the points of their lances. This small success may have done something to raise the drooping spirits of the Legion, and it confirmed their already low opinion of the Carlist cavalry.

CHAPTER EIGHT

The battle of Arlaban

The only important major action in which the depleted Legion partici-
pated from Vitoria was in January 1836. The commander-in-chief, Córdova,
had gathered a force of some 25,000 men. This was composed of regulars,
Spanish troops, mercenaries, 1,800 only of the British Legion, and the
French Foreign Legion under General Bernelle. A co-ordinated three-
pronged attack was planned, with the British on the right wing. The three
columns were intended to advance together in an attempt to open a pass
through the Arlaban mountains northwest of Vitoria, towards Oñate, where
Carlos and his court were in residence.

Co-ordinated actions between allied forces require the closest co-operation and unity of purpose, especially in severe winter weather. Lieutenant
Thompson had earlier written of the advantages which would have accrued
if each regiment of the Legion had had attached to it a company of the
Chapelgorris, 'but they will never do anything half so sensible'. If this system
had been adopted, he believed that 'all the contemptible jealousy and mis-
trust which had sprung up between the armies would have been obviated
and the split between the English and the Spanish generals likewise', since
there would have been an *esprit de corps*, with men and officers seeing themselves as members of a single body. This was very far from being the case,
and Córdova's behaviour, then and later, provoked justified criticism and
accusations of his jealousy of other commanders, especially of Evans and
the Legion.

The attempted attack ended in complete disarray. 'General Winter' fought
for Carlos; deep snowdrifts on the mountains and fog so dense that visibil-
ity was at times under twenty yards confused the Cristinos and confounded
Córdova's plans, preventing communication between the various parts of his
army. On 16 January the British column, with elements of the 1st, 2nd, 3rd,
7th, 9th and 10th Regiments,* and with some Spanish infantry and cavalry
under Evans, attacked the village of Mendijaz (fig. 8). Thompson describes

---

* Of these six regiments three were Irish, a testimony to the better health they had enjoyed
  in the epidemic of disease.

how his regiment, the 1st, fixed bayonets and charged into the village, supported by the other regiments, and quickly drove the Carlists out into the
plain below. Later the 1st advanced further with the 9th Irish, meeting little
resistance from the enemy, who abandoned their villages.

Any co-ordination of the venture was prevented by the foul weather.
Evans had received no further orders from Córdova and fog made any
movement of troops impossible. According to the local *Boletín de Alava*,
the fog was worse than any in living memory. The Legion suffered badly
from the cold, since few had cloaks and all were ill-equipped for the harsh
weather. Colonel Godfrey, lying out at night in a heavy hoar frost, found
his hair frozen to the ground on waking up shivering, and could not turn
his head to either side until extricated by some of his men.

It was said that Córdova had sent a messenger to advise Evans that he
planned to withdraw to Vitoria, but the message was never delivered, causing much confusion and acrimony.

On 18 January Evans could contain his impatience no longer, and set
off with a squadron of lancers to search for Córdova and his orders.
According to Captain Meller, Evans eventually found the commander-in-
chief within a mile of the gates of Vitoria. When they met, Córdova told
Evans that he was retreating to the city and that Evans should follow suit.
At midnight the Legion retreated, leaving bonfires burning in their abandoned camps to mislead the enemy.

Thompson calculated that the Legion's losses were one sergeant and
six to twelve men killed. They would have been higher but for the lucky
escape of the enormously fat Major Shaw* of the 10th, who could not keep
up with the others in the retreat. He was too heavy for the men to carry,
but the adjutant kindly lent him a horse, and he lived to fight another day.

Colonel Charles Shaw was cynically critical of the whole action. While
supportive of his behaviour in a very difficult predicament, he knew that
Evans now realised that he must think and act for himself, and that
Córdova had 'intended to lead him into a scrape'. Evans' retreat with the
Legion to Vitoria was managed in a simple, sensible, soldier-like way, for
which he deserved great credit. Another officer in the headquarters wrote
that Córdova was resolved that the Legion should not be brought into
action. Anglo-Spanish relations were at a low ebb.

* Major S. Shaw was no relation to Col. Charles Shaw.

Shaw commented also that in the quietest day in Oporto, in the Portuguese war, 'we had more firing in an afternoon than there was during these two days; but perhaps it may be magnified, not only into a battle, but into the glorious victory of Arlaban.' Shaw was wrong, and the Tory press predictably described the affair as a total defeat for the Legion. To make matters worse, Lord Londonderry told the House of Lords, quoting a letter from a correspondent in St Jean de Luz, that the soldiers of the Legion, returning totally drunk to Vitoria, had murdered 150 Carlist prisoners. This lie was typical of the calumnies directed against Evans by his political foes. Ensign Ball, who was present throughout the action, commenting bitterly on newspaper reports that the Legion were all intoxicated on 16, 17 and 18 January, wrote that 'it was like the fiddler's dog – drunk with hunger'.

Shaw also criticised Evans' decision to confer decorations on the Legion after the battle, writing to his brother, 'If we carry on with the system with which we began, namely decorating for the most trifling affairs, I assure you the officers must become regular Daniel Lamberts,* otherwise they will not have chests capacious enough to hold these decorations'.

By February 1836 shortage of money and 'every other thing that makes an army efficient, had reduced the Legion to near-destitution,' according to a correspondent of the *Courier*. The situation worsened when a convoy en route from Madrid with money for the Legion was by mistake or intention diverted to Logrono, to Córdova's camp. General MacDougall, the new quartermaster-general, swung into action. Thompson voiced the views of many when he wrote that MacDougall was 'the only clever man among our Brigadiers. Everything connected with the Staff has been miserably conducted, and yet these are the gentry that splash about in cocked hats on fine horses and run off with the pay for want of which the men are starving.' In this crisis MacDougall and Colonel William Wylde, the chief English Commissioner, set off for Madrid to complain to Mendizabal, chief minister to the queen regent, and to demand the three months' arrears of pay. On 12 March, as MacDougall wrote to Palmerston, Mendizabal solemnly promised to pay the arrears, to pay the officers and men monthly in advance, in accordance with British Army practice, and to establish

---

* Daniel Lambert (1770–1809) was, according to the *Dictionary of National Biography*, 'the most corpulent man of whom authentic records exist,' weighing 739 lbs. After his death he became a synonym for hugeness.

advance and reserve magazines of clothing and provisions with at least two months' supplies constantly maintained. Sadly his promise was broken.

MacDougall's appointment coincided with a radical reorganisation of the Legion necessitated by the heavy losses of men and officers suffered in the eight months since its formation. Thompson wrote to his father to describe the consolidation of the 1st and 2nd Regiments and the division of these and the 5th (Scotch) between the other regiments. His own regiment, the 1st, had been heavily reduced by typhus and the 5th, he believed, had been almost annihilated. 'If the Carlists only knew how we have died off like rotten sheep, they would attribute it to their general-elect, the Virgin Mary,* through whose interposition the heretics have been cut off like the host Senacrib [sic.].' He commented on the differing mortality among the various regiments, the Irish having suffered the least, though his statement that the 7th and 10th Irish Regiments had hardly lost any to speak of was over-optimistic. The ten regiments were to be reduced to eight plus the Rifle Corps, and would be formed into three brigades. Thompson himself was appointed to a company in the 9th Irish Regiment, whose colonel, Charles Fitzgerald, had a reputation as a good officer and a pleasant sort of man. He did not regret leaving the 1st Regiment as he would once have done, since 'most of the old hands who came out with me from England have died off or gone home and we have been flooded with officers from the 2nd'.

Colonel Shaw was delighted to be appointed to command the three Irish regiments, in his opinion the best and strongest brigade in the Legion, with the long-awaited rank of brigadier-general. Charles Chichester commanded the 1st (English), 4th (Queen's Own Fusiliers) and 8th (Highlanders) and William Reid the 3rd (Westminster Grenadiers), 6th (Scotch Grenadiers) and the Rifle Corps. The Legion was now a tougher and leaner body than before, having lost to disease many of the weaker vessels who should never have been enlisted, although fit men also had died in large numbers. The 1,800 men who made up Shaw's Irish Brigade were the toughest of all. In March 1836, when others lay huddled in their greatcoats against the cold, the spartan Irish were out in the early sunshine playing leapfrog and throwing stones.

---

* A reference to Don Carlos having appointed the Virgin Mary as Generalissimo of his army which, with her appointment also as chief medical officer to the Bavarian forces, had prompted the irreverent comment in a Protestant Irish newspaper that 'the goddess would have her hands full'.

About the middle of February the long-awaited supply of blankets, hospital clothing, baths, cooking utensils etc. obtained from the British Ordnance reached Vitoria, together with the medicines and medical stores orginally ordered *before the Legion left Britain*, that is, some seven months late.

CHAPTER NINE

Return to the coast and into battle; a costly victory, 5 May 1836

The spring of 1836 brought new hope and better health to the survivors of the Legion, and on 12 April Evans assembled them for the long return march to the coast, leaving many hundreds of their comrades in graves in and around Vitoria. Dr Alcock remarked on the wonderful change shown by the different brigades on the march, thinned though they were by the sick and the dead left behind:

> Even the sickly and the wan pushed gaily on, and the stronger marched with the elasticity and spirit of men who had shaken off all care. As for my friends the Irish, they looked as if they had never known care nor sickness either, and when they piled arms were as ready for a 'lark' as ever they had been at Donnybrook Fair.

An officer of the Irish Brigade confirmed the endurance and toughness of the Irish soldiers on the march to Santander, a distance of some seventy miles as the crow flies, which he believed was made in only six days, through rocky ravines and mountain gorges. The three regiments were quartered in different villages on their nightly halts, and great rivalry existed between them, especially the 10th and 7th, to be up and accoutred before daylight to steal a march on the others, though there was seldom a mile between them on the road.

Captain Meller of the 10th was in charge of the guard on the brigade's baggage and sick, 15 or 20 wagons, and 30 or 40 women and children. These camp-followers were not allowed to ride, and travelled with the sick in the wagons or trudged, bare-headed and bare-footed, twenty-one or twenty-two miles a day. Meller writes of the gratitude of the women if he took up a child on the pommel of his saddle. He took up on his horse a 13-year-old boy who foraged for food; little Johnny crowed like a cock or cackled like a hen, finding eggs for his master.

For Somerville it was a pleasant march at first; ten days took the 8th Regiment to Santander, but he became ill on the march, falling into a stupor which lasted eighteen days, and being carried the last two days in a bullock cart, so missing the bloody battle of 5 May. The Legion and their Spanish allies were taken by sea from Santander to San Sebastian, where Evans was preparing for an attack. It was 4 May before all had made the journey. The last to arrive were the 4th and part of the 8th Regiments, who were embarked on the *Phoenix* and *Salamander* war steamers, reaching San Sebastian just in time to join the battle which was already raging.

The division of the Carlist army encamped before San Sebastian and commanded by General Segastibelza was too small to blockade the town, which was always accessible by sea, and it lacked strength in artillery and other arms to besiege so strong a fortress successfully.* Nonetheless it tied down a strong garrison that might have been put to better use, and secured the country to its rear up to the French frontier.

The Carlists had, however, made some limited gains since the previous autumn, capturing the convent of San Francisco, where the Legion was previously billeted, and the wooden bridge over the river Urumea, which they had used to reach the convent, had been destroyed. The town itself was half-deserted, many citizens having crossed into France. The quays were heaped with turf through which cannon protruded, the streets barricaded and many windows shattered by the explosion of bombshells. There was none of the tumultuous welcome the Legion had received the previous year.

The Carlist forces were strongly posted within a series of entrenched lines, on a long series of eminences close to the town, the road to Hernani, south of San Sebastian, running through their centre. The position of the Legion's lines and those of the Carlists are shown in detail in a map published in Evans' own short account or 'memorandum' of the campaign, published in 1840.

Thompson, with the 9th Regiment, had reached San Sebastian on 24 April in good time for the coming battle. At 2 a.m. on 5 May he wrote briefly to his father about the proposed attack on the Carlist positions in a line of houses and a fortified farmhouse. The Irish Brigade, the 1st, 3rd, 6th and part of the 8th Regiments, the Chapelgorris and a Spanish regiment were involved. It was hoped that by attacking the houses in the dark they would drive the enemy out silently with the bayonet, and so gain the whole line of hills.

---

* During Wellington's siege and capture of San Sebastian in 1813, casualties amounted to between two and three thousand, with a high proportion of killed to wounded.

General Shaw, commanding the Irish Brigade, was another who put pen to paper on the eve of battle. He shared Evans' concern that part of the Legion had yet to arrive (and in retrospect it seems strange that the attack should have been launched while the Legion was below its full strength; one account even claims that the assault was originally planned for 4 May, but postponed because of severe weather). Shaw wrote of the danger of attacking strong lines with men who had never seen a shot fired, and was gloomy about his own chances of surviving the coming battle.

These letters were only just finished when the Legion marched off in the pitch dark into a countryside made wet and swampy by a week of rain. The army was deployed in three columns. The Light Brigade under General Reid was to attack the Carlists' right, and the Irish Brigade under Shaw the centre, while Chichester with the third brigade was to march along the shore and turn the enemy's left flank.

The battle of Ayete on 5 May was the first major conflict in which the Legion was involved, and the costliest in casualties. It was also an action in which they acquitted themselves bravely, far better than Shaw had thought possible for such untried troops, eliciting grudging praise even from hostile critics in England.

Two of the contemporary accounts of the battle are by participants, those of General Shaw of the Irish Brigade and Charles Thompson of the 9th Regiment, in the same brigade. Each man gives detailed descriptions of the action from his own perspective, and each refers in part to the role of the other. Thompson's account understandably devotes more attention to his general than does Shaw's to the junior officer, though Shaw refers to Thompson's creditable part in the engagement. The difficulty of any one man engaged in battle seeing more than the immediate events in which he is playing his part, while different scenes are played out all around him, so that a god's-eye view of the whole, complex, moving mosaic is almost impossible to achieve, has been well discussed by Keegan in *The Face of Battle*.

The advantages of the first-hand account of war over a second-hand report are obvious, but in this particular case the detailed and lengthy account given by Sergeant Alexander Somerville, who was not present at the battle but was told of it later by his fellow soldiers of the Highlanders and other regiments, gives a vivid impression and tallies in its details with the various eyewitness accounts. Somerville believed that, having made minute enquiries about the action, he could describe it as well as if he had been there. His analytical and psychological cast of mind contributes to the immediacy of his description.

Somerville takes up the story as the army marched out of San Sebastian in the small hours of the morning. They marched together by the main road as far as the convent of San Bartolomé. The Carlists' outposts occupied some houses two hundred yards beyond this, and the space between was neutral ground. Here they split up into their component parts. The Light Brigade under General Reid, with the Rifle Corps, 3rd and 6th Regiments and the Chapelgorris, took the right and seaward side of the enemy's lines, the Irish Brigade under Shaw the centre, and Chichester's brigade, with the 1st Regiment, two companies of the 8th Highlanders and about eight hundred Spaniards the left and most landward side.

Evans' orders to his men were not to fire, but to advance as close as possible and charge with the bayonet; this succeeded for a short time, until the first houses were cleared and the out-piquets driven back, 'but as daylight began to show each party their opponents, and as the fortifications of the enemy seemed impregnable to such a small force, it was necessary, in some parts, to halt and fire'. Somerville contrasts the differing modes of fighting of the Legion and the Chapelgorris. 'The bravery and determination of the Chapelgorris to fight, forgetting they were commanded by a general acting on a studied plan, now became a fault. Absolutely wild to get at the Carlists, when they could not charge with their bayonets, they fired even though ordered not to do so. It was very different with the 7th Irish; almost without firing a shot, they advanced in the face of vollies [sic], every minute some of them dropping down dead and wounded, but going steadily forward, with the indomitable Colonel Swan at their head.' The 7th must have presented an ideal target to the Carlists since, alone of the Legion, they wore white trousers, which showed up more clearly in the grey of the dawn. They captured the heavily defended windmill battery. Many of the enemy died in and about these houses, since they would not surrender, but fought with the 7th bayonet to bayonet. The conflict and slaughter for a short time was mutual, but the Carlists gave way. Shaw led his brigade on with great ardour. The first line of defences had fallen, and General Evans praised the Irish Brigade. 'You are doing nobly, Irishmen.' The second line of defences was now attacked with artillery. Several charges were made but repulsed by the enemy with great determination.

The Light Brigade, facing the enemy's right flank, was fully engaged. Encouraged by Evans, who mounted a parapet, drew his sword and called on his men to advance, and if necessary die like like Englishmen, they drove the Carlists from their posts. Colonel William Tupper, charging with his 6th Regiment, was shot through the arm. Hiding his wound under his cloak to avoid discouraging his officers and men, he led them on for two hours more, when, almost exhausted by loss of blood, he was shot in the head and died soon afterwards. He was buried where he fell, but his tomb now lies with other graves of the Legion on the slopes of Mount Orgull (where its inscription is one of the few still legible; pl. 16).

Sharing the dangers was Chichester's brigade. Somerville describes the reckless bravery of Colonel Fortescue of the Rifles, repeatedly engaged though wounded and with his clothes almost torn off, in hand-to-hand combat with the enemy. He earned the title 'Mad Fortescue', bestowed on him.

Descriptions of heroic, almost Homeric, episodes in the fighting are given by Somerville. In the Irish Brigade the 7th and 9th Regiments were repulsed three times, each time leaving many dead. At last a part of the 10th came to join them:

> Old Colonel (afterwards General) Fitzgerald headed the whole. A stone wall secured them, for a time, from the enemy's shot; and over the wall the old fellow* sprung, with a riding whip his only weapon. The men attempted to follow, but as they got over the wall, volley on volley poured onto them, and battered them down as fast as they got over. The first of them thus falling so thickly, the remainder hung back. All the officers of the three regiments who were over the wall fell, excepting Fitzgerald: he stood still, called them to come on – 'Irishmen! Tenth, Ninth, Seventh; Munster boys, bog-trotters, raga-muffins, come on with ould Charlie – I'll stand here by myself till I'm shot, if ye don't come.' On hearing these words one Irishman sprung over the wall, saying, 'Soul, and ye'll not die by yourself, ould Charlie.' This was a familiar way in which his men (who were devoted to him) always addressed him, and after that all who were there charged.

Several officers and a number of their men fell; among them, Somerville wrote, Captain Thompson of the 9th, a gallant, thorough-going fellow, was severely wounded. Fortunately, in this detail he was wrong, and Thompson was able before long to give his own account of events.

* Charles Fitzgerald was fifty years old.

Now the second line line of defences gave way to the determined onslaught, and the only important obstacle remaining was the fort of Lugariz. This was fiercely defended and the Legion suffered heavy losses in attacking it.

Just at this moment the naval ships *Phoenix* and *Salamander*, with the 4th and the rest of the 8th Regiments, entered the bay. Boats at once took them ashore, their knapsacks were thrown off on the sands, and the men were marched up along the seashore, rather than inland, on Evans' orders, to prevent their seeing the dead and wounded. The sight of the many wounded being carried into the town, however, could not be avoided, and had a chilling effect on the new arrivals. Colonel Godfrey encouraged them and they were welcomed by Evans himself, who told the Scots they would be proud to share the glory of the 6th.

The English warships *Phoenix* and *Salamander*, under the command of Lord John Hay, were anchored close to the shore, and now opened up a bombardment of ball and shell on the fort of Lugariz. At 1,600 yards distance, the shells were aimed with great precision, devastating the fort and its defenders. The Legion's artillery joined in, concentrating on one angle of the redoubt and opening up a breach through which the 4th and 8th Regiments stormed.

Among those killed was Captain J.W. Allez, Adjutant of the 4th Regiment, and one of three brothers commissioned in the Legion. While leaping a parapet he was shot at his brother's side. Seeing him fall, his brother paused only long enough to take his ring before charging onwards to capture the fort.

The Carlists' line was turned, and as the defenders wavered, the other brigades joined in the attack and carried the trenches at bayonet-point. By mid-day some 3,000 Carlists were driven out of the positions they had been consolidating for months, and the Legion captured a large amount of rifles, ammunition and stores. The Carlist commander was among their casualties.

Palmerston had obtained King William's approval for Hay's active co-operation with the Cristino forces in protecting ports held by the Queen and helping to recover any ports occupied by the Carlists. Hay therefore landed a Royal Marine battalion and some Royal Marine artillery, supplemented by small detachments of Royal Artillery and Royal Engineers, the combined force being under his own command.

This more active involvement of Hay and his marines in the battle, which helped in the capture of Lugariz fort, seemed inconsistent with

Palmerston's earlier decision that regular British forces would not be embroiled in the Spanish conflict. The Marines' intervention enraged Tory opponents of the Legion and of Palmerston's 'non-intervention' policy. Later the more intensive support given to the queen's cause by Lord John's ships and Marines prompted further criticism. At the time, however, Evans and his hard-pressed men must have been surprised and overjoyed by such timely intervention. Although any marines captured by the enemy could have been considered fair game for the Carlist firing squads, Don Carlos made an exception in their case. In July he decreed that officers and men of the Royal Marines who fell into Carlist hands should be respected and held as prisoners of war. Carlos was also anxious to obtain the services of men from the British naval force, putting a very high price on any who might desert. (It seems unlikely that any did so.)

Charles Shaw describes his own active involvement in the battle in command of the Irish Brigade, encouraging Fitzgerald and his other colonels in the attack. The 9th Regiment had ten of its officers 'knocked down' when Fitzgerald led them on, as described by Somerville. At one point the Carlists turned on part of Chichester's brigade which, led by Colonel Ellis and Captain Knight, Chichester's ADC, was charging them, seeing how few they were, and bayoneted all they could reach. Knight was one of the first to die. Lieutenant O'Connor of the 9th, described by Shaw as the most extraordinary leaper, and perhaps the most active man in Europe, had a lucky escape. Going to rally what he thought was a group of Chapelgorris, he found too late that they were Carlists. As one man turned on him with a bayonet and another raised his musket to fire, O'Connor parried the bayonet, knocked down both men and raced back to safety, leaping walls and ditches as he went. The Spanish governor of San Sebastian watched the episode through his telescope. Shaw lost many friends and colleagues killed and wounded in the battle.

It was two weeks before Thompson could write home, and his writing was shaky due to a wounded right hand. He describes how his company and another of the 9th cut down the hillside under a rattling fire of musketry from the breastworks on the hill opposite, seeing General Evans waving his sword and hurrahing on the men who wavered a little at the blazing fire which met them. Arriving at the bottom of the valley, he was astonished to find that half his company had vanished. Having hastily collected as many lost sheep of his own and other regiments as he could, he was ordered by Shaw to make his way to the breastworks and occupy a fortified house in the enemy lines. While slowly plodding up the hill he met Colonel Swan of the 7th, whose regiment had dwindled to about half a dozen men. Together they scrambled up among the apple trees, whose twigs and blossoms were cut off by flying shot, coming on the mortally wounded Captain Mould of the 10th, whom they could not stop to help. On reaching the breastworks they found that the Carlists had retired to the third line. They later counterattacked, recapturing the fortified house, which changed hands twice. The arrival of Shaw and Fitzgerald with reinforcements left the contested house in the Legion's hands. Thompson was now sent by Shaw to bring up as many men of the Brigade as possible. 'Belting downhill and falling headlong in the mud', he reached General Chichester and delivered his message. A number of men under Major Bruce Mitchell of the 8th were detached and returned with Thompson to Shaw who, now that he had a larger force, ordered the attack to continue. This was the point at which Fitzgerald sprang over the breastwork, as reported by Somerville, and advanced at the head of his men in the midst of the heaviest fire Thompson had yet seen. Thompson followed close at his heels, but had not taken six steps when he was shot in the left hip and knocked down 'flat as a pancake'. Here a second shot hit him in the fleshy part of his right thumb, just passing by the bone without breaking it. Rolling over on his back and tumbling head-over-heels in the lane below, he found himself in the presence of two villainous Carlists some thirty or forty yards off, who at once fixed bayonets and ran after him. Rolling and tumbling down the hill on hands and knees, he fortunately fell in with three members of his own company, who placed him on their firelocks and carried him off the field. The ball in his hand was cut out in the hospital, and he insisted on being taken to his own billet 'as the sights and sounds of the hospital were not very agreeable'.

This was understandable since the Legion had suffered very heavy casualties. One account gave 78 officers and 800 men killed or wounded, mostly wounded, although many of these wounds must have been slight, since Dr Alcock's hospital figures show only 382 wounded, with a death-roll of about a tenth of this figure.

In a letter to his mother, written under great stress on 6 May, Shaw wrote that the Irish Brigade had lost, in killed and wounded, about 400 men and 27 officers. Many of his fellow-officers were wounded, some severely. Shaw wrote that he was 'very fatigued and excited, and could cry,' clearly describing the post-traumatic stress so common in such situations, though little recognised at that time. Sorrow and anxiety spare only the rarest even among leaders, and Wellington himself had wept copiously after Waterloo.

An official return of casualties gave, as killed, 10 officers, of whom five were captains and five lieutenants (but seems not to include Colonel Tupper of the 6th, who was mortally wounded), five sergeants and 131 rank and file. Wounded officers totalled 65. Of these, Generals Reid and Shaw were slightly wounded, as was Lord William Paget, one of Evans' ADCs, and his Spanish ADC, Don F. Cotoner. Among officers severely wounded were Col. Swan of the 7th, Col. Considine, military secretary, and nine captains, lieutenants and ensigns.

Shaw had been slightly wounded. One officer who died of his wounds was Second Lieutenant Courteney Chadwick of the 3rd Regiment, who had been carrying the regimental colours when he and a comrade carrying the Queen's colours were shot. It was decided after this that the regimental colours would no longer be carried in battle, since they made such an easy target of those who bore them. Staff Surgeon Henry Wilkinson of the 6th later described the simple monument to Chadwick, who was buried on Castle Hill, with its quaint inscription, 'Sacred to the Memory of poor Court, who fell under his Colours, in the Battle of Ayetta, 5 May 1836. Beauty and Friendship Truly Mourn Him.' (Sadly, the monument is not among those that remain recognisable among the graves of the Legion today.)

Thirty-three NCOs and 594 privates were reported by Somerville to have been wounded. Most of their names are unrecorded. The weekly *Atlas* of 2 April reported that thirty of the wounded soldiers had since died, a statistic that seems very credible.

Among the many casualties of the Carlists was General Segastibelza, who was wounded on 5 May and taken to Hernani where he died on the 7th, the very day on which he had boasted that he would dine in San Sebastian after driving the English into the sea.

Hospital facilities in San Sebastian had been greatly improved since the previous autumn. A large building, designed originally as a cigar factory, well ventilated and overlooking the bay, had been converted into a hospital. This became the fever hospital for cases of typhus and dysentery, which continued to occur, though in smaller numbers. The large convent of San Telmo (pl. 6) was turned into a surgical hospital after the casualties of 5 May made a centre for the treatment of the wounded essential. The three higher floors of the main wing were dedicated to the care of gunshot wounds. Head, chest and abdominal injuries were concentrated on one floor, and amputations and gunshot wounds of the limbs, with fractures, on another. The grouping of patients by their type of injury made their care and management much easier for the surgeons and more effective for the wounded.

Alcock himself had been slightly wounded in the knee, delaying the opening of San Telmo hospital, which was under his care. In the first few days the wounded were therefore nursed in crowded conditions in churches and temporary buildings, but much help was given by the ladies of San Sebastian, who provided bedding, linen and other necessities, as well as nursing the injured men. Alcock pays tribute to their kindness of heart and feeling, and their courage and patience. Conditions were infinitely better than they had been for the sick in Vitoria. Alcock, ever anxious to learn practical lessons from the experience of war on the better management of the wounded, considered in detail the problem of transporting casualties from the scene of action. The Legion was supplied with twelve conveyances known as Cherry's Carts, which were on the whole found serviceable, though with disadvantages. Capable of carrying four wounded men able to sit upright, they needed more than one horse or mule on heavy roads and were liable to break down. Nonetheless they were more economical of man-power than stretchers, which might require eight, twelve or sixteen men to convey a wounded officer from the front far into the rear, and Alcock believed that their use as far forward as possible would be advantageous, not only in the current conflict but also to the regular British army in a wider sphere.

Evans' victory received a mixed press back in Britain. He was much criticised in the Tory newspapers for not having pressed on, after taking the Carlists' lines, to capture Hernani, which was only to fall the next year. The Legion and the Cristinos stopped before the venta or inn of Hernani, occupying all the heights from San Sebastian to the venta, and advanced no further. Three Carlist battalions arrived on 7 May to reinforce the garrison of Hernani. *The Times* of 14 May, after reiterating its disapproval of Lord Palmerston's 'non-intervention' in the affairs of Spain, wrote that it now had 'the more gratifying duty of bearing testimony to the valour of our fellow-countrymen, from the General Commander-in Chief to the private soldier serving in the cause of the Queen of Spain'. After this tribute to British bravery, the writer went on to consider the probable consequences of this action, which had been marked by so grave a loss of human life rather than what degree of valour had been evinced. Evans was accused of making a 'Bunker Hill' display and losing a frightful number of officers and men, without any further benefit except quieting for a time the anxious speculators on the London Stock Exchange. It was stated that the occupation of Hernani was the only object a skilful general could have proposed to himself, and that his personal valour in leading his men to death was no excuse for the want of combination and design as a military tactician.

Evans' decision not to press on and attack Hernani is understandable, despite pressure to do so from some of his officers, including General MacDougall, who resigned soon afterwards with several others. He was short of officers since many had been wounded, and was concerned that Carlist reserves might come down from the hills and cut off his lines of communication if he advanced too far. As it was, Evans could not hold all the ground he had gained, and the Carlists were able before long to resume the siege.

Rather less grudging praise for the Legion came from the *Cork Evening Herald* of 16 May: 'The news from Spain has been more interesting than heretofore. The British levies in the service of the Queen Regent have had an opportunity of displaying their courage with no small *éclat* in a sanguinary affair with the Pretender's forces, and, according to the accounts that have been obtained, their bravery and discipline were not unworthy of the fame of their countrymen in fields of war.' Surprisingly, there was no reference to the fact that the Irish Brigade, with many from the city and county of Cork, had suffered particularly heavy losses.

The *Spectator* also praised the gallantry of Evans and the Legion in storming the formidable fortifications built over four months by the Carlists and considered by many to be impregnable, capturing them after seven hours of almost incessant fighting. The editor believed that the victory would probably be decisive. He wrote that whatever might be its results, 'none could deny that these "ragamuffin mercenaries" – these "drunken dragoons" – these "diseased and cowardly wretches" – as the Carlist prints in London and the Carlist peers in Parliament have termed them, have fought with a coolness, gallantry, and success, which would add honour to Wellington's victories'.

Wellington himself, who could always be relied on for a pithy, if acerbic, comment, summed up the situation by saying that all Evans had achieved was to extend the evening promenades of the inhabitants of San Sebastian. Nonetheless the morale of the Cristinos and the Legion was greatly boosted. Villiers reported the effect of the victory in Madrid as magical. Córdova regarded it as 'a military achievement, the most gallant, and in its moral effect the most important event of the whole war,' while

Lord John Hay, who had contributed to the success, wrote of the proud gratification he felt at witnessing the gallantry of the Legion; 'the intrenched positions of the insurgents had seemed impregnable, but one after another were stormed by these brave men, in a manner that created a universal feeling of admiration.' The French general, Count de Harispe, wrote that the results of the combat did the highest honour to the British soldiers, and above all to their officers, who had given such brilliant proofs of devotedness and intrepidity. Evans' diplomatic reply described his pleasure in gaining the approval of a veteran general so distinguished among the heroic chiefs of the French Empire.

Somerville records that one shirt and a pair of boots were issued to each NCO and private in the Legion immediately after the battle. The men were charged eight shillings in their accounts for the boots, and credited with a gratuity of the same amount, but the arithmetic proved too difficult for most of them who, not understanding the book-keeping involved, believed that they had paid for the boots, which were issued by the quartermaster's stores but were actually a gift from the people of San Sebastian.

Greater unhappiness was created among the ranks by the decision of the Spanish government to award medals to all who had been in the engagement. For officers, the three different classes of the Medal of St Ferdinand were awarded, the 3rd Class for generals, the 2nd for colonels and the 1st for lieutenant colonels downwards to ensigns. Among the NCOs and men, some received the Ribbon and Cross of Isabella II, but this depended on the recommendation of their officers. Somerville was very critical of his CO, Colonel Godfrey, whom he greatly respected as a soldier, for distributing these honours widely in the regiment, believing that only two of the men deserved them, one of whom died before his award was announced. The medals had to be cast, and were not supplied until November 1836. They were the cause of endless disputes and envious mutual hatred, in Somerville's view, rather than an incentive to good behaviour and bravery. He was particularly critical of the award to the regiment's very unpopular adjutant, who ended up as a pawnbroker in northern Ireland.

The battle attracted the attention of British tourists; a letter of September 1836 from San Sebastian reported that Sir William Meade's yacht had left the port, and that of Mr Pelham had arrived, 'bringing several gentlemen from England to see the height of Ayete taken on the memorable 5th of May', and staying for three days (*Limerick Chronicle*, 13 August 1836).

CHAPTER TEN

Further fighting

The Legion were not given time to rest on their laurels, as hostilities resumed later that month. On 28 May they prepared to attack the Carlist positions again. At daylight Chichester's brigade, with General Jauregui's Spanish division, crossed the river Urumea at low tide, under cover of a heavy artillery bombardment, directed by Colonel Colquhoun, an experienced former regular officer in the Royal Artillery.

The Carlists were thrown into disarray, and the troops crossed the river almost without firing a shot, taking the positions on the far side at bayonet point. A bridge was then thrown across the river by Captain Maitland of the *Tweed* sloop of war and his sailors within half an hour, at a point where it was about 159 yards wide, deep and fast running. Somerville describes how the watching Spaniards were confounded to see the bridge rise as if by magic, and – with some exaggeration – considered the speed unparalleled in the history of war. The rest of the Legion and the Marines then crossed to the far side.

Meanwhile the *Phoenix* and *Salamander* under Hay, now firmly committed to supporting the queen's troops both by land and by sea, had sailed eastward four miles to the port of Pasajes, which was captured without difficulty.

As before, Evans was criticised for not continuing to advance, when the Carlists were on the run, to Hernani or Tolosa. Somerville believed that his limited manpower of only six thousand made such an advance inadvisable, since he would have had only about ten men for each mountain pass, and the Carlists would have come in behind him and cut off his supplies from San Sebastian.

On 6 June the Carlists again attacked in strength, hoping to retake their lost entrenchments and Ametza hill. General Eguia with his Navarrese regiments advanced at 7 am against Chichester's brigade, who repulsed them. They attacked again and were once more driven back. Three companies of the Marines were in action in support of some legionaries who were being driven back by the enemy, and their well-directed fire quickly caused the Carlists to retreat, but not without seven men of the Legion whom they had captured. The fate of these men was sealed under the Durango Decree. They were taken to Hernani and shot. The British press gave conflicting reports of their deaths. The correspondent of the liberal *Morning Chronicle* reported that they were executed particularly cruelly, being crucified, then shot in the feet, knees and bodies and left to die. The Carlist version is that they were shot in the ordinary way. Michael Burke Honan, an Irishman who was correspondent of the Tory *Morning Herald* accredited to Don Carlos' HQ, reported that he had met an Irish Carlist officer the day after the battle, who had interpreted for the seven soldiers. Six of them were English Protestants and one an Irish Catholic. The latter was spared long enough to make his religious confession. He had asked the officer if he would be shot, to which the answer could only be Yes. 'Worse luck then for Judy and the children,' the man said, and asked his compatriot to write a short letter to give to his wife. This the officer willingly did but, no doubt affected by the emotional situation, he forgot to ask the lady's address, so that the letter never reached the widow. She was only one of many who never learned the fate of their loved ones.

Somerville's account of the action of 6 June gives graphic detail. A group of the 2nd Irish Lancers found themselves surrounded by Carlist cavalry, infantry and artillery. Major Martin, formerly of the 8th Regiment but now serving with the Lancers, saw their desperate situation, and the hesitation of their colonel, and took over command; in a series of charges against the enemy's infantry and cavalry, he put them to flight. His Glaswegian soldiers of the 8th, to which he later returned, were full of pride and admiration for his exploits. An *esprit de corps* had developed in the Legion, as it does in most groups of soldiers involved in battle.

Somerville also describes an episode in which he and others of the 8th Regiment during this battle came under what would later become known as 'friendly fire'. They were fired on by men of the 4th Regiment, misled by the smoke and the noise of battle which drowned out the bugle calls into thinking they were Carlist troops. Several of the Highlanders were killed in this way. The first to notice that they were being fired at by their own men was a Private Aitken. A ball hit him on the outside of the left thigh, passed through and lodged just as it entered the right thigh. He held the ball in his hand as it lay inside his trousers, thinking he had only been hit on the right, and recognised it. 'It's an English ball. It's hardly torn my breeks,' he exclaimed indignantly. He was bleeding heavily, the ball having probably hit a major artery, and died soon afterwards. Somerville wrote that no mention of this tragic error had been made by anyone who had written an account of that engagement. Since Evans had spoken only faint praise of the 8th and 4th Regiments in the action, Somerville was anxious to give a true account to the public. He wrote that the 4th were unfortunate in their mistake, which led to a hatred between the two regiments which never wholly died away.

The cruelty of the Chapelgorris towards the wounded Carlists as they fled horrified the humane Somerville. The victorious Spaniards trod close on the heels of their retreating countrymen to kill and plunder, especially the officers, who gave better hope of rich pickings. They committed atrocities on the wounded after stripping and plundering them. Their cruelty, he admitted, was equalled by that of the Carlists towards Cristino prisoners. Somerville insisted that the Legion always treated its prisoners with respect, but freely describes their delight in plundering when battle was over and opportunity arose. A much wider area had been taken than on 5 May, and the scope for looting was correspondingly greater. The men and women found in the captured houses sought to curry favour with forced cheers for the English and the queen, but this did not save them from pillage. The spoils were mainly food – bread, flour, pigs and poultry. Amidst this scene of plunder, General Evans was to be seen galloping from house to house, doing all he could to put a stop to the looting.

Somerville believed that the Carlists lost nearly a thousand men in this engagement, and the Legion and Spanish Cristinos about half this number. Most of the British casualties were in his own 8th Regiment.

Despite their heavy defeat the Carlists took the offensive again on 9 June, this time on a height east of the port of Pasajes. The height had been heavily fortified and the Carlists attempted to take it by night by scrambling up the rocks. An officer of the Marines' guard was visiting his sentries just as the enemy was first glimpsed. Holding their fire until the Carlists had surrounded the garrison, the Marines were able to kill or wound most of them with one volley of musketry and artillery. The Carlist chief, Eguia, exasperated at the capture of Pasajes, was desperate for a victory for his brave Navarrese troops. An attack on the western part of the Legion's lines, where General Shaw commanded the Irish Brigade, was repulsed by the 10th Regiment, but principally by Colonel Colquhoun's gunners and their canister shot. The necessary precautions that had to be taken with such a small force on lines extending so widely were 'very hard work for the troops,' as Somerville wrote, 'though amounting to nothing with the readers of foreign news'.

An anonymous account of the British Legion by 'a volunteer in the Queen's service', published in 1837, is one of the few other accounts of the war, besides those of Somerville, written from the viewpoint of a private soldier. The author details the Carlist attempt to retake a large chapel and piquet house at Alza on the left of the lines. Twelve legionaries, who had mistaken the Carlists for reinforcements of queen's troops, had stayed behind in an upper room. All were massacred, except for a 16-year-old boy, who feigned death, was stripped and pricked with bayonets. The youth saw a Carlist soldier dash out the brains of his father with his musket in the same room. The same soldier wrote of another episode in August 1836, when 'a party of Rifles and Irish' had made a bold inroad into the enemy's lines. They were said to have surprised a company of Carlist officers at dinner in a large house, and to have cut off their heads and left them on their plates in retaliation for their cruelties. This report does not seem to be confirmed by any other writer. If true, it would seem to be one of few atrocities committed by the Legion, who were noted for their efforts to mitigate the vindictive ardour of their Spanish allies.

The 18th of June 1836 was the twenty-first anniversary of the victory of Waterloo. It was traditional on that day for 'Waterloo men' to be entertained at the expense of their old officers in honour of the battle, and the custom was faithfully followed in the Legion. Evans himself had fought at Waterloo, and there were altogether three or four hundred in the Legion who wore the honours and could tell the tales of the Peninsular battlefields. Though he respected, even revered, an old soldier, Somerville thought there were not three hundred fools in the Legion more contemptible, boorish and of greater hindrance to the efficient services of the younger men than these, who pretended to know everything. Nonetheless he believed there were a few noble old veterans. He mourned the death on 6 June of old Sergeant Deans of the 6th, who fell not twenty yards from the grave where he and others were now buried. Deans was a remnant of the 42nd Regiment, a survivor of Egypt and Waterloo; he wore four different honours of the English service, had a pension, came out to Spain, fought gloriously on 5 May, was foremost all day on 6 June and fell dead with two musket balls in his temples, almost when the last shots of the engagement were fired. 'What a career!' Somerville wrote. 'Egypt and Waterloo had spared him, and he fell here, as they will say in England, without glory!'

The 11th of July saw another offensive by Evans, this time on the walled town of Fuenterrabia, further east of Pasajes and near the French border. Its capture would probably have made it possible also to take the town of Irun to the south, so closing Carlos' supply route from France. Although both towns eventually fell to the Legion and the Cristinos in 1837, this first attack was a failure. One reason was that Evans, seriously ill at the time, was in such pain that he could not take personal control of the operations, so that General Reid was the effective – though cautious – commander. Incorrect intelligence had told Evans that the Carlists were about to abandon Fuenterrabia, so that he took no artillery with him. His plan required the Legion to capture the bridge over the river Bidassoa between Irun and Fuenterrabia, but delay on the way let the enemy reach the bridge first and, although the Legion took it from the Carlists, lack of ammunition forced them to retreat some hours later.

Evans' force of five thousand included a detachment of Marines, the 10th and 6th Regiments of the Legion and the Chapelgorris under the direction of General Shaw. The Legion's Lancers were also involved. Hay's ships at sea kept up a heavy fire but, according to Somerville, their fire was directed where it did much less harm that it would by falling any-where else. He believed the steamers could easily have battered down Fuenterrabia, and that therefore the intention was not in fact to take it. The Carlist losses were nearly three hundred killed and wounded, and the Cristinos' about one hundred. Colonels Beatson of the 10th and Ross of the 6th Regiments of the Legion were wounded. Evans was so ill that he could not ride and had to be conveyed back to San Sebastian by sea.

Although Somerville defended Evans against criticism of the 'Fuenterrabia affair', which he did not think should be called a defeat, his own officers included some critics of his handling of the action. Soon afterwards a dispute took place between some senior officers over an account of the 'Fuenterrabia affair' which had appeared in the London *Courier* and was believed to have been written by General Shaw. Though loyal to Evans, Somerville did refer to 'this fruitless, fatiguing and inex-plicable excursion'.

Shaw's letters to his family in July and August make frequent refer-ences to the *Courier* letter, which some had interpreted as expressing a hope that he would succeed Evans as commander-in-chief. Correspondence between Shaw and Evans continued until 29 August, when Shaw finally tendered his resignation, which Evans accepted. Shaw had commented on how ill Evans had appeared during the fighting before Fuenterrabia, and how at one point he looked the very picture of death and later had to be brought home by steamer, seriously ill, but recovered. He wrote that he pitied Evans, who had many enemies, and regretted that several officers had resigned from the Legion, yet his own repeated complaints must have added to Evans' burdens at this difficult time, so that his resignation may have come to Evans as a relief. It is today difficult to understand how officers fully committed to their men and to the cause for which they fought could simply resign halfway through the two-year period of their engagement, leaving the men bereft of their leaders. Had the men themselves expressed a wish to resign they would have received short shrift, as deserters understandably did. Indeed, it was at this critical time in the life of the Legion that misunderstandings or mistakes which might be attributed to Shaw himself during his recruiting in Scotland began to bear bitter fruit. In the case of the Scottish regiments, unlike the others, there was confusion as to the length of the engagement the men had entered, so that many of the Scots believed that by the summer of 1836 they had fulfilled their contracts.

This led to a mutiny of the 8th Regiment, which spread to involve others including the 6th and 10th and some of the Lancers. On the morning of 16 August, Somerville tells us, the 8th were paraded to march to the height of Alza, two miles away, to relieve the 1st Regiment. While waiting for Colonel Godfrey, much whispering developed in the ranks, despite their officers' commands to be quiet. Somerville then learned that a mutiny was planned; he had been kept ignorant of this by his comrades, who thought he would not take part in it, but would try to prevent it. Godfrey rode up at 9 o'clock, paused to take his customary pinch of snuff, and ordered the parade to attention. This order, and the order to dress ranks, were obeyed, but at the command to shoulder arms the only two to obey were Somerville and his corporal. When threatened by Godfrey, the individual sections of the Grenadier Company obeyed his order to shoulder arms, but the other companies made it plain they would not obey. When Godfrey asked the reason for the mutiny he was told it was the want of pay, but another man raised the question of their having to serve for another year, for which he was punished. On the issue of pay Godfrey admitted it was a great grievance, but that he also had not been paid, and had laid out £300 of his own money on the regiment. At 3 p.m. General Chichester addressed the 8th, asking them what they wanted. An Irishman named Conolly spoke up for the men, saying that they had fought on 5 and 28 May and on 6 June, and been praised for their conduct, having suffered hunger, frost and snow before. When asked if they would do their duty if they were paid, the whole regiment agreed, and Chichester promised to raise the money that very day. His promise was kept, and at six in the evening the regiment again fell in in the presence of the paymaster and a mule laden with a heavy bag of dollars. Although the money, or part of it at least, was there, the men had resolved to go nowhere except to San Sebastian until they were paid in full. The management of this delicate situation was not ideal since Chichester and Godfrey disagreed on how to handle it.

Matters were made worse by trouble in the 1st Lancers. Although most of them had enlisted for two years, sixty men who had hurriedly joined the others before leaving England had not engaged for the full period, so that their situation resembled that of the Scottish regiments. When their CO, Colonel Kinloch, asked for the names of those not wishing to serve more than one year, sixty men answered. Their horses, arms and accoutrements were removed, they were marched into San Sebastian and later marched out by four companies of the 10th Regiment to be tried by court-martial. Twenty-five lancers were charged with mutiny. The preliminaries had been completed and the first man was being tried when the 8th Regiment armed themselves and broke in to free the lancers. Colonel Kinloch demanded that the officer in command of the 10th, who were outside, should disarm the mutineers of the 8th, but the 10th refused to interfere, their officer saying that he must have higher orders before he could act, and the men shaking the priming out of their pans and unfixing their bayonets.

Bad though the situation was, it now took another ludicrous downturn. The 8th Regiment was taken by sea to Santander where twenty-five men were chosen allegedly to mount a guard, but in reality to be imprisoned on board the naval frigate *Castor* as ringleaders in the mutiny. Despite reports of their 'cruel treatment' in the English newspapers they were, as Somerville reports, very well treated, being given excellent food, clothing, hammocks and blankets, luxuries they had not enjoyed since leaving Scotland. After three weeks of imprisonment they were visited by Colonel Godfrey, who offered to pardon them if they would promise good behaviour, the alternative being a Spanish prison. Godfrey easily obtained this promise.

Eventually the Spanish government transferred £12,000 to San Sebastian and the men were paid. Godfrey, well aware of how they would spend the money, warned them sternly against the dangers of drink, offering to remit their pay to London. The money was paid out by the paymaster to the officers in charge of companies and thence to their men. Captain Sheilds and Sergeant Somerville got about £100 in all kinds of Spanish coin for their company. When the money was given out there were loud complaints from those who had sold their uniform and clothing to raise cash, and had appropriate deductions made from their pay. 'You've *ninepence* to get, Jock,' Somerville informed one Scot, who could not understand this when some of his friends were getting £3. He was told, 'You've had 17 pairs of shoes, 20 shirts, 4 pairs of trousers, besides many other things.' 'What did you do with all these?' the captain enquired, but got no answer.

No sooner had Somerville completed the paying than the mayhem Godfrey had feared began: 'Those who had got pounds were lying drunk and pennyless. Some who had got none had fifty dollars. For three or four miles around, the roads to the wine-shops were crowded. Through the fields and on the roads they were lying dead drunk.' Wine cost about fivepence a quart, enough to intoxicate any one. Hosts of beggars and Spaniards with food and articles for sale came flocking from far and near. Some of the men bought whole pigs, and roasted them on bonfires. Colonel Godfrey rode about, commandeering all the bullock carts to carry the drunken soldiers back to their quarters.

Such was the state of the regiment for six days. On the fourth day Godfrey proclaimed that his indulgence had ceased, and that any men not on parade next day would be considered absent without leave and punished accordingly. It was not until the sixth day that some soldiers returned under a guard of Spaniards, and were court-martialled. All were ordered two hundred lashes, but only the first received his punishment, the others being pardoned. An amnesty of one day was declared for those still absent. All were heard to say that they would rather serve without pay than have a repetition of such a riot.

Meanwhile, back in San Sebastian there had been a mutiny of the 10th Regiment, who for nearly a week refused to do any duty, and the 6th Scottish Regiment, having completed their year's service, demanded to be discharged and sent home. General Shaw, who had brought the Scottish regiments out without a clear contract, was in an embarrassing situation; nonetheless he urged 'prompt measures' on General Evans in dealing with the 6th, meaning that they should be forced to serve longer by the threat of force. The failure of this approach had already been seen in the affair of the 8th and Evans wisely avoided it.

The mutiny of the 10th Regiment in mid-August 1836 was certainly taken seriously by Evans. Several of the soldiers had threatened or struck their officers, including their adjutant, Captain Wright, Captain O'Dell, Lieutenants O'Donnell and McIntosh and Lieut. Colonel de Lasaussaye. Details of the court-martial at San Sebastian were naturally given prominence in the Irish newspapers; the *Cork Evening Standard* of 12 September carried an extract from the general orders of the Legion of 31 August. Six privates and a sergeant of the regiment were tried and all but one convicted as charged. Four were sentenced to death, but Evans commuted this to transportation.* One man was sentenced to two hundred lashes and another to three weeks of solitary confinement. Evans cautioned the men of the 10th against letting themselves be 'betrayed by the effects of intoxication into acts of insubordination, mutiny and outrage' and attributed their behaviour to the maddening effects of liquor. The account of the episode in the *Clonmel Advertiser* of 17 September was less detailed. It reported that about 45 of the 10th had rebelled and gone up to the Castle (to be imprisoned). The regiment was said to number not more than 350 men. The report continued 'They say that Col. O'Connell brought them out, and now he has deserted them.' This refers to Colonel Maurice O'Connell, who was later to be briefly commander-in-chief of the Legion and who seems, from later events, to have been as devoted as any to the welfare of his men. The explanation of the charge of deserting the regiment probably lies in the fact that, as recorded in the same issue of the paper, O'Connell, with Lieut. Colonel Cannan of the 9th, had recently left London 'to proceed overland' to San Sebastian. (The Channel crossing and travel through France presumably had more appeal for them than another venture in the Bay of Biscay.)

The situation in the Legion at this time was very unhappy. The *Standard* referred to General Shaw's much-discussed resignation. Desertions, it wrote, were frequent, and the officers, 'having no chance of fighting the enemy (a questionable statement) are fighting duels with each other'. Among other officers resigning were Colonel G.C. Swan of the 7th Regiment, a half-pay

* In the British army, of the seventy-six death sentences passed on soldiers between 1826 and 1835, thirty-five were commuted to transportation [Holmes, 2001].

British officer who had fought bravely in the action of 5 May, when he was severely wounded. The promotion of Colonel Godfrey over his head was quoted as the reason for his resignation. The paper commented that Godfrey was a 'Portuguese officer and out of the British service', indicating the bad blood existing between the two groups of officers.

Duelling had been quite common between officers in the Legion, but it assumed major proportions at about this time. The correspondent of the *Clonmel Advertiser* wrote on 1 September that 'we have had some severe skirmishing, but unfortunately, not with the enemy'. Colonel Lasaussaye, deputy quartermaster-general, and Major Richardson, late of the 4th Regiment, had recently had a duel. Three shots each were fired, fortunately without effect, an explanation took place by Major Richardson, and the parties left the ground. The previous day, Captain Parkes of the 10th had fought with another officer, who was slightly wounded. If this is true, Parkes was something of a fire-eater as well as a good shot, since he had also 'gone out' with Captain O'Connor of the 3rd, 'who was dangerously wounded and it is said has since died'. Parkes had also had a skirmish the evening before, and there was to be a court of inquiry the next day, which certainly seems merited by his score of one dead and one wounded.* The paymaster of the 3rd had 'hit one of his subalterns slightly'; the *casus belli* was not mentioned, but the unfortunate paymasters of the Legion were probably unpopular due to arrears of pay, as scapegoats for the Spanish government, the most dilatory of paymasters.†

---

* More blood-thirsty still was Cornet and Riding Master T. Murphy, of the 2nd Lancers, described by Somerville as 'a great character', who shot and killed Capt W.A. Smith of the same regiment in a duel. Formerly a troop sergeant major in the British 3rd Light Dragoons, he went on to kill two Carlist peasants and fifteen soldiers, some of whom had been promised quarter.

† In August 1836, the financial problems of the regular Cristino army aggravated the troubles of the queen regent in her summer palace at La Granja. Discontented over arrears of pay, and encouraged by leaders of the Progressives, a group of sergeants in the neighbouring barracks staged a revolt. Defying their commanding officer, their regimental band played Diego's hymn, the anthem of the Liberals, and were at once arrested. The sergeants then took command of the troops and marched on the palace, shouting for the Constitution of 1812. Cristina received a three-man deputation led by Sergeant Alejandro Gomez, who demanded restoration of the Constitution and dismissal of the unpopular ministry. Resisting these demands at first, she later agreed to meet a larger group. Many of these had been drinking heavily, and their threats forced Cristina to agree, signing a decree that the Constitution should be published and promising to change her ministry. Such a promise she knew she could not break without disastrous results. She had survived a hazardous ordeal as well as possible. The Carlist campaign meanwhile was flourishing; General Gomez had captured the city of Córdova and reached the Mediterranean, but Carlos himself, determined on nothing less than absolute power, took no diplomatic advantage of the sergeants' mutiny to exploit the split in the ranks of his enemies.

CHAPTER ELEVEN

The Legion repulses a massive Carlist attack, 1 October 1836

This troubled short period of mutiny and duelling gave way to a more settled, though brief, phase for the Legion, as far as the enemy would allow. They returned to San Sebastian on 10 September with perfect order now restored, and passed their time in drilling twice daily on the sands of the bay, in guard duties and piquets. New uniforms were issued. Colonel Apthorpe, on one year's leave from the East India Company, took over command of the 8th Regiment from Colonel Godfrey, who was promoted brigadier-general in the place of Shaw, who had resigned.

The period of calm lasted only about three weeks. Taking advantage of the departure of three thousand Spanish troops from Evans' force and their embarkation for Santander, leaving no more than six thousand bayonets to defend his extended lines, the Carlists again took the offensive. On 1 October they began a heavy bombardment of San Sebastian from Ametza hill, and later columns of Carlist infantry drove back the Legion's piquets with a murderous fire. An advanced piquet of thirty men of the 3rd Regiment, Westminster Grenadiers, stationed in a house and courtyard, maintained their position with great valour, despite the death of their officer, Lieutenant Jackson, early in the action. The house later became known as the Westminster piquet-house, and when the battle was over the Legion were able to visit the building, amusing themselves by counting the holes made in its walls by the Carlist cannon balls. Evans took the trouble to count them and came up with a tally of over seventy.

It fell to Colour-Sergeant Somerville to mobilise his company. He describes how the bugler, given no time to dress, was running around stark naked, shouting for his bugle and, having found it, continued running in a state of nature, playing 'Turn out the whole'. Adjutant O'Driscoll 'chased the poor bugler from house to house along the riverside, making him blow the alarming rouse at every door'. To the boom of cannon and rattle of musketry, mounted officers, including Evans, galloped back and forth on the road to San Sebastian.

It was a deserter from the Legion, named Wilson, who had previously served in the Royal Artillery at Woolwich, who directed the Carlist artillery, resulting in its unwonted accuracy at a distance of 1,200 yards.* This was the first occasion the Carlist guns had proved effective, perhaps because Wilson had only recently deserted, dazzled by the lure of Carlist gold. A group of Legion officers stood in the path of a cannonball from Ametza hill. Major Hogg saw it coming and saved himself and his horse by springing to one side, but others were less fortunate, or less agile. About six men were knocked down and several wounded. One man was cut in half. Somerville describes a bizarre episode in which a cannonball hit a group of four – a mounted officer, two Chapelgorris behind him and an Englishwoman further back. 'The ball carried away the horse's nose, then entered its breast, explored the regions of its inside, and made its exit behind, leaving the rider unhurt. It next took off one of the Chapelgorri's legs, he being on higher ground. Then the one behind him, on lower ground, was knocked dead at once, and the ball, travelling a little further, came in contact with the woman, committing an inexpressible injury. Her wound, though not fatal, was extremely dangerous, and I believe afforded the medical officers an experiment, perhaps without parallel in the history of surgical operations. It was only due to Mr Alcock, and another eminent gentleman of the hospital, that they at all times exerted themselves to save the wounded, and that in this case they did so particularly and were eminently successful.' The correspondent of the London *Times* adds further details: the injured woman was an Irishwoman 'who was in the family way, and had another child in her arms'. The horsemanship of the rider of the dead horse, Adjutant Foreman of the 4th, was compared by the reporter with that of Squire Osbaldeston. Although he escaped unscathed, beyond a rather smart shock to his nervous system, Lieutenant Foreman was mentioned as being slightly wounded on the list of casualties in the same edition of *The Times*.

The Royal Artillery was now working closely with the Legion, and again displayed its superior gunnery. Colonel Colquhoun was directing the artillery and quickly scored hits on the Carlist position, according to Somerville, a mile distant, and later on their guns on Ametza hill, killing the turncoat Wilson and silencing the guns.

The balance had swung in favour of the Legion, and their cavalry now came into action. Under Lieutenant Colonel Wakefield, the 1st

* Evans, in his report, estimated it at no more than 500 yards.

Lancers were summoned by the trumpet-call 'Boot and Saddle'. They charged on the south east side of Ametza hill, to the north of which was the 8th Regiment with Somerville. The Carlists gave way, retiring behind their breastworks where the cavalry could not follow them, and retreated under heavy fire. The 8th Regiment was not engaged in the action that morning, and Somerville had a good opportunity to see the charge of the Lancers. Their horses were in fine condition and many of the men had served in British cavalry regiments, while others were Polish soldiers of fortune, and noted for their bravery. The sight of horses returning without riders, and men without horses, showed only too plainly the losses they had sustained. Somerville admired the way the Lancers went through their evolutions in beautiful style, as if on a field-day, but regretted that there was only one point on the line of attack where the use of cavalry was practicable, and that only partially so, 'else the Carlists might have suffered much more than they did'. The Spaniards, he believed, did not know of the tactic of forming squares to receive cavalry or, if they did, seldom practised it, preferring to fight in light infantry style, always with a natural or artificial defence to fall back on. Similar comments on the limitations of cavalry in the campaign were made by Thompson in his letters. The correspondent of the *Cork Evening Standard* wrote on 2 October: 'Cavalry are of no use in this country. We lost 18 horses yesterday out of two troops that were out.' (He did not mention that they also had two officers and ten men wounded.)

Next the infantry went into action. The 6th Scottish Regiment advanced over the same ground when the Lancers had charged. The Carlists fell back and the 6th took their position with trifling loss. Their dog Briton, already twice wounded, led the charge, 'in conformity with his military character, only once being heard to bark'. He was accompanied by a Spanish dog 'which fell and retreated on three feet, while Briton held his ground with a determined bow-wow until a ball silenced him by cutting him slightly in the throat, when he returned to his companion in hobbling retreat, and tried to turn him to advance, but the Spaniard sat on his hunkers and looked mournfully on, when all at once he was shot dead by a ball going through him. Briton at the same time got another wound on his head, and came out and got his wound partially dressed. Then, impatient to get away, he went to the dead dog, trying to make him rise, howling and attracting the men's attention to his dead companion – but unattended to, as there were other matters of importance going on.' There is something heartwarming about this little incident and its importance for those who saw it 'in the valley of death'.

Details of the human casualties are given in Somerville's narrative and in the press reports of the battle. Captain H.G. Backhouse of the artillery, an enthusiast in his profession, decided to approach close to the enemy, galloped forward with other rocketeers, dismounted, and took up a new position, 'firing a rocket with dreadful vengeance, slaughtering along a line of a battalion, previously screened'. He had prepared another and was in the act of setting it off, when he was shot through the head. *The Times'* correspondent had met Backhouse in another part of the field an hour before his death, and after a hearty shake of the hand asked him how he was getting on, to which he replied, 'Oh damn it! We are knocking them about like bricks.'

Somerville's comrade 'Muckle Jamie' was badly wounded but refused to go the rear, declaring, 'I say, Captain Sheilds, are ye not gaun to gie me my siller afore I gang into the hospital to die?' When finally seen by the surgeon his trousers and shoes were full of blood.

General Evans himself, riding about with the greatest imaginable cool-ness from one regiment to another, was slightly wounded, a ball grazing his right ear. Somerville commented that a thousand balls must have passed near Evans that day, yet this was the only one that touched him. Whatever their criticisms of him, no one who saw Evans in battle could question his courage; some in fact spoke of his foolhardiness.

Recollecting a moment of relative calm in the battle, Somerville com-ments how a certain spirit of kindness comes over the spirits of men when under fire. He and his company found themselves in a very snug corner behind a wall while their artillery behind bombarded the enemy:

> A high wind carried over the blue smoke, and the sun, shining in his usual way, on the opposite side of the river, appeared so common and unconcerned-like, that on looking over to it, no one would have thought that the scene of smoke, fire, bustle and noise, between that side and us, was that thing that is called a battle. It went on and on, the same, long continued roll of thun-der, the Rifles, 3rd and 10th Regiments, who had been all day at the work, still kept hard at it. The others had all a share, but were generally relieving each other, such as the 8th relieving the 4th and so on.

General Fitzgerald's brigade, *The Times* reported, was constantly engaged under fire, and firing from five o'clock in the morning until noon when, from the complete exhaustion of the men, and their muskets having become foul from the frequent discharges, they had to be relieved by General Chichester's brigade. From noon until 6 p.m. Chichester's brigade carried on with equal fortitude.

The Times' correspondent could see no substantially beneficial result to the Legion from this long day's fighting, during which several hundred shot, shells and rockets were expended and some three hundred thousand rounds of ball cartridge on both sides fired away. The only satisfactory result seemed to be that it gave incontestable proof of the high degree of efficiency and soldier-like conduct in the field that the Legion had reached through so many obstacles, preventions and discouraging circumstances. No better proof could be given than the eagerness of the men, after being engaged in the field and under fire for thirteen hours, to charge up the steep sides of Ametzagana hill and storm the deep entrenchments and high breastworks of the enemy on its ridge. This feeling almost expressed itself in murmurs among some of the regiments at being prevented by Evans from attempting this feat. The *Spectator*, as before, supported the Legion, writing that they had had another opportunity of proving that bad fare and shabby treatment had not affected their gallantry and discipline, despite the fruitless fighting on this occasion.

In his official despatch to General Rodil, the reinstated Cristino commander-in-chief, Evans wrote:

> Our troops were full of ardour and confidence, and we might probably have seized on the enemy's cannon, but having already gained a decisive success, and inflicted a severe punishment on the rebels, I did not desire to throw away for an inadequate result 400 or 500 additional men in killed and wounded, which it might have cost us to storm the steep and entrenched heights before us, particularly as it does not enter into my plan to retain possession of that position.

Though no ground was taken in this costly engagement, which was purely one of defence, the Carlists had been repulsed and severely defeated, with heavy losses in killed and wounded. Evans believed these must have amounted to at least one thousand; one of their own officers said that they had lost 'the flower of Guipuzcoa'. The official return of the Cristino casualties gave 236 British, of whom 56 were killed and 180 wounded. The Spanish units had 19 killed and 121 wounded, a total of 140, making 376 combined casualties. The three British officers killed were Backhouse of the Artillery, Lieutenant Jackson, 3rd Regiment, who was killed early in the heroic defence of the advanced piquet, and Lieutenant Gartland, 10th Regiment, much lamented by his men. On 3 October the coffins of Backhouse and Jackson, bearing their arms covered with crepe, were carried in procession up the steep path that wound (as it does today) round the side of the castle hill to the plateau within a few hundred feet of the summit, where they were buried. The coffins were followed by General Evans and his staff, all the principal officers of the Legion and as many others as were not on duty. Colonel Colquhoun read the funeral service and a farewell volley fired over the graves. Lieutenant Gartland,* being a Catholic, was allowed burial in the Spanish cemetery, to which his remains were accompanied by the officers and men of the 10th Regiment, many of whom would also have been of the 'Old Faith'.

Of the seventeen wounded British officers, seven or eight had severe wounds. These included Colonel Kirby, 1st Regiment, Lieutenant Middleton, 1st Lancers, Captain O'Connor, 3rd Regiment, Captain Asgill, 4th Regiment, Captain Robertson, 8th Regiment, Captain Atkins or Atkyns, a County Cork man, and Lieutenant McLean, both of the Rifles. (Two years later, in December 1838, Lieutenant Colonel Atkins was called before a medical board in Dublin for a pension for severe wounds received in the attack on Ametza hill, among hundreds of former members of the Legion, officers and private soldiers.)

The Order Book of the Legion for 1836, incomplete though it is, gives figures for the deaths in hospital in the General Military Hospitals in San Sebastian (San Telmo) and Santander. In the month of October it records seventeen deaths in San Telmo from the 2nd onwards, the day after the battle. Five men died on 2 October, two on the 4th and one or two on many other dates that month. It seems likely (though the causes of death are not given) that most of these deaths followed injuries suffered on 2 October.

---

* George Borrow in *The Bible in Spain* describes his visit in May and June 1837 to the hospitable Dr Gartland, head of the Irish College at Salamanca, 'a genuine scion of the good Hibernian tree, an accomplished scholar, and a courteous and high-minded gentleman'. It is possible that he was a relative of young Lieutenant Gartland, perhaps an uncle.

The men of Somerville's company and no doubt all the Legionaries were much occupied on the day after the battle in writing to their families at home. Many were illiterate, and Somerville, who functioned as a father-confessor or elder brother to the powerless and weak, was in demand to write letters for them. He and another educated Scot whose own description of the battle appeared to aspire to Miltonian heights, were overwhelmed by appeals to pen letters for their comrades. Having written a dozen letters, Somerville excused himself from further commissions, pleading his official duties as colour-sergeant: he had 'all the regimental and general orders to copy, returns for rations, ammunition, boots, shirts, trousers, 5th of May medals, and other things to write, besides a number of articles to enter into the ledger, before tattoo.'

This same day, 2 October, was the date when the yearly allowance of clothing referred to in Somerville's agenda was served out to the Legion. With the meticulous detail of a quartermaster he explains that, between the gratuitous clothing and that charged to the men's accounts for articles which they had sold or destroyed, the *average* for each man was now one greatcoat, and either a second greatcoat or a blanket; 2 dress coats; 3 jackets; 3 pairs of cloth trousers; 5 pairs of white trousers; 4 pairs of Blucher boots; 14 pairs of shoes; 12 shirts; 2 flannels; 4 pairs of worsted socks; 2 pairs of mitts; 4 forage caps; and all the other necessaries that make up a soldier's kit. Some regiments had items peculiar to them; the 6th Regiment had their second and third tartan plaids. The British government at about this time sent out one English blanket for each man as a gift. Though not over-generous, these blankets were a valuable present since the Spanish government had never provided the Legion with any bedding. Though the situation at this time was far better than in the previous harsh winter, many items were still in short supply. A request for more blankets, surgical instruments and hospital stores for the Legion was sent to London on 25 October. Such requests continued throughout the life of the Legion.

CHAPTER TWELVE

Rest and recreation:
a quiet Sunday in San Sebastian

It is comforting to know that life in San Sebastian at this time was not without some pleasures and relaxations. At this point in his narrative Somerville describes a sunny day in October in San Sebastian 1836 when he accompanied a young Scottish medical student on a tour of the town. It was a Sunday, and began as usual with the Spanish colours being hoisted on the citadel and walls, and a few extra cannon being fired at the Carlist lines. They had entered the town early and commented on the difference between the streets of a Spanish town and those of their own country. No congregated drunkards in public houses, or dirty idlers lounging about the streets, were to be seen. The church bells tolled early and every Spaniard, male and female, rich and poor, rose from their beds before the sun and joined soberly together in religious worship. About 7 o'clock the shops opened and continued trading until nearly noon. They entered the church as soon as the city gates were opened, finding it crowded, with many worshippers, unable to enter, kneeling outside. This magnificent church, probably the church of San Vicente, adjacent to San Telmo, was at that time the only one in the town used for religious purposes, the others serving as stores and magazines. Somerville's companion was struck by the beauty of the young Spanish women, demurely veiled, and later saw them in the streets in more coquettish mood. At this point General Charles Chichester emerged from the church; a zealous Catholic, he went to church with all the devotion and regularity of a Spaniard. The young visitor was impressed by his fine, tall, military figure, 'but wondered how he could be a Catholic'. Somerville seemed amused by the insular bigotry of the young man, who was shocked by all the buying and selling on the Sabbath morning, and gently pointed out the contrast between what they saw there and the situation in the high street of Edinburgh, where two-thirds of the people were still snoring in their beds after the excessive drinking of Saturday night.

Strolling along to the vegetable market, the visitors' attention was drawn to a perfect specimen of Spanish beauty presiding over a stall with 'haughty consciousness of superiority'. Her story, as Somerville tells it, was a romantic one: the daughter of a peasant in Estramadura, she had come to the north 'to wait the opportunity of committing a deed'. A general of Spain, now high in command, had shot every tenth man of a regiment, and her brother was one of them.* 'What do you think of that one?', Somerville asked his friend. 'That's the tragic muse personified,' he answered. 'Has she to sell greens for a living?' 'I don't know,' I replied; 'but we must be off.'

Moving on, they encountered various senior officers of the Legion, including the adjutant-general and the dandified quartermaster-general who had replaced MacDougall. Neither of these, nor other officers, had a copper to pay for their cigars or their brandy-punch, but Somerville and his friend were in funds, and discomfited the dandy by being able to pay for the drinks they bought from two attractive French ladies. Although the men had been paid in August, the officers were still in arrears of their pay, and it must have been a galling experience for those normally able to pay their way without difficulty.

Passing through the gate the couple then visited the lines, seeing the 70-foot high wall, the ditch, forts, more ditches, further forts and drawbridges which made San Sebastian's strength. They crossed the river by the new wooden bridge and visited one of the batteries. At the Queen's battery they met Lieutenant Skedd, an old veteran of twenty-eight years in the British Royal Artillery, who had until a few weeks before been sergeant-major of the 8th Regiment and a close colleague of Somerville. General Chichester then joined them and asked Skedd what the Carlists were doing throwing up works so close to his lines. 'Send a shell over among them,' he said. This was done at once and, Skedd being a clever gunner, the visitors having a telescope, were able to see 'how a shell was fired – how it bursted, and how heads were blown off, and how unconcernedly the Carlists began to work again while a few carried off the dead and wounded'. Another shell was then fired which killed the wounded Carlists and those who carried them, upsetting the young medical man, who thought it 'a d——d shame'. Worse followed when a Legion soldier raised his head at the wrong

* In a later chapter Somerville explains that rumour had it that the lady was the sister of one of those Chapelgorris executed by General Espartero as punishment for plundering and profaning a church. If so, she never enjoyed her revenge, since Espartero lived to see the accession of Alphonso XII, Isabella's son.

moment, to have it blown off by another of Skedd's shells. Chichester's comment was pragmatic: 'It can't be helped, Skedd, but I'll put another sergeant on duty there, and he shall be answerable for every man's head being clear of danger, else he shall lose his own head.'

'"Come, bury that body now, and get on with your work; don't make an ado about that," the officer of the working party called out, and the body being buried, thus passed one scene of the drama of the Legion, and I observing to my friend that he saw we had a curious life of it, and he answering, that he thought some of us had a curious death of it, we left the tragedy and proceeded to the glacis to witness the grand melodrama of the Sunday afternoon.'

Here they found regiments going through their evolutions and exercise, drilled by officers conscious of the crowds watching them. On the sands horseracing was in progress, and in the fields beyond there was steeplechasing. The Spanish observers, especially the young women, were entranced by these English sports. The reckless Colonel Fortescue rode about, accompanied by his wife, whose freedom and grace on her prancing steed, 'characteristic of the English lady of fashion, drew forth the admiration of the fair maidens of Spain, who it must be known, ride only in baskets, two being carried on a mule at once in panniers that hang on each side of the animal'.

The tall figure of Colonel Apthorpe, Somerville's CO, and his lady attracted their attention, with several other officers, some with their wives and families. Somerville pointed out Colonel Cannan of the 9th riding a fine chestnut mare. The elegantly dressed officers were identified in turn to the young visitor, who commented on the contrast between them and an old grey-headed man like a farmer, in blue jacket and coloured trousers, without a sword, who was saluted by all the officers who passed him. 'For goodness' sake,' said Somerville, 'don't make a remark on that old fellow, where any of the Irish will hear you, for that's Old Charlie, General Fitzgerald, and these are his sons, Major and Lieutenant Fitzgerald; the first one he flogged when he came to the country was his son, to let his regiment see what like the cat-o'-nine-tails and a blistered back were.' This brave and picaresque Irishman would always stand out in a crowd, and after the war continued to live an adventurous and unconventional life, never shirking a fight or a quarrel.

Next, on a grey stallion an officer of about sixty, with a large cocked hat which had seen better days, large red moustachios with snuff lying on them, and in a uniform richly trimmed with gold, rode by. His entourage consisted of two aides-de-camp and an officer 'the exquisite of military dandyism', who was identified as Colonel Jockmus, a Frenchman and the Legion's new quartermaster-general. The principal figure was General Godfrey, Somerville's previous CO. His keen eye noticed one of the 8th with a button off his new dress-coat. Reprimanded, the man excused himself saying he had no thread and no money to buy any. He was sternly told to go to his captain and say that General Godfrey had sent him to get half a pisetta to buy thread.

Somerville's sharp eye for the ridiculous found plentiful entertainment among his officers, many of whom were military dandies. Colonel Gilbert Hogg, who later commanded the 8th Highlanders, came in for critical comment. 'Fancy the clever Colonel Hogg, with his corsets, tight uniform, boots that pinched his corns – his sharp-grey eye and his yellow hair – fancy him with three young ladies.' The colonel might not have written the excellent character reference he sent Somerville two years later from Gilstown, Co. Roscommon, if he had known of his sergeant's view of him.

The parade of personalities in the Cristino army continued with the appearance of an old fat man, his belly lying on the front of his saddle, with the Spanish lancers riding after him, as the embryonic doctor described him. This was General Jáuregui, known to the Spaniards as *El Pastor*, the Shepherd. He was one of Zumalacárregui's old chiefs, and one of the Cristinos' most successful generals, who had been fighting since the start of the war. A man of humble origins, originally a shepherd, he had been in turn half-shepherd, half-soldier and guerrilla (robber), was commissioned in the army and rose rapidly. He had many relations in the ranks, but had promoted very few of them. An excellent horseman, and familiar with every mountain path and pass and every guerrilla haunt, he was much loved by his men, but suffered from the jealousy and backbiting of the more aristocratic officer corps of Spain, among whom jealousy of their colleagues was a besetting sin, as Wellington had noted in his Peninsular campaigns.

The naval element next hove in sight. Commodore Lord John Hay, whose intervention by sea and land had been invaluable to the Legion, and was to be again, passed by; he had earlier lost one arm in battle and the empty sleeve was pinned up to his breast. The English sailors seemed the gayest and most heartwarming of the motley crowd. Their uniforms, hats with the words *Phoenix, Tweed* or *Royalist* and a sweetheart on one or both arms, gave evidence of the unchanged and unchangeable Jack Tar of Old England.

Spanish dances were going on in several groups, but the graceful, slow movements of the fandango, danced by the Spanish girls to the accompaniment of the guitar, were 'too lazy and intellectual for a sailor'. Several of them broke through the ring of spectators and pushed aside the partners to take the females by the hands, dance, caper and kiss at a rate of speed and with an enthusiasm of mirth that put the Spanish onlookers into convulsions of laughter.

The mingling of the various colourful characters in festival mood, English and Spanish, male and female, young and old, military and civilian, produced an atmosphere of carnival in deep contrast to the grim experiences which the soldiers had endured and would endure again. Somerville, savouring again in retrospect the carefree and lively experience, ended his account. 'Fancy these things and the Spaniards going all early to bed, and the Sunday of San Sebastian as we saw it nearly complete.'

CHAPTER THIRTEEN

Relief of Bilbao: a second winter at war

Life continued fairly peacefully for the Legion until 17 November 1836, when a minor action took place. The 6th Regiment were ordered to cross the western boundary of their lines, and burn some houses which the Carlist piquets had long occupied, and from which they often came down to attack the sentries of the 6th and other regiments or men gathering water, as well as attempting, often with success, to entice men to desert. The houses were situated on a hillside, separated from each other by small cornfields and orchards; bombarding them with balls and shells had been ineffective, and it was decided that more direct and drastic action was needed. The men of the 6th forded the river 'at knee and neck deep', drove back the Carlists, took possession of their houses and set them on fire. The small action was bravely carried out, but Somerville refers feelingly to the heart-sickening scene of war's other side. One cottage, beyond reach of the Cristino cannons, was still occupied by a family consisting of grandmother, daughter and grandchildren, with their poultry, pigs, goats, cow and calf grazing and browsing in the orchard and on the green. The old woman took the pigs and poultry into the house, which was barricaded. Although the Carlists rallied to defend the house, they were driven back by the 6th. When the men broke into the house to loot the livestock they found only the old woman, and rescued her while the mother and children were hidden in a garret. Only when the house was set on fire was it realised that they were still inside, but it was too late to save them. 'Smoke and a crackling blaze, with the noise of the pigs, hens and other animals, ended that dreadful act.' It was said that the old woman was sometimes seen lingering about the ruins of her house. This distressing episode was crudely illustrated in Somerville's History by an artist whose work was a deep disappointment to the author.

Meanwhile in other theatres the war continued with waxing and waning intensity. The capture of an important northern city had long been an ambition of Don Carlos. Bilbao would have been a glittering prize, if it could be taken. Its unsuccessful siege by the Carlists the previous year had cost them the life of Tomás Zumalacárregui, their most successful general

– an important factor in reducing their chances of ultimate victory. Now funds were again running low in the Carlists' war chest. Foreign bankers might be persuaded to lend more money if Bilbao were captured. Carlist operations against the city began on 22 October. The siege was mounted by the count of Casa Eguia, and General Villareal was to prevent the Cristinos from raising the siege.

The task was harder for the Carlists than in 1835, when the garrison of Bilbao had been much smaller. The Cristino general, San Miguel, now had a garrison of about six thousand men including artillery and national militia, the inhabitants were determined to defend their city and the outlying houses and convents, occupied by the Carlists the previous year, were now held by the queen's troops. Evans had been asked to send troops from San Sebastian to help in defending Bilbao, but was in no position to spare any men from his own meagre force. By capturing forts on both sides of the river Nervion, Eguia was able temporarily to cut off Bilbao from the sea, but his attempts to enter the city failed. The Carlist bombardment, starting on 25 October, opened up a breach of two hundred yards in the wall, which was stormed by three battalions, who were encouraged by the promise of four hours of pillage if successful. Their two attempts at the assault were repulsed with losses of two hundred dead and wounded. The defenders were pleased to find that the greatest damage done by the bombardment was in a street mainly occupied by citizens of Carlist sympathies. The blockade of the river was partly lifted on 31 October when an English gunboat forced its way past the port of Oliviaga through a heavy fire of musketry. General Espartero's relieving force was daily expected at Bilbao, a report from San Sebastian on 1 November stating that he would reach the city that very day. This was over-optimistic: Espartero's advance was delayed by bad weather and muddy roads, and he was forced to transport his troops from Castro (Urdiales) to Portugalete by sea, so that he only reached Portugalete, on the seaward side of Bilbao, in late November. There he concentrated his forces and did not start his final advance until 20 December. His approach was co-ordinated closely with Lord John Hay, whose naval squadron was involved in the relief of Bilbao. Ten heavy guns from HMS *Saracen* were landed and transported on sledges to cover Espartero's advance along the right bank of the river, and officers and men from the *Saracen*, the *Ringdove* and the *Comet* fought beside the Cristino troops, supported by Colonel Colquhoun and the Royal Artillery, equipped with field artillery and mountain howitzers. Espartero captured the bridge of Luchana and broke through the Carlist lines. On Christmas Day

1 Portrait of Assistant-Surgeon Morgan O'Connell, 10th Munster Light Infantry, 1837.

2

3

4

2 The Legion in Vitoria, 1836 – an unflattering caricature.
3 The French Foreign Legion in action against the Carlists.
4 Beggars in scarlet. From a drawing of 1810 ('Choral Symphony') by Edwyn Gill.

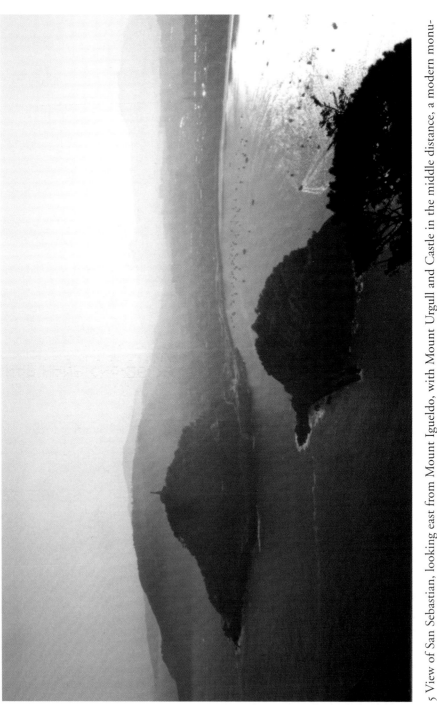

5 View of San Sebastian, looking east from Mount Igueldo, with Mount Urgull and Castle in the middle distance, a modern monument at the summit, Santa Clara Island in the foreground, and the Bay of La Concha to the right.

6 The former convent of San Telmo as it is today.

7 View of San Sebastian in 1835, looking west, showing the castle and town, the bridge over the river Urumea in the foreground, and convent of San Francisco at bottom left.

8 Vitoria with Legionaries in the foreground.

9 Hernani – with lancers and infantry of the Legion in the foreground.

10 The siege of Irun, May 1837. The bridge of Behobia with the Legion's Rifles firing at Carlists in the church.

11 Fuenterrabia.

12 The Town House of Irun, which survives today.

14 Gravestone of Col. Ebsworth on Castle Hill, San Sebastian.

13 Defaced monument to the British dead of Wellington's siege of San Sebastian, in the first Carlist war.

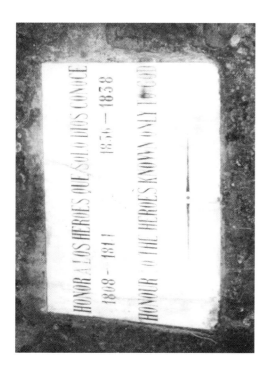

HONOR A LOS HEROES QUE SOLO DIOS CONOCE

1808 – 1814   1836 – 1838

HONOUR TO THE HEROES KNOWN ONLY TO GOD

15 Plaque in honour of British soldiers who died in the Peninsular War and the First Carlist War.

16 Tombstone of Col. William Tupper of the 6th Scotch Grenadiers.

17 The church at Andoain, where officers and men of the Legion defended
    themselves until promised quarter, and were then killed.

18 Medal for the action
of 5 May 1836 awarded
to Dr O'Connell.

19 Medal for the action
of March 1837 awarded
to Dr O'Connell.

the relieving force entered the city. Carlos' second failure to take Bilbao low-
ered his stock in the eyes of the hard-headed bankers of Europe, making them
even less willing than before to sink their funds in his faltering cause. The
effect on Cristino morale was uplifting, and in Britain and mainland Europe
the betting changed in favour of the queen and her party. Cristina decreed
that the town of Bilbao should add to the titles of 'Very Noble and Very
Loyal' which it already possessed that of 'Unconquerable and Unconquered'.
Titles were showered on the municipality of the town and decorations on the
army and the citizens involved in the defence and relief.

Writing in 1877, Major Francis Duncan of the Royal Artillery used
powerful metaphors to illustrate Espartero's raising of the siege:

> A chapter of accidents, a chapter of carnage – a time of vacillation,
> and yet a time of marvellous fortune in a brave general's life – a ray
> of light in a dull sky – an ambitious wave rising out of a grey sea,
> and courting the brightness of the lighthouse of public interest.

For General Evans and the Legion the news must have been welcome,
but their own situation was still grievous. The reports from San Sebastian
of the siege include mention of urgent despatches brought out by the
Rhadamanthus from Palmerston to Evans. The adjutant-general of the Legion,
the report states, was going to England with the return despatches, charged
by Evans with a very strong representation to Lord Palmerston 'of the very
painful and precarious position in which the Legion is placed, in consequence
of the apparent utter inability of the Spanish Government to pay the arrears
due, or fulfil its other engagements with the Legion'. This would be followed
by an attempt to get Palmerston to propose an arrangement to the Spanish
government by which the English Treasury would undertake to pay the
Legion (it was hoped on good and solid security from Spain). Should the
plan prove abortive, either by Palmerston's unwillingness to entertain it, or
by the Spanish government's refusal to agree, then Evans was firmly resolved
to embark himself and the Legion, and return to England.

A correspondent of *The Times* at this date showed more sympathy than
usual for Evans in his predicament.

> General Evans is well aware that he has now nothing to depend
> upon but the good faith of the British Government. The with-
> drawal of 5,300 Spanish troops from San Sebastian, with the

avowed purpose of intercepting the Carlist General Sanz in the Asturias, was in reality by a trick, to expose the Legion to the whole power of the Carlists, and so ensure its destruction. We state this advisedly. We know well that the majority of the Queen's generals would prefer the loss of San Sebastian to its preservation by General Evans. The Gallant Member for Westminster is as honest and high-minded as he is brave – this is his crime in the eyes of the intriguing gang who monopolise all honors in the ranks of the Constitutional army. Rodil would sacrifice Evans as readily as he has done the gallant Flinter* if he had opportunity.

These comments echo strongly those of the astute Somerville on the malicious motivation of Córdova at the time of the Legion's involvement in the battle of Arlaban the previous January. It was a situation of extreme difficulty for any commander, and it is hard to see how anyone could have coped with it any better than Evans had, and continued to do in the remaining months of the Legion's contracted service. *The Times* writer was quite correct: the Carlist attack of 1 October had followed only a few days after the 3,000 Spanish troops were withdrawn from Evans' command.

December and January of the winter of 1836–7 were kinder to the Legion in San Sebastian than the previous winter in Vitoria. Fortunately there were no epidemics, though isolated cases of typhus and other diseases occurred, taking their toll of officers and men.

---

* Brigadier-General Flinter, described variously as an Englishman and as an Irishman of good family (*Annual Register*, 1838) had fought for the queen from an early stage of the war. In 1834 he had written graphically of the privations of the queen's troops, poorly supported and led by their officers. He contrasted this with the superior quality of the Carlist light infantry, whose officers were men covered with scars from the War of Independence, practical and brave. In October 1836 Flinter was at Almaden, site of the rich mercury mines controlled by the Rothschild brothers, with 1,150 men and orders to dispute the entry of General Gomez into Estramadura. Vastly outnumbered by Gomez's forces, he had written to a friend that he intended to sell his life dearly and that 'you may depend that the honour of Old England will not be tarnished'.

He lived to fight on and defeat the Carlists in the mountains of Toledo. Despite the Spanish government's dislike and suspicion of him as an Englishman, public opinion, recognising his successes, resulted ultimately in his being appointed field-marshal in 1838 and placed in charge of the provinces of La Mancha and Toledo. Flinter's theatre of action was remote from the northern provinces, and it does not seem that he met Evans or had any dealings with the Legion. His advice would have been very useful if they had met.

Flinter committed suicide in Madrid in September 1838.

Somerville sketches the life of the Legion at the turn of the year. On Christmas morning the snow lay two feet deep, drifting into the ruins of the Antigua Convent, the billet of the 6th Regiment, the worst housed of all. The 8th occupied the Convent of St Bartholomew. The two Scottish regiments kept Hogmanay in uproarious style after celebrating Christmas quietly, but Somerville and his friends later kept the feast of Hansel Monday in traditional style, with theatricals, singing, card games and drinking. No less than eight taverns, established by those married women of the Legion who had survived the hardships of the former year, catered for the needs of the drinkers, dealing in 'akadente' (*aguardiente*: brandy) and other spirits as well as groceries. In the 8th only two of the ladies would condescend to do the laundry of the Legion, their conventional work, since they were so keen to set up in business. Colonel Ross and the officers of the 6th made a present of new gowns and mantles to the females who did *not* sell akadente, hoping that they would continue to do their washing.

Somerville singles out for special praise one soldier of the 6th whose representations of Scotch characters and 'cries of Edinburgh' delighted them all. The same man was to figure in a tragic episode later in his Narrative.

The 7th Irish occupied a 'city of huts' where they were crowded, drinking and making merry. Their huts were too small for the fighting and dancing, indispensable to the 7th, according to Somerville, which took place outside. 'Any member of another regiment who approached would either be dragged into the hut and forced to drink and be merry, or be knocked down outside, perhaps both; but it was certain he could not go through Irishtown unmolested.' On the other side of the river were stationed the 9th and 10th Irish Regiments, 'with many a genuine Irishman full of frolic and mischief'. Further away (and the separation of the ethnic elements was wisely designed) the English regiments lay in a village and some scattered houses, where they had made their quarters into a little London, with a Westminster, a Cheapside and a miniature Covent Garden. Extra money was allowed and everything possible was done to ensure a few good dinners. It was a very different Christmas from that of the previous year.

Despite a general order prohibiting any parley with the enemy, the rule was often broken, soldiers from the two sides meeting on neutral ground to exchange gifts of tobacco, from the Legion, and food and wine from the Carlists. Men of the Legion would also often go down towards the Carlist lines to get firewood from the ruined houses. In early February 1837 seven unarmed legionaries came down early one morning for firewood. The Carlists had hidden in a neighbouring house and, rushing out, captured five men. One of these was allowed to escape by his Carlist captor, but the other four were taken to Hernani where the Carlist general, under the Durango Decree, condemned them to death. One of the four was Neil Cunningham, the soldier of the 6th whose theatrical performance had so enchanted his audience a few weeks earlier. Playing now on a different stage, he was fortunate as the only Catholic among the captives in being shot dead at once. The fate of the other three, if the reports Somerville heard were true, was dreadful. It was said that their fingers, ears and other parts were cut off, they were wounded with scissors and then tied to posts and left to die. One man was said to have lingered for forty-eight hours.

After this time, Somerville tells us, and the English newspapers confirm, nothing of importance happened until 10 March 1837. All was a regular routine of military duty, and a daily expectation of an advance on the Carlists. The private correspondents of the English papers wrote impatiently of the inactivity of the Legion and 'No news from Spain' was a common headline, with explicit or implicit criticism of Evans. Somerville himself criticised the tendency of the press to give 'white a tinge, and black a darker shade'. He referred to Michael Burke Honan, correspondent of the *Morning Herald*, who was in the court and camp of Don Carlos, and whose account was the best description of that side of the war yet written: it was Honan who had given details of the sad fate of the men of the Legion captured by the Carlists.

CHAPTER FOURTEEN

Oriamendi

'Soldiers are citizens of death's grey land,
drawing no dividends from time's tomorrows.'

Siegfried Sassoon, *Dreamers*, 1918

In March 1837 the men of the Legion had only three months of their contract still to serve, and it seemed unlikely that many of those who had survived the perils of battle, disease and starvation would hasten to re-enlist, unless some notable victory could be achieved. Since 1836 there had been three major offensive operations from San Sebastian against the Carlists, which could only be described as of limited success. Their full benefit had been denied the queen's cause by failure to follow up with further advances, a failure criticised by many at the time, but which in the hindsight of history is understandable. Determined attacks on the city had been made by the enemy, and repulsed by Evans' forces, often with great heroism. The difficulties of effective collaboration with their Spanish allies were all too evident to Evans and his men, with a pattern of betrayal and lack of support dating back to the abortive advance on Arlaban in January 1836.

Nonetheless there was heavy pressure on Evans and the Cristino generals to mount a massive combined operation, making use of the Legion while it was still available. General Sarsfield, then captain-general of Navarre, suggested a plan for a three-pronged advance against the Carlists. Sarsfield's own column was to advance from Pamplona towards Tolosa, that of Espartero would advance from Bilbao towards Durango, while Evans' forces would attack the Carlist lines at Hernani and Irun.

In theory the scheme seemed sound and promising and, under different conditions, might have succeeded, but many must have had grave reservations as to the chances of a successful combined operation. Evans knew from bitter experience that he could only depend on himself since trust bestowed on his allies would probably be betrayed. The assessment of the situation at this time, given in Francis Duncan's retrospective account of *The English in Spain* in the two Carlist wars, published in 1877. Duncan had written a history of the Royal Artillery and had read the letters and journals written by brother officers who had been employed under the English Foreign Office as commissioners with Queen Isabella's armies between 1834 and 1840. The most distinguished of the seven gunner officers was Colonel William Wylde, whose name occurs in many accounts, particularly of the siege of Bilbao and the Eliot Convention. Colonel Colquhoun, whose gunnery contributed so much to the Cristino successes, was another. Three officers of the Royal Engineers also played an important role with detachments of their men. Duncan pays tribute to them: 'The terms of the Eliot Convention would have been but empty platitudes had it not been for the ceaseless labours of these English officers, who for the first time in Spanish history organised that which reads like a paradox – philanthropy in war.'

Familiarity with the letters and despatches of Wylde and his colleagues gave Duncan a fuller insight into the motivation behind the actions, and inaction, of the key players in the war. His review of the manpower situation confirms that Evans' force was quite inadequate for any single-handed operation. Even with Sarsfield's force from Pamplona he would have needed further reinforcements from Espartero totalling at least 6,000 to 8,000 men to be of any use. In supplying these reinforcements to Evans, Espartero was checked by General Oráa, his indecisive chief-of-staff. Wylde's powers of persuasion, however, managed to obtain reserves from Espartero, and 5,000 men embarked at Portugalete for San Sebastian early in February, followed on 2 March by a further 1,500, in transports provided by Lord John Hay.

Duncan believed that the plan for a triple advance against the Carlist lines in Guipuzcoa was sound and thoughtful. If Evans were to attack the centre of their lines near San Sebastian, and if the right and left were simultaneously attacked by Espartero and Sarsfield, he believed there would have been a great probability of success, but co-operation was rare among Spanish generals, and jealousy was common: 'Sarsfield shone in excuses, but their quality was inferior to their number.' Writing to Evans in February 1837, he pleaded lack of funds as an excuse for not moving. He suggested that Espartero, rather than he, should take the initiative, and should have taken Durango before he himself should leave Pamplona. Sarsfield also claimed, untruthfully, to be outnumbered by the enemy in front of him, although he had at least 15,000 men. Evans himself, in his Memoranda of the campaign, recorded that he had told Sarsfield on five occasions in March of his intention to move out on 10 March. In his letter dated 9 March, but received by Evans on the night of the 11th, Sarsfield wrote, 'You may rely that I shall advance probably before 48 hours.' Evans made the point that, though Sarsfield had never been in England, he spoke and wrote the language perfectly, so that there was no linguistic excuse for misunderstanding.

Sarsfield's excuses and delays allowed the Carlists to strengthen their positions, especially Hernani, the target for Evans' attack. The Carlist commander, the Infante Don Sebastian, son of Don Carlos, following the introduction of conscription of all men between eighteen and fifty in the Basque provinces and Navarre, now had an army of some 32,000 men. He could see clearly that he had little to fear from Sarsfield in Pamplona, but much to fear from Evans. By the end of February Don Sebastian had no fewer than 17,000 men strongly entrenched in front of San Sebastian, with no sign of movement from either Espartero or Sarsfield. 'General Winter' again brought his battalions into play and snow lay a foot deep round San Sebastian. It was not a position in which any commander should have been placed, but Evans knew once more that he was on his own and must act without support.

His mixed force consisted of about 3,300 men of the Legion, including Lancers, 5,000 Spanish troops, about 450 Royal Marines with their own artillery, and a small detachment of the Royal Artillery made up of four or five officers and about a hundred other ranks. The regular British troops, though led by Evans, were under Commodore Hay's command.

On 10 March, according to the agreed plan, Evans moved off from San Sebastian to attack the Carlist lines before Hernani. His aim was to reach the same position as he had held on the right of the river Urumea before his attack on Fuenterrabia in June 1836. This involved capturing the heights of Ametzagana, or the Ametza hill, which had been taken by the Carlists and strongly fortified. Its recapture was achieved at considerable cost to Evans' forces. The left was then pushed forward to some rocky heights near the high road from Astigarra and Irun, which was held by Evans against vigorous Carlist attack until night, when he withdrew the troops to the neighbourhood of Alza.

Somerville devotes many pages in his narrative to the action of 10–17 March. The 4th, 8th, 9th and 10th Regiments advanced under the command of Generals Chichester and Fitzgerald. Somerville's account of the spirited attack on 10 March describes how Major Cotter of the 9th galloped in front of his and the 10th Regiments, and in a few minutes was at the top of the Ametza hill, single-handed among the Carlists, waving his sword and hurrahing while the Carlists retreated helter-skelter, and the infantry advanced up the hill, covered by the continuous heavy fire of the queen's artillery, until 'the furze bushes and trees covering the hill were scorched and at last the mountain side was in a universal blaze, and divided the combatants from contesting that part. There were dead and wounded of both parties left, and the lingering life of the dying was thus extinguished by the spreading flames. The wind rose high, and the fire blazed furiously. Noise, death and destruction continued. The very elements seemed to love the strife and, aiding the destroyers, said, "Well done, war! wreck! ravage! and kill, and we'll help ye."'

When darkness fell and the firing gradually died away, most of the infantry bivouacked for the night in the open air. Next day the sun rose to show the river, clear and deep, winding its way through the valley, as if nothing unusual had taken place, but the black, burned mountain looked dull and dreary, and the hospitals were filled with men groaning in their wounds. Somerville thought that upwards of one thousand men in Evans' army were killed or wounded, and that the Carlists must have had many more casualties, since they had been exposed to artillery and rockets, unlike the Cristinos. The fate of the wounded must have been grim. Dr Alcock does not refer to this in his account, but burns and the effects of hypothermia on those lying out in the March night would have added to the usual toll of bullet and cannonball.

March 11th was a day without action, apart from moving the artillery up to the captured heights, from which they opened heavy fire on all the houses within range, dislodging the Carlists, so that Somerville's brigade was able to cross the river and gain much ground, reaching behind the cover of their guns.

The triple plan, as far as Evans was concerned, had gone well. The results of 10 March had been better than expected, and on the 11th Evans waited, according to the plan, for his Spanish allies to fulfil their parts. At first optimism prevailed amid rumours that Espartero was on his way from Bilbao to Durango with twenty-eight battalions, and that Sarsfield had promised to advance if provided with a few days' rations. Sarsfield should have joined Evans for a combined attack on Hernani, Tolosa and other Carlist towns, but there was no sign of him. He had actually left Pamplona on the 11th but after one night had returned to his base because of bad weather. The Annual Register recorded that he returned to Pamplona, having encountered nothing worse than a severe wetting!*

---

* Alexander Ball provides a plausible explanation for Sarsfield's behaviour. He believed

The Carlists' intelligence network was highly effective and Don Sebastian, quickly realising that the field was clear as a result of Sarsfield's defection, made a forced night march of twelve leagues (about thirty-six miles) to Hernani on the night of 15 March. Another part of the Carlist army, freed from the need to shadow Sarsfield, proceeded instead to Hernani by rapid marches. The failure of Espartero to fulfil his part of the plan, advancing only to Durango and retiring to Bilbao on 21 March, was perhaps less disastrous for Evans than Sarsfield's defection, though equally inglorious.

March 12th, Somerville tells us, was a day of pouring rain, but the Legion advanced nonetheless. After describing the twisting, but generally northward course of the Urumea, he relates how the Legion and the Marines crossed the river by a bridge of boats near the village of Loyola. Driving the Carlists back at the cost of a few wounded, and all soaked to the skin, they took up quarters in the houses left by the Carlists and Spanish civilians. The Marines were occupying part of Loyola, having crossed the river in the afternoon. Relations between the Legion and the Marines were generally good, despite some jealousy of the soldiers over the Marines' regular rations of tea and rum. Somerville took pride in the fact that, when exposed to the same toil and wear and tear in makeshift quarters, the Marines looked no better than the Legion.

March 13th was a peaceful day, with parades and the sharing and smoking of a quantity of tobacco, bought with the proceeds of a wager between Evans and Chichester as to whether the Legion or the Spaniards would take most ground. Chichester had won the bet and rewarded his men by treating them to tobacco all round.

March 14th saw some action, with a fresh advance, but Somerville had time to note and comment again on the appearance of Colonel Hogg, who was 'so genteel in his uniform that he had crippled his feet with tight boots'. Somerville allowed that, as well as being a conspicuous ladykiller, Hogg was also a dashing, clever soldier. Events were soon to show that Hogg's choice of footwear in no way hampered his activity in battle. The Rifles, 3rd, 4th and 8th Regiments advanced along a narrow ditch-like road as the Carlists retreated. At night they retired to nearby houses, leaving piquets ahead. The rain fell without cease while the men

that he took opium for a medical complaint and had tendered his resignation, which had not been accepted.

waded to their knees in water and mud. Somerville's company was crowded into a large, well-furnished country house whose furniture they burned for firewood.

On **March 15th** the fighting intensified. Somerville was advancing with the 8th Regiment among whin bushes three feet high, which suddenly exploded with fire and smoke from a straggling volley. His officer, Captain Sheilds, ordered him to 'fire, damn you, Somerville, fire'. In a bizarre twist, his ramrod disappeared from his hand, hit and bent by a ball. The bugle played the 'advance' and the men went on to reach a road under cover of a bank, from which a rattling fire was returned. At this point Colonel Hogg galloped up and fiercely ordered them to cease firing and keep their heads down, ready to advance when the order came. Hogg himself stood quite exposed as the balls were chipping off the earth on the bank and topping the twigs of furze around them. One of the Scotsmen commented to Hogg that he thought he wanted to get himself shot, but Hogg merely smiled. Somerville wrote that Hogg was a vain man, but that vanity would be pardonable if all coxcombs would show it off at such risk as he did.

Obediently, the men lay inactive for nearly half an hour but, despite the order to hold fire, Charles Scott, a Hawick youth who fancied himself as a crack shot, fired at and hit a Carlist officer on horseback. Somerville had time to admire the beautiful way in which the Royal Artillery gunners performed all their manoeuvres, serving their small mountain guns, about three feet long and carried by mules, and lying loose on small frames off which they leapt at every shot.

It was now about 3 pm and the engagement had become general. The 1st, 3rd and 10th and three Spanish regiments were to the left of the 8th, and the 7th and Chapelgorris on their right. The Carlist guns on the Venta hill had stopped firing. Captain Coyle with the first company of the 8th was sent out skirmishing down through a deep hollow, firing for almost an hour until their ammunition was exhausted. They then advanced with bayonets fixed, Coyle with drawn sword, and his company yelling and hurrahing, when the Carlists, twenty times their number, precipitately retreated. Somerville criticised Coyle for advancing without ammunition, but admired his decision to keep a position he could not defend by attacking those who were coming against him. 'Who could have done it better?' he asked. His verdict on Coyle was that he was a daring and qualified officer.

General Chichester, though he and his horse were both wounded, was very cool. He asked Colonel Hogg (the tone scarcely warrants the word order), 'Just go through that wood and take possession of it – you'll be fired on, I believe; but – but just go up, and use your bayonets; and stay there in spite of them.' As colour-sergeant of his company, Somerville would have been close enough to hear the conversation. He went up with Hogg and his fellow Scots, accompanied by the Chapelgorris on their mission, sustaining a minor wound to the left arm and seeing his Major, Wilson, also wounded, having his wound partially dressed (the surgeons were clearly in the front line) and refusing to retire to the rear. The company advanced. The Carlists had been dislodged from positions which they had been defending all that afternoon. The 9th, 10th and the Spanish regiments had taken the positions and were advancing about 400 yards south of Hogg's men, towards the Venta hill, or Oriamendi. This was regarded as the greatest obstacle and the greatest prize facing Evans' forces since it was the last barrier between the Cristinos and Hernani. The 8th advanced quickly as far as a stone wall over which the men of the 7th had been, and were still, firing. Breastworks and barricades covered the entire side of the hill, which was surmounted by a battery. Protected by these defences, the Carlists were ranged and ready to receive attackers.

General Evans, who seems to have been ubiquitous on that day, now appeared and told Hogg not to go forward with only one regiment, but to wait for the others which he had ordered up to come to his assistance. 'Oh, allow me, General, to go; I'm sure we'll go through these breastworks,' Hogg replied, and appealed to his men, who cheered, 'and,' Somerville writes, 'for the first time in my life, I heard what I had heard in history, but scarcely ever believed, of men calling to their leader to be led on.' 'Go on then, my brave fellows,' said Evans. Godfrey, who had earlier commanded the regiment but no longer had any connection with it, joined Hogg, 'for he said he gloried in the way he had answered the General'.

'"Forward, the 8th. Hurrah! Hurrah!" Hogg called, and galloped on with Old Wilson, with swords drawn, and the brothers Major and Captain Sheilds. Twilight caused flashes to glance to so vividly, that the world within view of us seemed to be bursting into thunder and fire.' Major Sheilds was hit. Godfrey's grey stallion was killed under him. Somerville's brandy bottle was broken and his finger cut by the glass. The first barricade was reached, and Hogg was on top of it, waving his sword and calling his men on. It was ten feet high where it crossed the road. Captain Sheilds got up on it, and a few men were scrambling up.

The Legion fought their way up the Venta hill, driving the enemy from one breastworks after another. It was only after a five-hour conflict, according to the Annual Register, that the Carlists, finding themselves on the point of being outflanked, abandoned their last defence on the hill and fell back to Hernani. The first to reach the posts on top of the hill was Cotter of the 9th, who had just been promoted to colonel. He was followed by a mixture of all the regiments involved in the assault. The bugles sounded 'Halt' but some were determined to see the top of the hill and pushed on. The first acts of the Legion were to get in and take possession of four pieces of cannon and pull down the Carlist flag. They found the battery formed by a circular wall of turf 15 feet high, enclosing a space 60 feet wide. Unfortunately, a barrel of wine and another of spirits were discovered, and discipline broke down, with an immediate scramble for the drink. The farcical scene deteriorated when an ingenious Irishman of the 9th, eager to take advantage of the situation, shouted that there was a powder magazine with a match burning in it. The truth was that he had scattered his own ammunition around, put a light to it and exploded it amongst his comrades intent on the wine-barrel, in the hope that he could keep the spoils to himself. With victory at this point secured and the enemy – for the moment – in full retreat, this collapse of discipline did not lead to the disaster which might have followed in a more critical situation. The Scots and Irish were able to enjoy their hard-won plunder once the panic caused by the false alarm had died down.

Night had now fallen and the regiment was reformed after the confusion of battle and Bacchic excess (in which the sober Somerville took no part). The Legion spent the night in the open, occupying a range of heights, with Hernani about a mile below, the high rocky hill of Santa Barbara to the west. This hill had cost Wellington a six-weeks siege with nine thousand men to capture from the French. Officers and men alike asked themselves why Evans did not storm his way into Hernani that night, but Somerville supplied the answer, in the hazard to the army if they had taken the town, with the inevitable plunder that would have followed, in defending themselves against the Carlists who would have poured down from the heights the next day. Nonetheless the men were congratulating themselves on the success of the day's fighting, and many believed they would be able to walk into Hernani the next day. Their hopes were to be dashed.

March 16th, shaken awake at dawn, Somerville heard the sound of cannon and musket, saw the reddening clouds on the frontiers of France to the east, and started to his feet as Colonel Hogg rose from his dyke-side, putting on his sword and calling for his horse. A tot of akadente was served to all. It was a delectable mouthful 'before which the chilling frost of teetotalism would have melted into dew!' Few of his comrades can have analysed their feelings that morning as did Somerville, who ventured that 'it was partly drunk in anticipation of the demoniacal performances of the day; it was the devil giving his children a sweetening mouthful to please them, while he sent them out to play on one of his holidays!'

Colonel Colquhoun's guns were pounding Hernani, and chimneys, steeples and roofs flew into the air, until he was ordered to stop by Evans, unwilling to take possession of the ruins of the town. The Carlists had thrown up a redoubt outside Hernani with four pieces of cannon commanding the Cristinos' approach. Despite this, the 4th and 9th Regiments of the Legion went down almost to the walls and drove back twice their number of Carlists behind the town. The 6th and 8th Scotch Regiments were held in temporary reserve.

Now the price of the perfidy of Evans' Spanish allies was to be paid, when Carlist reinforcements from Durango arrived. Don Sebastian emerged from a gorge in the hills 'as if by magic' according to one account, with 10,000 infantry and 300 cavalry. Their arrival was decisive and disastrous. The Carlist forces now outnumbered Evans' army by many thousands. Column after column marched up in front of the Legion. Their superior numbers and the wide extent of country they could command allowed them to come round on Evans' flanks. The Rifles of the Legion drew in their skirmishing companies when they could no longer stand out against the advancing battalions, and kept their ground with part of the 3rd Regiment, though the Carlists had almost surrounded them, attacking them from the front and two flanks. They were outflanked on their left when the Spanish regiments posted there gave way and then retreated, despite efforts by their own officers to drive them back into battle; Somerville saw two Spaniards cut down by an officer who tried to turn them. On the extreme left of Evans' forces the 1st Regiment of the Legion were dangerously isolated and Somerville writes that these were the first and only regiment of the Legion to retreat without orders, but that they later 'made a noble and daring stand, which was more than sufficient to redeem their fighting character'.

The Rifles were singled out in Somerville's account for standing with obstinate determination, but he noted also that 'our brave Irish brethren were not idle at this time'. The reckless manner in which they let themselves be slaughtered should have silenced the critics of the Legion at home. Colonel O'Connell of the 10th repeatedly led on his men and met the Carlists hand-to-hand. Colonel Cotter of the 9th was equally resolute and reckless and his 'Cork boys' did not leave it all to him. In running his sword obliquely into the breast of a Carlist and withdrawing it, he broke it, leaving eighteen inches in the victim's body. As he wheeled his horse and retreated in search of another weapon, he escaped with no more than a ball through his left leg. This did not send him off the field. His tragedy was not played out – he wanted a sword, and Somerville goes on to tell how he got one.

A man of Somerville's company, who had advanced too far and found himself surrounded by Carlists and unable to retreat, fired at the Carlist general, who fell from his horse, apparently dead. A dead Carlist colonel yielded one sword. Meanwhile the general who had seemed to be dead was trying to escape in the hubbub of fire and smoke, but was seized and taken prisoner by a Scot, who relieved him of his sword and silver scabbard, which General Godfrey offered to buy from him, promising to pay him later. The canny Scot wanted immediate payment. When Cotter appeared with the stump of his broken sword and ready cash, a bargain was instantly struck; two dollars changed hands and soon after Cotter, at the head of some companies of the 9th, was again in action. At least three thousand men confronted them, for the Carlists at that point were three regiments deep.

> Cotter played a noble part. With the sword of their own general, he dealt about blows that split heads, and knocked the muskets and bayonets as they came against him to the ground. He was completely surrounded, and so was part of the 8th at the same time; but in front and rear of his body, with his noble horse springing wildly amongst clashing bayonets, smoke and fire, he dealt his blows about. At last the charger fell, and the gallant rider, exhausted with wounds, sunk below as many bayonets as could be dashed into his body at once!
>
> There and thus fell Colonel Cotter! I have not overcharged a sentence. – A thousand eye-witnesses still live to testify the truth of what is here written. That day has been called national disgrace! I should like to see what page of history contains a name more honourable to his country, if the death of a hero is any honour.

Reviewing the rapidly worsening situation, Somerville comments that reserve regiments sometimes have the best, and often the worst luck. If their side is successful they do not fight. If a town is taken and plundered they seldom get a share, being kept outside; but during a retreat the reserves have the worst part of the fight. So it was with the 6th, 7th and 8th Regiments on March 16th. Since the 7th Irish were a considerable distance from the 8th, Somerville did not see them in action, but all the reports he heard of them were favourable and he had no doubt that, though outflanked and driven back, they made their opponents pay well for their advantage.

When the enemy began to gain ground the 6th Regiment was moved off first to strengthen the positions towards the right. Only one company of the 6th was visible to the Carlists, the rest lying in 'dead ground'. The entire Carlist cavalry came boldly up on them, sure of an easy victory, but the 6th fired a volley 'that sent riders and horses in a confusion never excelled, in slaughter'. The howitzers of the Marines' artillery showered them with grapeshot, rockets and shells before they could retire to reform. They never did reform, so great was the destruction dealt out to them: 'They came up a dashing, gallant-looking corps; in five minutes they went back to where they had started from, the greater part of men and horses being left dead and dying.'

Colquhoun's artillery were now almost surrounded by the Carlists. The Lancers made repeated charges to save the guns, with severe losses each time. Two companies of the 6th were the only infantry that could be spared at the time to assist, 'and never did any soldiers go more devotedly to be slaughtered'. Commanded by Captain McKellar and Major Wood, they held the pass of a road for half an hour, attacking the Carlists furiously, so that the enemy gave ground a little, while the guns caused them heavy losses.

Soon after the first engagement of the 6th, the Spanish regiments on the left had retreated. This left the Legion's units to the left of the 8th exposed to crossfire, compelling them to abandon the ground on which they had fought all that morning. The 8th, last of the Legion's reserves, was now called into action at a critical moment when all the regiments within sight of the 8th were giving way. The 8th lay hidden in a wooded hollow. They were thus unaware how far the Carlists had advanced on their left, but at the same time the enemy did not know that a fresh regiment lay in wait in the wood, which they had nearly surrounded. Colonel Hogg had not wished to move without an order, though he understood the situation well enough, and General Chichester, knowing that the 8th still had one side open, left them alone as long as he could for a last throw of the dice. The Spanish regiments were making off in a very disorderly fashion, but the extent of the Legion's defeat only became known to the 8th when wounded men of the Rifles came by with news that two hundred wounded English and Spanish troops had been captured in a house where they were awaiting evacuation to hospital and, soon afterwards, bayoneted by the Carlists.*

As the bugles sounded the advance the 8th moved out of their wooded hollow into more open terrain. The adjutant-general, Le Marchant, galloped up to urge them to stand fast and keep their ground. The men cheered, and Hogg called on them to charge towards a low stone wall ahead of them, behind which were massed ranks of Carlists, many of them coming over the wall. Somerville wrote afterwards that he now, for the first time in his life, found himself in danger without any feeling of fear. 'Death seemed inevitable; therefore no other thought entered the mind but to slaughter to the last.' They had no time to load, and fought bayonet to bayonet. But now the bugles had sounded retreat; the regiment could not have stood, as all would have been dead in five minutes. Hogg is said to have called on the men to save themselves as the Carlists were threatening to surround them. Another attempt was made to drive the enemy back, but without success. Captain Coyle, leading the first company, fell dead by a shot in the head, their lieutenant, Butler, having previously been wounded and carried off. Hogg ordered Lieutenant O'Driscoll to take over command of the company; this he did, but a few minutes later got his death wound, dying two days later. Another who fell in this harvest of death was Colonel de Lancey, one of Evans' staff officers.

General Chichester himself escaped injury, but his horse was wounded. Remounted, he was conspicuous in the fight as if courting death. His concern for his horse gave Somerville material for a bizarre story. Among the officers round Chichester was a diminutive ensign named Darking. The general told the little man to fetch a surgeon to look at his horse. Darking offered to see to the animal himself, explaining that he was a doctor.

---

* Writing to his brother on 19 March, Assistant-Surgeon Morgan O'Connell, who had been tending the wounded English and Spanish soldiers in the house, described how he escaped; as the Carlists suddenly dashed in at one end he 'rushed out' under their fire at the other untouched and fought his way to his brave regiment, 'sorely lamenting the cruel butchery which awaited those brave sufferers I left. The savage enemy bayoneted every wounded man' (*Limerick Chronicle*, 1 April 1837)

Pulling out a case of instruments, he began to work, despite Chichester's disparaging remark that he would be able to get into the wound himself and find the ball. He extracted the ball, 'arranged some of the arteries and other vital parts, closed the wound skilfully, all in a few minutes, and the horse recovered. Shortly after, when necessity gave him liberty to operate on as many men as he chose, he did it most successfully, and altogether, I must say, he was a clever little fellow; only, he was so small that the surgeons, previous to that, denied his belonging to the profession. The officers thought him nobody, and the men made sport of him.'

This incident took place at about the time of Cotter's death. Soon afterwards, the pace of battle accelerated further, and a part of the 8th, ordered to hold a position in the corner of a wood at all costs, became completely cut off by the Carlists. Somerville was among them and recollected afterwards how men can continue to fight when all hope has gone. The men encouraged one another to fight to the last and not let themselves be taken prisoners, knowing that death would inevitably follow their capture. They were saved by another charge of the Lancers which threw the Carlists into disorder. There were a few moments of mutual destruction and 'then one of the Navarrese regiments and the Tolosa volunteers of the Carlist force advanced from behind the stone wall, and would have given the Lancers a volley and ended our share in the war, but just as they rushed forward, a rebound, then two, three and four bursted loud above the other noise, and that dreadful new invention, spherical case shot,* from our artillery, then just got to that part of the road, mowed down the Carlist regiments. Never was a sound so sweet as that burst of our own cannon to our ears.'

An escape route from the trap was now open for the 8th. 'There was not a moment to think. From where we were a retreat or a useless death was inevitable, and a good many of us were only brought along by getting hold of the Lancers' stirrups. I had hold of one and was getting out to the road, when the poor fellow by whom I held got a ball through his thigh.' Pausing for a few minutes, Somerville noticed two legionaries, one with a

---

* This was the shrapnel shell, named after its inventor, Henry Shrapnel (1761–1842) of the Royal Artillery. It consisted of a spherical case filled with balls, fused to explode approximately 50 yards above and 100 yards in front of a target, and was effective up to a range of 1,000 yards (Robertson, 2000). It had been used with great effect against the French in the Peninsular War, but still retained an aura of novelty. Foreign Office despatches for 1837 record the concern felt that 'spherical cases should not fall into other hands but those of British officers'.

wounded arm who was trying to save a comrade who had lost both his feet. Three minutes later the Carlist bayonets were in them both.

The regiment, shattered as it was, suffered another severe attack as it retreated. The appearance of Colonel Hogg, Captain Sheilds and other offi-cers at this time was almost demoniacal, and so was that of many of their men, being wild and seemingly careless of their fate. The Chapelgorris, whom the 8th now joined, had had many killed; this was the first time they had ever retreated. They had an excellent rapport with the Legion. They refused to move or fire a shot if the Spanish regiments were put beside them again, having been deserted three times by regiments of the southern Spaniards. When told to go alongside an English regiment, how-ever, they hurrahed, fixed their bayonets and waited impatiently to begin again. They and the 8th, with some companies of other corps, were ordered to hold a position, and did so, but with dreadful loss. They were much encouraged by the determined drumming of an elderly Chapelgorri, about four feet high, who had served as drummer-boy, soldier, guerrilla, outlaw and drummer again, for a period of forty years. Standing fully exposed, he rattled his drum before his regiment. A bugler joined him, and the two stood in front, answering the Carlist 'advance' until the bugler fell dead. One of the drummer's sticks was shot away but, seizing the bugle, he rat-tled with it instead of the drumstick until he too was killed.

Somerville now discusses a controversial aspect of the retreat of the Legion. He writes that, at this part of the retreat, the Royal Marines were engaged for a short while. They had been standing on ground to the right of the Venta hill, and rather in front of it, all the morning, and it was now midday. Until then they had not been within shot of the enemy. They fought only for half an hour and performed their share of the fight by dis-charging a few volleys from the ground where they stood, then advancing about twenty yards into one of the narrow byroads and firing fifteen or twenty rounds, partly under cover of its bank. They fronted a space of 100 yards or less, while the engagement was spread over a distance of two miles from right to left, and Evans had to spread his small force over the whole extent. In describing the assistance of the Marines 'in this negative tone' Somerville stresses that he does not mean to depreciate them in any way in order to enhance the character of the Legion. He writes:

> They had 18 men wounded and <u>none</u> killed, out of between seven
> and eight hundred. If ordered to stand where they were, or to enter

the fight earlier when it was at its hottest, they would have done so, and have stood until slaughtered or ordered to retire. But Lord John Hay said, 'No, the Marines shall not be engaged any longer, General Evans, while 3,000 Spaniards have turned their backs on the enemy, and while 4,000 have not been engaged at all, but are lying there in the heights looking on! You, of course, will order your own English regiments as you choose, but I shall withdraw the Marines.' This is a part of the conversation that passed between His Lordship and General Evans about mid-day. For the precise words I cannot vouch, but this was the meaning conveyed, and immediately acted on. I am as sure as I was then of existence that Lord John Hay thus addressed Evans, for at the time of their conference I had assisted in carrying a dying man to the surgeons in the rear, and while I was holding him until an attempt was made to take a ball from his inside, the two chiefs stood for a few minutes within five feet of the operation.

Therefore the Marines did not '*cover the retreat of the Legion*'. Somerville's account is circumstantial and precise. He was well aware, when he wrote some time after the events, of the emphasis placed by the press on the role of the Marines in saving the situation or at least preventing a complete rout. The correspondent of the *Morning Chronicle*, reporting on 18 March from Bayonne on the 'disastrous defeat of the Cristinos', wrote that a battalion of the English Marines alone held its ground and protected the retreat. The *Cork Standard* of 29 March reported that the English Marines succeeded in saving the artillery. The Annual Register of 1837 recorded that during the disorderly retreat of Evans' army their Carlist pursuers had nearly reached the spot where part of the artillery was placed, and were on the point of getting possession of the guns and cutting off the retreat of the Cristinos when

> they were met by a barrier not easily surmounted; for the British Marines, 400 strong, who had been drawn up upon the road, seeing what passed, made a charge upon the advancing Carlists; they, however, did not wait for their approach, but moved off to the right and left, in search of some more impressionable part of the line. The Marines themselves, when nothing more remained for them to do, moved slowly off the ground in companies, and marched into St Sebastian in good order.

Evans himself, in his Memoranda, wrote that at about midday Hay decided to withdraw the Marines and all the artillery, which agrees with Somerville's timing, and despite his own protests and those of Colonel Wylde, actually withdrew them at three in the afternoon. Evans considered that Hay's action was no doubt attributable to the threats of attack held out in Parliament against the employment of Marines in inland operations. 'No one,' he wrote,'could have been more constant and truly devoted in his support of the Queen's cause on all occasions than the noble and gallant officer alluded to.'

A different account was given in his diary by Richard Steele, an officer of the Royal Marine Artillery, according to whom the Marines stayed long enough to save the day when British and Cristino troops were falling back in disorder. He was convinced that, but for the Marines, Evans' army would have been completely routed with tremendous loss. Edgar Holt, one of the few twentieth-century historians of the war, writing in 1967 and reviewing the evidence, believed that the claim that the Marines had covered the Legion's retreat to San Sebastian was not credible, since they were certainly withdrawn before the battle ended, some time after 6 p.m., when darkness would have fallen. They were fighting on a very narrow front and their casualties were few. If they had stayed until some hours after 3 p.m., this would have meant that they had gone back on Hay's very firm decision of midday.

Francis Duncan, writing forty years after the battle, saw the situation in a similar way to Steele and the British press; he wrote that the retreat was prevented from degenerating into a rout by the admirable steadiness of the English Marines in the centre, and by the efficient fire of the Royal Marine Artillery. It is unlikely that Duncan had read Somerville's account, to which he does not refer, and he was perhaps disposed to accept the received version of the time, which saw the Legion in an unfavourable light. The gallantry of the Legion's Lancers in their repeated, costly charges to try to save the guns was acknowledged by contemporary writers, although the infantry were seldom given the credit they deserved.

Somerville goes on to describe how 'we continued fighting for three hours after the Marines were withdrawn'. The same unremitting slaughter did not continue all the time, since they had fallen back on the Venta and the heights on a line with it which they had taken the night before, and from which they had descended that morning. From there they opposed the Carlists all the afternoon with heavy fire, and it was from this time that most of the confusion of regiments was seen and that unmilitary conduct, if any, occurred. The retreating Legion had as far as possible to carry their wounded with them, since they would otherwise be killed by the Carlists.

He writes that at about 6 p.m. the Venta and all the adjacent heights were abandoned, and the Legion returned to the quarters they had occupied before they set out on the 10th, where they again mounted piquets as before. On leaving the Venta the 8th and any other regiments which he saw marched home as regularly as if coming off parade, except for those like himself who were carrying the wounded. He remarks on the great kindness of the women of San Sebastian towards the wounded, contrasting this with the behaviour of 'our own women', those of the Legion, but without enlarging on his criticism.

Somerville was dismayed because Evans in his general orders of 17 March, St Patrick's Day, which were widely reported in the press, gave an account of the affair that was not strictly true. He neither blamed those Spanish regiments which had retreated, as he should have done, nor denounced Espartero and Sarsfield as he might have done. For this Somerville felt he could excuse Evans, unwilling to stir up hostility with the authorities before he could honourably withdraw the Legion from Spain, but he thought that Evans was also motivated by a wish to flatter Lord John Hay and the British government, and even by a desire to conciliate his political enemies at home, to attach more importance to the intervention of the Marines than was consistent with strict truth. It was particularly galling to the officers and men of the 8th Regiment, who had fought bravely and suffered heavy casualties, that Evans had not mentioned the Regiment at all. When Colonel Hogg and other officers approached Evans with their resignations he issued an 'after order', apologising for having been misled with reports about the 8th, and stating that he had found their conduct strictly honourable and their services most efficient. Hogg was justifiably upset; his own conduct, as in earlier battles, had been heroic, as had that of Captain Coyle and many officers and men, living and dead. One feels grateful that Somerville's detailed narrative survives to set the record straight.

His feelings towards the carping and critical comments of the press on this, as on previous occasions, were bitter. 'From the Conservatives to the ultraest Democrats, the same ungenerous feelings are manifested towards the late unfortunate Legion and its more unfortunate chief. They forget that the same charges were made against the men who fought in the wars of Wellington,' he wrote later, asking, 'What is there, or what can there be different in the young men of this day from those of the days of the Peninsular War? Had Espartero done his part, or half of it, the war in Spain would have been ended by Evans at the time of his retreat from Hernani.'

As with the actions of 5 May the previous year, and others, the British newspapers vied with each other in their criticism of Evans. The *Cork Standard* of 29 March wrote that the conduct of General Evans towards the poor fugitives whom he has cajoled into scenes of blood and starvation was condemned by men of all politics here, for it was regarded as totally unwarrantable in him to have seduced a body of men into a disastrous war, which at best could only terminate in pensionless glory. In attacking Evans the writer was clearly hitting vicariously at Palmerston and the Liberals. He referred to the 3rd Regiment as diminutive cockneys, the scrapings of Westminster and Whitechapel, contrasting them with the Marines and artillerymen, heroes of the hour, for whom Don Carlos was now offering a £20 bounty for each man who would desert to him. The Tory *Morning Herald* gave grudging praise to the 7th Irish Regiment which under Colonel Beckham had supported the Spaniards promptly, having forty or fifty wounded. The editor of the *Spectator*, more critical than before, believed that General Evans's personal gallantry was doubted by nobody, but that his generalship was now more than ever questioned, and that a series of unsuccessful *offensive* operations must ruin the reputation of any commander.

In a debate in the House of Commons on 17 April Sir Henry Harding criticised Palmerston and the government for having issued the Order in Council which led to the Legion's formation. On 16 March, their *dies irae*, the Legion had no rations to eat, but there was a ration of rum, and men resorted to it, so that half the Legion were intoxicated. This, Harding claimed, was a strong argument for revoking the order (which had only some two months to run) and for making provision for the proper treatment of the men until their return to Britain. The hypocrisy of his argument contrasts with the laissez-faire attitude of most politicians towards the Legion up to this point, and their continued dismissive stance over its remaining unhappy existence.

General Jáuregui, *El Pastor*, last encountered on a peaceful Sunday in San Sebastian, attempted to retrieve the honour of the queen's army over the flight of the Spanish regiments on 16 March. On the 17th a court-martial for investigation of cowardice of certain Spanish officers took place. They were found guilty and were shot. In the Legion procedures were more diplomatic; the *Cork Herald* on 5 April published a letter of 23 March from Spain describing the court-martial of Lt Col. Harley of the 4th Regiment 'on certain charges', as General Evans delicately termed them. The colonel 'made default', escaping with his skin intact, and was accordingly deemed absent without leave and dismissed the service by an order of the day. Several other officers were dismissed the service at this time, as happened soon after other major battles. Somerville wrote that these officers 'immediately became historians of the retreat from Hernani'.

Evans' state of mind after the battle was extremely distressed. Somerville reports that he wandered about the glacis on the banks of the river that night, giving way to the most poignant grief. One correspondent wrote that Evans was 'narrowly watched by those about him lest he should commit any rash action himself'. Somerville felt the deepest sympathy for the general since he himself, 'with not the thousandth part to grieve for that he had, laid himself down in his billet, buried overhead in his greatcoat and blanket, and wept bitterly'.

Many senior officers resigned after 16 March. Somerville records that General Godfrey resigned, and that he never saw him again; his tone is regretful, since he had a great respect for his former commanding officer, and for General Le Marchant, who also resigned, being replaced as adjutant-general by Colonel Maurice O'Connell.

Somerville himself spent twenty days in hospital, seeing many of his comrades dying from their wounds. Many of the men needed poultices on their shoulders, swollen and blackened by the recoil of their muskets. He himself needed to have incisions made in his right shoulder 'to let out the bruised blood'.

News of the battle, sometimes confusingly known as the battle of Oriamendi, from the heights overlooking Hernani, was slow to reach Britain. Many early press reports were inaccurate and all were critical. On 19 March the *Cork Standard* published a violently hostile report of what it called Evans' disastrous defeat. Relying on the Cristino forces, it continued, Evans had embraced a shadow. Ill-paid, worse fed and deficient in zeal, they had dastardly abandoned him and the Legion.

The writer estimated the Legion's losses at over seven hundred killed and wounded. Though unable to know the exact losses of the Spanish Cristino forces, he believed that 1,480 wounded men had entered San Sebastian on 16 March, nearly one-third of the army.

Evans' official general orders dated 19 March and published in *The Times* gave figures for the Legion's losses similar to those suggested by the journalist, with a total of 61 killed, 640 wounded and 82 missing. Three officers were named as killed, including Colonel Cotter of the 9th and Captain Coyle of the 8th, whose deaths Somerville had witnessed. Colonel Oliver de Lancey, formerly of the 75th Regiment, a Guernseyman and cousin of Colonel Tupper of the 6th Scotch (killed on 5 May 1836), was dangerously wounded. A bullet lodged in his cerebellum and he died six days later, an autopsy being performed by two regimental surgeons. Captains Fielding of the Rifles and Mostyn of the 4th died on 21 March. Lieutenant O'Driscoll, whose death Somerville had also seen, was wrongly listed as severely wounded. Eleven officers were listed as severely or dangerously wounded. Those slightly wounded included General Chichester.

The casualty figures of horses of the 1st Brigade show, among four officers', including Chichester's, three animals killed and eight wounded. The 1st Lancers suffered the loss of four sergeants, seven rank-and-file, with sixteen horses wounded and three killed.

The tally of the equine casualties is followed by that of the Spanish Cristino troops, put at one thousand or more killed, wounded or missing, of whom 120 were officers. Another estimate, in a letter to *The Times*, spoke of two thousand or possibly four thousand. Most of those 'missing' could be presumed dead since Cristino and Legion prisoners were unlikely to be spared.*

Another casualty of the queen's forces was the Marines' regimental dog, Dash, as brave as the Legion's dog, Briton, the previous year. Dash went into action with the Marines on 10 March and again on the 16th, and was twice wounded. After the battle the Marines 'knighted' him for gallantry and awarded him a medal made from a Carlist bullet. Sir Dash survived the war and returned to England with his unit.

---

* One dramatic exception which came to light later was the case of Sergeant Peter Kean of the 9th Regiment, who was among a group of men captured by the Carlists on 16 March at the same time as Colonel Cotter was killed by the Carlist lancers. The correspondent of the *Morning Chronicle* on 18 January 1838 wrote that Kean and his fellow soldiers were taken before Don Sebastian at Hernani, who ordered them to be sent to Tolosa, there to be shot. Fortunately for Kean, he recognised among Don Sebastian's staff a Colonel Murray, whom he had known in Dublin. Murray interceded for him and his life was spared. Kean was later included in an exchange of prisoners at Vitoria and arrived in San Sebastian in January 1838, some ten months after his capture, to the astonishment of his comrades, who had long since considered him in his grave. These were members of the much smaller Legion which remained after its third reorganisation.

CHAPTER FIFTEEN

The taking of Hernani, Astigarraga, Irun and Fuenterrabia

After the losses of the Legion before Hernani from death and injuries, with the additional drain of officers who resigned or were dismissed, a major re-organisation was needed, as it had been after the heavy casualties of 5 May the previous year and the earlier heavy toll of disease in the winter of 1835–6 in Vitoria.

The three brigades were reduced to two. The 7th Irish Regiment was incorporated with the Rifles and, with the 1st, 4th and 8th Regiments, formed one brigade under the command of General Chichester. The 9th and 10th Irish Regiments were amalgamated and styled the Consolidated Royal Irish, which with the 8th Highlanders formed the second brigade under General Fitzgerald, whose two sons continued to serve in the 9th Regiment, or Irish Grenadiers. Colonel O'Connell took over the adjutant-general's department. The general orders of 20 March record the distribution of the officers of the 7th Regiment among other regiments, and the names of twenty officers placed on the retired list, 'in conformity with the orders of the government for the reduction of the force'.

The few remaining months of the Legion's service in Spain were eventful, and their actions went some way to redeem their tarnished reputation. The huge numerical advantage of the Carlist armies had now been reduced by the concentration of most at Estella far to the south of San Sebastian, with only small forces left to defend other positions.

Between 23 April and 6 May Espartero's army was ferried by sea from Bilbao to join Evans: 23,000 of them landed at San Sebastian, mostly conscripts from southern Spain, men for whom the fiery Chapelgorris had the greatest contempt. Many were poorly clothed and all looked ill, yet they were under strict discipline from their officers in gaudy uniforms with gold rings and rich sashes. Somerville comments that they were never seen intoxicated, in contrast with the men of the Legion, who were very often under the influence of drink.

Hernani (pl. 9), the prize that had eluded Evans before, remained a vital target, and the army moved to attack it again. On 4 May the first attack on Hernani took place by Evans' forces only, while Espartero's army was held in reserve. On the 5th, the anniversary of the action of the previous year, the Legion wore laurel wreaths and their 5th of May medals, and many of them were drunk. Somerville's account of the fighting over the ten or twelve days of the attack on Hernani charts the succession of events. On 6 May the Carlists opened a heavy cannonade. Thirteen prisoners were taken by the Chapelgorris and immediately put to death, but seven others, captured by the Legion, were spared and taken to the castle.

Colonels Colquhoun and Howe did great execution with their spherical case shot on the Carlists, who had not realised how close were the artillery. Just before twilight, with the cannonade at its height, a heavy black cloud appeared above the battle, followed by thunder and lightning, so that heaven and earth seemed to be at war. Next day the Carlists withdrew their guns from their positions.

On 14 May at daybreak the Legion's artillery reopened fire in torrential rain, causing the Carlists to retreat and make a stand on the Venta hill, from which the 6th and 8th Regiments with the Chapelgorris drove them into a hurried retreat to the heights of Santa Barbara.

The 6th Regiment, on coming up to a house which they had defended on 16 March, where they had buried some of their dead, found the bodies dug up and the bones scattered, having been smashed and cut into pieces with hatchets not an hour before the Legion's arrival there. In that house of death a half-ration of akadente was doled out to the men of the 6th, who grumbled that it was not a whole one. It was now eleven o'clock and the rain had poured incessantly on them since one in the morning.

The attack on Hernani now began in earnest. The Irish regiments, Rifles and Artillery advanced by the main road while the 6th and 8th and the Chapelgorris, commanded by Colonel Ross acting as Brigadier, with Colonel Martin as his ADC, went forward on the west side of the Santa Barbara heights and took these from a Carlist force equal to theirs in number, suffering some casualties. The impulsive Colonel Hogg was put under arrest for having advanced further with some companies of the 8th than he was ordered, being nearly cut off by the enemy. Skirmishing continued into the afternoon and next day. Many inhabitants who had fled on the Legion's approach now returned to their houses. The men were not allowed to enter Hernani that day, but occupied houses outside. Two rash foragers were shot by the enemy and found stripped naked next day. The following night allowed the Legion a good night's sleep, and Hernani and Astigarraga were finally taken.

Evans' next target was the fortified town of Irun near the French border. Today an industrial town, it retains little of its former character. Somerville describes the advance and attack on Irun. The army marched through the north gate of Hernani on 16 May on the road towards France, crowded with fifteen or twenty thousand men two regiments abreast, Spanish and English. They passed through villages where they were given water and cider by the women to propitiate them, most of the men having fled, and through the little town of Oarzun, which had been abandoned by its garrison and threw its gates open to the army. From here they could see the fields of France four miles away and, half hidden at the bottom of a mountainous ridge, along which they marched, the town of Fuenterrabia,* just north of Irun. On the ridge and on other heights the army of General Espartero lay in reserve.

Two miles away could be seen the battery in the Fort del Parque which defended Irun, with the red flag of No Surrender flying over it, a very discouraging sight to the assailing army. The fort stood on a commanding eminence with steep scarps, ditch and embrasures. The Carlist artillery, with eight pieces of cannon, had been trained by Prussian engineers and was the best which the Carlists had so far produced

An ADC of General Evans galloped up with orders. 'Colonel Ross, move up the Scotch brigade; General Fitzgerald, march on the Irish; the 6th and 8th by yon lane behind the General, and the Irish through this field; regimental surgeons will keep their ambulance in rear of these houses, and the hospital wagons stay on the road.'

The May morning was loud with birdsong: 'The incessant call of the cuckoo in its untiring egotism mellifluously repeating its own name, and the innumerable larks and linnets that sang as if Spain was a happy land, ceased as the guns of Irun opened fire.' Very soon Evans' cannon opened up on the town and the battery. The 7th Irish, now forming a single rifle regiment with the original Rifles of the Legion, and the united 9th and 10th Regiments advanced, with the 1st Regiment, towards the batteries, while the 3rd and 4th, with the 6th and a few thousand Spaniards lay behind in reserve.

The most dreadful and unremitting cannonade which they had ever heard now raged on both sides of the Legion and over them, as they darted

* Known as Hondarribia in the Basque language.

to get under cover of the enemy battery, but so low as not to be seen. The only mistake the Prussian engineers had made in planning their battery was to have allowed their opponents to approach so near to it under cover.

Until half-past three in the afternoon there was not a moment's intermission in the mutual bombardment. Scaling ladders had been brought up and the 'forlorn hope'* was ordered to be performed by the 8th Regiment, when Colonel Cotoner, one of Evans' Spanish ADCs, rode up with a white flag and a message from Evans for the Carlists, offering to suspend hostilities if they would surrender. The message, on a scroll stuck on the end of a musket, was hauled up to the enemy. The garrison of the battery consulted with the garrison and governor of the town, General Soroa. It was learned later that, while the former were willing to surrender, the latter were not, perhaps persuaded by a deserter from the Legion, fearful for his own skin, on whom they relied for advice, or an English Tory newspaper correspondent, that the Legion would put them all to indiscriminate death.

The atmosphere was tense. Half an hour had elapsed. 'Adventurers of different sorts' had come in as far as the Legion, among them no less than three correspondents of the London newspapers, anxious to get the first news.

> Dead silence continued. Not even a whisper was heard, in our anxiety to hear what answer had been given, and no other sound, until a solitary cuckoo put forth a note and then stopped, as if in trial to find if it was safe to begin; the war seemed to be over, and the sweet bird went gaily on. But the party with the flag of truce had scarcely got to the position of our nearest artillery, when off bounded a cannon from the battery which had been slyly ranged along the roadside, elevated to that point during the cessation. The ball killed a horse – a man – wounded two – carried the wheel of a gun carriage – threw a 'London correspondent' into a ditch, and half covered him with earth.

Somerville's account conveys the pleasure he felt at this sight.

---

* Derived from the Dutch 'verloren hoop', the lost squad or troop, this refers to a body of men chosen to begin an attack, especially a group of volunteers who first entered the breach or scaled the walls in storming a defensive fortification. The more modern meaning of a 'faint hope' or enterprise with little chance of success has resulted from a wordplay or a mistaken etymology [Brewer, 1992].

The same instant, all our guns being ready, blazed off at once, and more determinedly than ever. The bombardment went on as one long roll of thunder, until the darkling twilight caused both parties by mutual consent to leave off.

The Legion spent the night on the roadside, wet and cold since no fires could be lit, Somerville in more comfort than most, since he gathered stones to build a bed to keep him out of the mud and enjoyed a sound sleep.

Somerville quotes extensively from the notes made by an intelligent and observant Rifleman on the actions of the regiments on the eastern side of Irun during the evening of 16 May and the next morning. The Rifles came under heavy fire and suffered many losses, but reached the east gate of the town. Unable to enter there from lack of scaling ladders, they gained entry to a nearby church (pl. 10), where a hundred of them spent the night while the rest occupied adjacent houses. A neighbouring hotel yielded a plentiful supply of wine, and the writer bought a bottle of champagne for four coppers. Some men found their way into the belfry and rang the bells until a late hour, while others played the organ, contributing to a bizarre musical interlude in the midst of war. At daybreak the Carlist gunners and the Riflemen bellringers resumed their orchestrated cacophony, soon interrupted by loud cheering coming from the town gates, which were already partly open, with men of the Rifles and the 1st Regiment scaling the walls of nearby houses to enter through the windows. Barricades between the houses were taken one by one, the Carlists retreating to the strongly fortified Town House, or Town Hall (pl. 12), which held out to the last. Among the Rifles' casualties were the popular young Lieutenant Wheat, their bugler and bugle-major. When the strong barricaded door of the Town House was rushed, the Carlists finally surrendered (fig. 9).

Another witness to the taking of Irun was the Reverend Thomas Farr, an English traveller in Spain, whose reminiscences were published in 1838 and who praised the clemency and humanity shown by Evans and the Legion in their hour of triumph. Evans, well knowing the ferocity of the Chapelgorris, who neither gave nor received quarter, had the forethought to send them some way off to occupy a hill, on the pretext that two Carlist battalions known to be nearby might try to turn his positions in the confusion of the attack on the town. (Somerville, however, who knew the Chapelgorris better than Mr Farr, commented that that would not have stopped them from being in at the kill, and they did not remain on reserve as ordered.)

Somerville, never niggardly with telling detail, continues his eyewitness account of the action by extolling the bravery of General Arbuthnot, Evans' brother-in-law, who commanded the storming party at the eastern side or Behobia gate, in attempting to blow it up. The first to mount the barriers by the scaling ladders at the gate was Captain Pierce of the 1st Regiment. He stood exposed to the full fire of the Carlists, waving his sword and encouraging the men who followed him up the ladders. The first of these was an Irishman who had been taunted for cowardice by his comrades and wanted to disprove the slur. He was shot dead as soon as he reached the summit. Pierce, with great presence of mind, dragged his body inwards so that it would not fall down on those climbing the ladders, lowering their morale.

Captain Roberts of the 8th was another officer whose bravery Somerville reported. He and his men were preparing to burst open the east gate when an old man handed him the keys. The gate was unlocked and Roberts and his troops entered.* The old man was terrified, but gained confidence and believed himself safe, when a party of Chapelgorris broke in on the Legion and dashed their bayonets into him before they could be stopped. Many examples of their barbarity were noted by Somerville, who described a Chapelgorri capering merrily along a street with the foot of a man, severed by a shell, stuck on his bayonet.

Many of the victorious army entered the houses in search of plunder, only to find some desperately defended by men expecting no mercy and determined to sell their lives dearly. Somerville was about to climb the stairs in a house he had entered when the Spanish sergeant eagerly pushing in front of him fell dead from a shot. He himself was hit by a bullet which barely missed his shoulder, entered the folds of the greatcoat strapped to his back, and passing through it lodged among his books. Shots were fired up the staircase, and in an upper room was found the corpse of a Carlist.

In another house which had belonged to a man of means, a Broadwood piano from London was found, on which a comrade of Somerville attempted to play with untutored fingers and child-like pleasure, until his

---

* A rather different account of this episode was given by the correspondent of *The Times* on 3 June, who wrote that a corporal of the Rifles, who had got into a house adjoining the gate, came into the street and managed to open the gate with a pickaxe, under tremendous fire from the barriers and houses behind him.

mate dropped a 24 lb cannonball which he had brought up from the street through the instrument. Twelve or more of his company were seated round a table in the same house, drinking wine, when some of their Chapelgorri allies entered and upbraided them for being idle. One of them carried the severed head of a Carlist by the hair, and with this he swept the glasses off the table before throwing it at a mirror, 'perhaps deeming that its reflection rebuked the fearful realities of the scene,' as Somerville commented.

Evans and his officers worked desperately to protect their Carlist prisoners. General Chichester, who had been in the hottest of the street fighting, was conspicuous in opposing the Chapelgorris and other Spaniards who sought to kill their captives. After securing their safety, he was next employed in running from house to house and street to street, causing the wine and other liquors to be run out to prevent drunkenness. A ball would be fired into a cask of brandy or a pipe of wine, above and below, leaving it to empty itself at leisure. Those in search of drink would fill a china or other vessel, or even a shoe or a boot. Every shop and house was ransacked and, despite Chichester's efforts, the streets ran with cider, wine, akadente, brandy and blood. Reassuringly, Somerville tells us, the latter came *mainly* from slain cattle, sheep and pigs, all of which met an unceremonious death, a steak or chop being taken off the beasts by anyone who chose. An Irishman of the 9th had secured probably the most valuable plunder of all – the official coat of the *alcalde* or chief magistrate, decorated with silver and gold and the date 1600. The man wore it on top of his own clothes 'and capered with it at a great rate'. He meant to take it home with him but later, when hard up, sold it from a strong desire for a taste of akadente. Somerville's own hopes were raised when he found a promising-looking box in a bookseller's shop, sure that it was full of silver and gold. Instead it contained lead bullets and musket balls, newly made on the premises – 'evidence of the universal devotion of the people of those provinces to Carlos'.

The Carlist prisoners were in mortal danger from their victorious countrymen, and only the strenuous efforts of the Legion's officers saved most of them from death. Officers were to be seen guarding the three or four hundred helpless prisoners who were found hiding in cellars and houses. Somerville saw one Carlist surrounded by Colonel Hogg and Captains Roberts, Sheilds and Forbes of the 8th Regiment, covering him with their own bodies. Hogg was walking backwards and holding him as if embracing him, with Sheilds nearly riding on his back while the others brandished their swords round him to keep off the Chapelgorris, 'one of whom sprang from side to the other, trying to poke his bayonet into the trembling Carlist'. Similar scenes occurred throughout Irun, but not all were as successful in saving their prisoners. Some of the 1st Regiment had a prisoner in their charge and, seeing two Chapelgorris following them, closed round their man, telling them to keep off. The latter replied that there was no need to keep them off as they were also following to protect him. This put the Englishmen off their guard, at which one of the Spaniards plunged his bayonet into the prisoner saying, 'The English do not know how to take care of prisoners.'

Somerville devotes several pages in his History to the case of the ambiguous Captain Dickson, who was found among the Carlists at the capture of Irun. A half-pay captain in the British army, the son of an English admiral, he had gone out to Spain 'to see what was passing between the contending parties'; he had declined to serve either under Evans or Don Carlos. He spoke perfect Spanish, and would have made a good correspondent for the English newspapers or, indeed, a useful spy for the Carlists. He had distinguished himself earlier in rescuing Captain Hamilton of the Legion's Artillery in an engagement with the Carlists, and this was to be his own salvation.

When passing through Hernani on his way to Irun (which was still in Carlist hands) Dickson had been accosted by the Cristino General Gurrea and asked to carry a letter to General Evans. Having undertaken this task rather unwillingly, he was captured by the Carlists and was lucky to escape with his life, being imprisoned in the Town House of Irun, where he witnessed its siege and capture. By reasoning with his captors that their lives would be spared if they surrendered, he persuaded them to abandon the fight and put out white flags. His problems were not over, however, since being found with the Carlist forces he was regarded as a traitor and a Tory, and had to be protected from the bayonets of the victors by officers such as Captain Pierce and Colonel Ramsey, who knew of his services to the Legion*.

---

* The above is based on the account in Somerville's 'History' of 1839. His 'Narrative' of 1838 gives a different version, referring to an Ensign Dixon who was captured in the Town House, having tried to dissuade the Carlists from surrendering by telling them that they would be slaughtered by the Cristinos (which would have happened but for Evans' intervention). He also wrote that in June 1836 Dixon had visited the Legion in San Sebastian, posing as a gentleman on his travels, had got into the good graces of many of its officers and gathered as much information as he could. He was caught sketching the defences and was found to have corresponded with suspected Carlist agents in Bayonne. The Spaniards wanted to kill him as a spy, but Evans succeeded in getting

1 Contemporary cartoon representing Spanish patriotism striking Joseph Bonaparte to the ground, his mask of hypocrisy by his side, with a portrait of King Ferdinand VII above and a lion, symbolic of Castilian strength, attacking the French eagle.

2 Queen Cristina of Spain, wife of Ferdinand VII and mother of Isabella II.

3 Ferdinand VII, king of Spain.

4 Isabella II, aged 13, on assuming powers.

5 Don Carlos, brother of Ferdinand and claimant to the Spanish throne.

6 Entry of Cristina into Madrid in December 1829, escorted by Don Carlos.

Lt. Gen. Sir G. De Lacy Evans
G.C. St. F. and K.C.B.

7 Lieut. General George de Lacy Evans, commander-in-chief of the British
Legion (from a contemporary portrait).

8 The British Legion and their Cristino allies in action against the Carlists at Arlaban, in January 1836.

9 Capture of Irun by Generals Evans and Esparrero, May 1837.

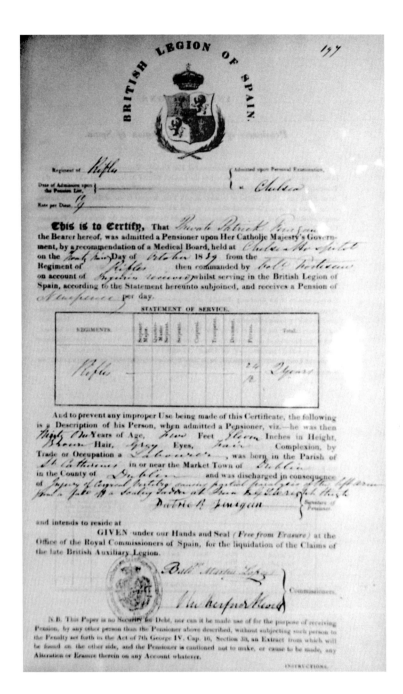

10 Pension certificate of Dubliner Private Patrick Finegan of the Rifles, who was awarded a pension of nine pence a day for injuries sustained at the siege of Irun in 1837; signed by Dr Alcock.

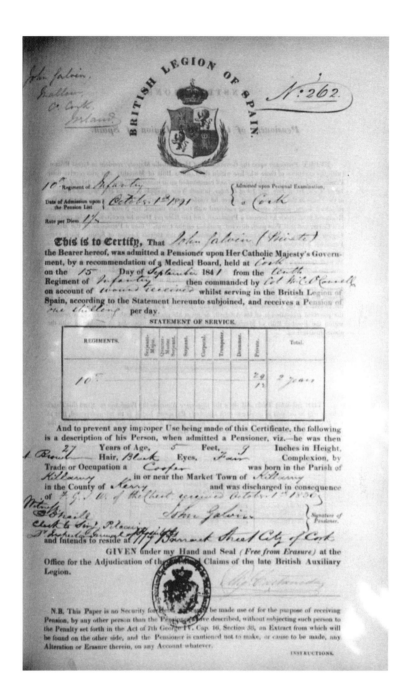

11 Pension certificate of Private John Galvin of Killarney of the 10th Regiment, who was awarded a pension of one shilling a day for gunshot wounds to the chest received in October 1836.

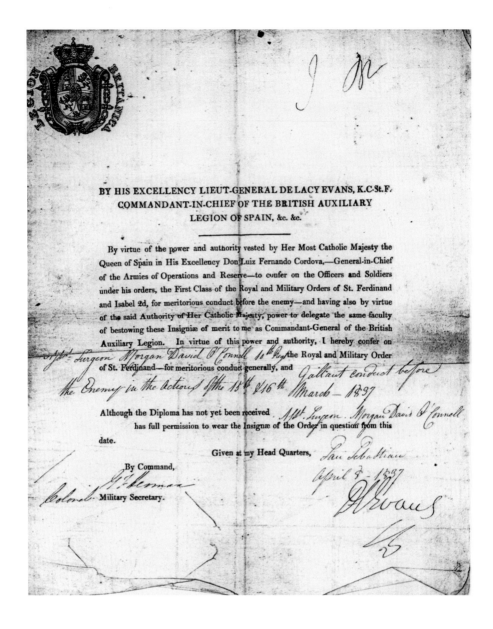

BY HIS EXCELLENCY LIEUT.-GENERAL DE LACY EVANS, K.C-St.F.
COMMANDANT-IN-CHIEF OF THE BRITISH AUXILIARY
LEGION OF SPAIN, &c. &c.

By virtue of the power and authority vested by Her Most Catholic Majesty the
Queen of Spain in His Excellency Don Luiz Fernando Cordova,—General-in-Chief
of the Armies of Operations and Reserve—to confer on the Officers and Soldiers
under his orders, the First Class of the Royal and Military Orders of St. Ferdinand
and Isabel 2d, for meritorious conduct before the enemy—and having also by virtue
of the said Authority of Her Catholic Majesty, power to delegate the same faculty
of bestowing these Insigniæ of merit to me as Commandant-General of the British
Auxiliary Legion. In virtue of this power and authority, I hereby confer on
Asst Surgeon Morgan David O'Connell 10th Regt the Royal and Military Order
of St. Ferdinand—for meritorious conduct generally, and *Gallant conduct before
the Enemy in the actions of the 15th & 16th March—1837*

Although the Diploma has not yet been received *Asst Surgeon Morgan David O'Connell*
has full permission to wear the Insigniæ of the Order in question from this

date.

Given at my Head Quarters, *San Sebastian*

April 8 - 1837

By Command,

G. Herman

Colonel Military Secretary.

Evans

12 Citation for award of the Order of San Fernando to Dr O'Connell for the action of
March 1837.

13 Burial place of British officers on the Castle hill of San Sebastian.

NOTES

ON THE

MEDICAL HISTORY AND STATISTICS

OF THE

BRITISH LEGION OF SPAIN;

COMPRISING

THE RESULTS OF GUN-SHOT WOUNDS, IN RELATION TO
IMPORTANT QUESTIONS IN SURGERY.

BY

RUTHERFORD ALCOCK, K.T.S. &c.

DEPUTY INSPECTOR GENERAL OF HOSPITALS, WITH THE AUXILIARY FORCES
IN PORTUGAL AND SPAIN.

LONDON:

JOHN CHURCHILL, PRINCES STREET, SOHO.

MDCCCXXXVIII.

14 The title page of Dr Alcock's *Notes on the Medical History and Statistics of the British Legion in Spain.*

ERECTED
TO THE MEMORY OF
COLONEL SIR DUNCAN MAC DOUGALL, K.C.S.F.,
OF SOROBA, ARGYLESHIRE.
BY THOSE FRIENDS AND COMRADES TO WHOM HIS PUBLIC SERVICES AND HIS PRIVATE WORTH
WERE BEST KNOWN.

HE SERVED WITH THE 53ᴿᴰ AND 85ᵀᴴ REGIMENTS AT THE CAPE, IN THE PENINSULA, AND IN FRANCE;
AT THE SIEGES OF BADAJOZ, BURGOS, AND Sᵀ SEBASTIAN;
AT BAYONNE, AND AT THE BATTLE OF SALAMANCA,
WHERE, THOUGH WOUNDED, HE GALLANTLY SAVED THE COLOURS OF HIS REGIMENT.

IN AMERICA, HE WAS AT THE BATTLES OF BLADENSBURG, BALTIMORE, AND NEW ORLEANS,
ALSO AT THE CAPTURE OF WASHINGTON.

HE FINALLY COMMANDED THE 79ᵀᴴ HIGHLANDERS, UNTIL HE RETIRED FROM THE BRITISH ARMY,
TO JOIN THE BRITISH AUXILIARY LEGION IN SPAIN,
AS QUARTER MASTER GENERAL UNDER HIS FRIEND SIR DE LACY EVANS,
AND RECEIVED THE ORDER OF Sᵀ FERDINAND FROM QUEEN ISABELLA II.

IN HIS LATTER YEARS HE RAISED THE LANCASHIRE ARTILLERY MILITIA,
AND WAS AMONG THE FIRST TO PROMOTE THE VOLUNTEER MOVEMENT.

HE WAS A CHIVALROUS SOLDIER, AND A WARM HEARTED FRIEND.

HE DIED ON THE 10ᵀᴴ DECEMBER 1862,
IN THE 76ᵀᴴ YEAR OF HIS AGE.

15 Memorial to Col. Sir Duncan MacDougall in the crypt of St Paul's Cathedral, London. MacDougall served as the popular quarter-master general in the British Legion as part of a varied military career. (By kind permission of the Dean and Chapter of St Paul's Cathedral.)

16 Emblem of the British Auxiliary Legion.

At equal or greater risk was the correspondent of an English Tory morning paper who narrowly escaped death when found among the Carlist garrison. Somerville believed that, if this man had been executed, his blood would have been the most justly shed of any spilt in Spain. There was evidence that he was not only a witness of the Durango Decree butcheries of English prisoners, but was also 'one of those who continually represented to the Carlists the savage disposition of the Legion, and fabricated the stories of our putting prisoners to death'. The men of the Legion would have needed no help from the Chapelgorris to avenge their murdered mates, and it was as well for the Legion's good reputation that the wretched man contrived to escape.

The *Cork Standard* of 22 May in its report on the capture of Irun paid tribute to the very fine conduct of Evans in avoiding bloodshed. It also referred to an Anglo-French collaboration in which the French army helped with the care of the Legion's wounded. At Evans' request, the commandant of the 20th Military Division provided a moving hospital and a wagon, and also sent some of his surgeons.

Hernani and Irun had now fallen, and the remaining target was Fuenterrabia (pl. 11), unsuccessfully attacked by the Legion the previous July. Fuenterrabia lay only a few miles north of Irun, and its capture would finally close off the Carlists' supply route from France. The correspondent of the Tory *Morning Post* had predicted on 19 May that Irun and Fuenterrabia would prove hard nuts for the Cristino army to crack, but the very next day had to report the capture of both towns.

The army halted within 800 yards of Fuenterrabia and cannons were brought up to bombard the town, while Lord John's gunboats sailed up the Bidassoa river ready to batter it from the other side.

The Reverend Farr takes up the story. General Evans, hoping to prevent unnecessary bloodshed, sent a flag of truce to Fuenterrabia to persuade the garrison to surrender. According to Carlist precedent, the surrender should have been the signal for a massacre. Fearful for their own lives when captured, and assuming that the garrison of Irun had been put to death, they replied that 'they might as well die fighting, as be butchered in cold blood'. When told that the garrison had been spared they refused to believe it, and insisted on ocular proof. Two of their officers were

---

him off on Dixon's promising to return England – a promise which he broke, determined, for whatever reasons, to remain near the scene of the action.

allowed to ride to Irun where they found the garrison alive and well treated. Though convinced by this, they continued to procrastinate, insisting now that they could not surrender unless an article were inserted in the capitulation to the effect that they should be the first prisoners to be exchanged. These terms were agreed to, but Evans' patience was finally exhausted when a Carlist ADC returned with a message that they would not surrender unless one of their officers, accompanied by an English officer, went to the headquarters of Don Carlos to seek his consent to the capitulation. Evans granted the garrison five minutes grace; if the capitulation were not brought to him signed by them, and the gates of the town opened, when the five minutes had expired the fire from the batteries would commence. He had his answer after four minutes, when the gates opened and the garrison began to file out and deposit their arms on the glacis.

The 6th Scotch Regiment under Colonel Ross was ordered to march into the town and take possession of it. Mr Farr, anxious to be part of this historic event, was allowed to accompany Ross. When they were within about a hundred yards of the prisoners General Chichester ordered Ross to halt his regiment and addressed them, asking them not to cheer or show any signs of exultation. He felt sure they would 'have no wish to triumph over, or hurt the feelings of a fallen enemy'. It says much for the men and their officers that they observed this request to avoid triumphalism at a time when they had at last some real cause for rejoicing. Mr Farr compared this honourable restraint with the heroes of Rome and Sparta, and did not exaggerate, in view of the murder of eleven of the Legion captured earlier, before Fuenterrabia.

Farr asked Colonel Shaw, commanding the Artillery, the number of guns and quantity of ammunition taken since he was writing to a general much interested in the Legion who had been with Wellington at Waterloo and all the Peninsular battles. He was told to tell the general that, whereas it took the duke three days to get his army in order after Badajoz was taken by assault and given up to plunder, the men of the Legion were perfectly sober and steady, under complete order and discipline, and ready to take another town the day after one had been taken by storm and given up to plunder. It is doubtful whether the duke or many of his countrymen ever read Farr's praise of the Legion, but Somerville's anxiety to redress the record is very understandable. He himself describes how the Royal Irish, one of the regiments who formed the storming party, marched out over 700 strong, drums beating and colours flying, only thirty men being absent when the muster roll was called, perfectly sober and under the most perfect order and control. He contrasts this with the mayhem that had followed the capture of Ciudad Rodrigo in 1813, and the fall of Badajoz.

The one-eyed General Soroa, commandant of captured Irun, attested further to the humanity of the Legion. He addressed a memorial to Don Carlos in which he described his vigorous defence of the town and, when death seemed inevitable, the approach of officers of the Legion 'who with the greatest generosity offered us quarter'. An offer so unexpected surprised them for a moment; 'but they pledged their honour, and resistance being madness, we laid down our arms'. Soroa begged Carlos to order his generals to treat with all humanity the individuals of the Legion who might fall into their hands. 'Nearly 700 families of those who composed the garrison of this town and Fuenterrabia, would have mourned the death of their fathers, brothers, relatives and friends – they all live, and live for Your Majesty, by the noble generosity of their enemies.'

The British press gave unusually generous praise. The correspondent of *The Times* of 3 June 1837 wrote that on Sunday 21 May, exactly one week after leaving San Sebastian, the Legion marched back again with eight hundred prisoners, 'having taken four strong towns and fortified positions, and 22 guns besides'. The *Standard* of 30 May commented on the taking of Irun, 'In the History of War we can find no more honourable trophy than this.'

A garrison of Marines and Marine Artillery was put into Fuenterrabia, and the Legion returned to Irun where they remained for the next three days.

Somerville took the opportunity, with the help of a French officer, to cross into France. The man had spent four years in Edinburgh and was very critical of the servile attitude of the Legion towards their officers. On 24 May General Espartero moved south to besiege Tolosa with his Spanish troops and the artillery of the Legion. It was in these operations that General Miguel Gurrea, the Cristino field-marshal whose son, Captain Ignacio Gurrea, was one of Evans' ADCs, was killed. *The Times* reported that he was shot through the head while encouraging by his example his column to pass over a bridge swept by heavy fire from the other side of the river Orio. He was described as one of the queen's bravest and most upright officers. His tombstone on Mount Orgull at San Sebastian was erected by his family and his friend, 'General Lacy Ewans' (*sic*).

CHAPTER SIXTEEN

Disbandment and repatriation of the old Legion: a cold reception

The Legion's term of service expired on 9 June. Few of the private soldiers would have wished to prolong their stay in Spain by a day more than necessary.

General Evans, anxious to return to his Westminster seat, had left for England on 3 June, calling en route at Paris, where he was received by King Louis-Philippe. Many senior officers also left for home, including General Chichester. The Spanish government, however, hoped that the Legion would continue to fight for the queen in Spain, and it was announced only days before the 9th that Britain had renewed the order in council for another year. Colonel Wylde, the senior British commissioner with the queen's army, was given the task of persuading the legionaries to sign on for another year of service in a re-organised Legion under the command of Colonel Maurice Charles O'Connell, who had performed gallantly in the previous two years and was now promoted to brigadier-general.

Wylde addressed the Legion on 7 June, telling them of the opportunity to re-enlist, and encouraging the men to do so. He spoke first in their praise, and this must have been music to the ears of men who had been more reviled than lauded by their fellow-countrymen.

> I have seen you in arduous situations [he said] and I can tell you – and I am not telling you so to flatter you – that no soldiers could have done better than you have done. I am proud of you, your country is proud of you, and it would be a blind mistake of you, men, to go home just now. Nearly one-half of the working population are out of employment, and cannot obtain it in England. Now I do think, men, you could not, under these circumstances, do better than stay.

The picture Wylde painted was grim but true, and the situation in Ireland, Scotland and Wales was no better. Somerville believed that the military and moral character of Colonel Wylde was considered a guarantee that the Legion would be fairly dealt with.

To the surprise of all, the Spanish government now produced the money to pay the privates and NCOs – but not the officers – of the Legion their long-awaited arrears, and arrangements were made to pay off the regiments.

Many officers who were awaiting their pay felt obliged to remain in Spain, fearing that once they went home their chances of settlement would diminish, if not evaporate. Some who had not intended to enter the new Legion changed their minds for financial reasons.

The comments of Somerville at this point, as usual, are relevant and illuminating. Showing an old soldier's cynicism as to motivation, he points out in his History that, if there had been no intention of raising a new force out of the old one, it would have been more prudent to have kept the money and paid the men on their arrival in England. As re-enlistment was going on, however, it became necessary to resort to the common practice of recruiting – that mode which was always, when levies of men were needed with regiments in Britain, in order to get them to volunteer for the regular army, namely that of giving men money and every facility to wallow in drunkenness until it was all spent. Every facility was indeed given to spend the money and, when it was spent, five dollars were offered to all who would re-engage for another year. Some who had longed for 10 June found themselves on that day claimed by the officers of the new corps, having taken the bounty while drunk.

Scenes of chaos developed, similar to those following the payday of the previous July. Fighting broke out between the regiments. The 8th Scotch were paid on 8 June, and some other regiments, especially the Royal Irish, 'made harvest of them' as they passed through the Irish billets on their way to celebrate in San Sebastian. Some paid protection money to men of the 9th. In a battle between the 9th and the 6th and 8th Regiments, a Scot fired a fowling-piece and an Irishman retaliated with a pistol. One of the 9th was dangerously wounded and several others severely injured.

No officers were to be seen during these affrays. Most officers of the 8th were busily engaged in trying to persuade men to re-enlist, since on their success in this would depend their future rank in the new Legion. Though pressed hard by Colonel Martin (who became a paymaster in the new Legion) Somerville refused to sign on. Colonel Hogg who, though a clever soldier and brave man, was unpopular, could only persuade six men of the 8th to join his new corps. About a hundred of the 8th did re-enlist, but specified that they should not serve in his regiment. It was for this reason, Somerville believed, that Hogg refused to recommend the men for their full gratuities. The conditions were that the men would receive a gratuity of two, four or six months depending on the recommendation of their commanding officer. Somerville himself was given the full gratuity, but thought the colonel's behaviour 'very disreputable to his character'.

Some men had taken a bounty three or four times by going to officers who did not know them personally, and then after all escaping. Others gave the names of Legionaries who had no intention of taking the bounty, but were nonetheless claimed to have enlisted.

Their new-found wealth was spent by some soldiers on costly and inappropriate clothing. An Irishman of the 9th paid eighteen dollars for a cocked hat with feathers, boasting that he would return home 'a bold general', until hunger forced him to sell it for a tenth of its cost. Another, whom Somerville later saw begging in the streets of London, cut a dash for a few days, keeping two liveried servants. Some bought donkeys to ride on, guns or pistols, while others flaunted rich Spanish dresses and fancy uniforms. Even the prudent Somerville took a sudden fancy and had a suit made of Spanish cloth, wearing it with pride and noting 'the mortification of the poor devils of officers who had got no money'. This suit may have saved his life two months later.

During the month or more in June and July that Somerville and his regiment, like others, were awaiting transports to take them home, they had only scanty rations which they supplemented by buying small amounts of food. He had deposited money in a bank in San Sebastian, perhaps the only man in the Legion to do so, though he also banked small sums under his own name for his comrades, drawing on it from time to time, and lending money to some on the security of their papers. So generous was he that he lent all but the price of his treasured suit. On 11 July the men of the 8th Regiment embarked on the *Prince Regent* transport. Colonel Martin again urged Somerville to re-enlist, and finally persuaded him. The parcel containing his suit had already gone on board but could not be found. Somerville went on board to retrieve it, intending to return and sign on with the new Legion, but was not allowed to go ashore again as the ship was about to sail. Many of the men and officers among whom he would have served were murdered at Andoain two months later. Had he died with them we would have been deprived of one of the main sources of information about the Legion.

The logistics involved in providing transports to convey the Legion to Britain were complex and difficult, and there were long delays in the arrival of the ships. These, when they came, were often unsuitable and dirty, sometimes small trading craft on which a hundred men were crammed with great difficulty. Somerville may have been right, however, in his cynical belief that the delay was deliberate, to allow more time to recruit from the unwilling soldiers, whose blankets had been taken from them when disbanded. The Legion had been provided with new items of uniform shortly before disbandment, but these became worn and dirty during the long wait for transport, and some men sold clothing to raise money for food.

Somerville was at pains to explain in his Narrative that the idea of the Legion being left naked was a misunderstanding, since he believed that during the two years of their service as much clothing was given to each man as a soldier in a British regiment would receive in five years. The issue of shoes, boots and trousers exceeded by seven or eight times the allowance of a regular British soldier. These items had all too often been sold for cash when pay was in arrears.

Foreign Office despatches had been received in London regularly for the previous two years concerning the affairs of the Legion, but it was only in late May that these began to refer to the need for transports to convey the men to Britain. On 25 May a letter from Lieutenant Colonel Reid referred to taking home men 'who may wish to leave the Spanish service on June the 10th next'. On 31 May despatches mentioned British transports to be placed at the service of the Spanish government to convey to England those wishing to return. The wording of these despatches conveys no sense of urgency and suggests that the numbers expected to return were small. It was some weeks before any arrangements were made. The *Prince Regent* transport was ordered to embark 500 men, natives of Glasgow, and convey them to Greenock on the Clyde; she sailed on 11 July with Somerville and his comrades of the 8th on board.

The men of the 7th Irish Regiment were so anxious to get away that they waited on the quay at San Sebastian for six days and nights, even in the rain, so as to be the first to get on board an English brig, which was delivering a cargo. The men busied themselves in carrying sand for ballast and water, hoping to speed her departure. Dirty and disagreeable as it was to lie outside, all hoped they would soon reclothe themselves when they got their £10 each on landing.

Somerville describes how the desperate legionaries who had waited three or four days on the quay were mistreated by the captains of two ships. The men manned the boats and pulled as if to get the vessels clear of the bay, while the steersmen brought the ships back at every tack to their previous position, to the great amusement of their own sailors, as well as the crews of five or six English and French warships lying at anchor close by. Their officers seem to have completely deserted them in their hour of need.

The *Prince Regent* was one of the best British troop ships, yet she was 'a vessel wretchedly rigged, manned and accommodated to her trade of carrying troops'. Only two of her crew were able-bodied seamen, the rest having been taken on for wages. Designed to carry only 280 men, she had been to the Mediterranean with regular British troops, and was on her passage home *uncleansed* when she took on board 520 men of the 8th Regiment, including Somerville. As the men went on board they were distributed to the berths by NCOs, and the filth and stench were intolerable. 'Fleas and lice, bugs and other vermin nestled in every seam and splinter.'

The ship's destination was Greenock on the Clyde, and though they had been told this, scepticism was rife as a result of the men's grim experiences, and some of the more credulous among them believed the mischievous rumour that she was bound for the West Indies, where they would all be sold as slaves. Somerville found the consternation among the ragged crowd in the hold ludicrous to witness, but he tried to reassure and comfort them.

The *Prince Regent* logged and rolled in the Bay of Biscay for three weeks, but eventually made progress and at last a 'snoring breeze' sent her dashing through the Irish Sea.

> Never, I believe, will five hundred beings, as dirty and forlorn as we then were in appearance, wear such light hearts as we, when the shores of Ireland on one side and Galloway on the other flitted past. It was a battering rain and boisterous wind, but that was all nothing, the Craig of Ailsa rock got three cheers as the bending masts groaning beneath their canvas carried us along. There was not a height or hollow in the land on either side which was not described by some one or other who claimed acquaintance with the locality; and with gladness, though rough and wet, that night passed over.

The next morning was a lovely one. The ship had anchored during the night and when she weighed anchor a gentle breeze bore her into the Clyde, for the men to disembark at Greenock with full hearts.

The *Cork Standard* of 4 August 1837 carried a report of the arrival of five hundred men of the Legion, destitute, in Glasgow. It also reported that the brig *Caroline* of Swansea, which had left San Sebastian for England five or six weeks earlier with two hundred Rifles of the late British Legion, Captain Cook and two other officers on board, had not been heard of since. Two boats were shipwrecked, one off the coast of Brittany and the other on the English coast, with the loss of almost all hands. One of these vessels was probably the *Caroline*.

Another transport carrying men of the Legion, in difficulties near the Scilly Isles, landed three boatloads of troops. They terrorised the inhabitants, who locked themselves in their houses while the soldiers looted their barns and orchards. 'They seemed the roughest, most ferocious outlaws that had ever been seen.' In extenuation, the looters would probably have died of starvation had they not helped themselves to food. Relief was slow to come; on 26 August Home Office records referred to a bill for £46 4s. 5d. for provisions for use of the British Legion at the Scilly Islands. In September three anxious Justices of the Peace at St Mary's were told that application would be made to the Foreign Office for payment of the same bill, and in late November were reassured that the money would be paid on application. It is unclear when the bill was paid, or how long the men had to wait before being taken to the mainland.

Their return to their native land was a highly emotional event for Somerville and his fellow Scots, with mingled feelings of sadness and hope. Sadness must have been prominent, for the comrades they had left in Spanish graves. Somerville calculated that of the 2,300 men who had left Greenock about two years before, less than a thousand survived. To the 520 on the *Prince Regent* were added 200 more who had returned to Portsmouth and another 200 still serving in the Legion, of whom over 100 were to die at Andoain in the coming September. Duncan gives the strength of the Scotch corps in the new Legion on 1 July 1837 as rank and file 289, sergeants 25 and officers 25.

On landing the men were accosted by the friends and relatives of the dead and missing, asking after their loved ones, and even more enquiries were made by the crowds when they reached Glasgow. All were anxious about their gratuities, which they had been told would be paid by agents upon landing. Three Legion officers went ashore at Greenock to ask about the arrangements for this and for other help, but no news as to the gratuities could be obtained, and the men stated that the officers had deserted them there, telling them to go on to Glasgow (*Cork Standard*, 7 August 1837).

The provost and magistrates of Greenock, anxious to be rid of the ragged troops, hired two steamers to take them to Glasgow without delay. On arrival at the Broomielaw they were greeted by immense crowds. In the absence of any officers, Somerville and three others went to the office of the Spanish vice-consul, Mr Reid, and thence to his house, where Reid sent them away. They then went to see the lord provost of Glasgow, Mr Mills, but were told that he could do nothing for them. They were met by Captain Miller of the police, who went back with them to the provost who now, under pressure, gave them some food and agreed to arrange food and temporary accommodation for his unexpected and unwelcome visitors. The men were marched to the bazaar in Candlerigg, fed and given sleeping quarters. Next day they were marched to the cattle market, given breakfast and a pass with sixpence – the latter to save them from the vagrancy laws, and the pass to let them travel on to their destinations. In his Narrative, Somerville ends his account of the return of the surviving Scots soldiers of the Legion: 'gradually the whole dwindled away. Some found their friends, who immediately restored them to the fustian jacket of civil society; others got kind strangers to pity them; and some, who had none of these, began to exercise their wits.'

Those who had disembarked in England fared no better, and sometimes worse. Far from being welcomed as heroes, they were shunned and feared by respectable citizens, who saw them as a threat to property and health. Penniless and unable to obtain work or lodging, most had to choose between beggary and banditry. The ragged red coats of the ex-legionaries soon provoked antipathy rather than sympathy in the upright citizens of the entire kingdom. The *Blackburn Standard* in August 1837 printed the local news, reported a few days later in *The Times*, that 'the men of the Legion are infesting the roads of this town and its surroundings, where they are operating like the roughest outlaws of the past. They are making the highways unsafe for those who travel alone or unarmed.' A correspondent in Portsmouth reported:

> The current situation in Portsmouth and Portsea is extremely dangerous, both for the moral welfare and the health of the inhabitants

of the two towns, owing to the large number of ex-legionaries –
the Scots and Irish in particular – who have landed here and are
infesting our streets. There are about 2,700 in the most deplorable
state of filth and misery. The police are watching them day and
night. It was not possible to prevent them from leaving the harbour area, and now there are hundreds of them dossed down in
the streets. They are the cause of fight after fight in which the glint
of knives is immediately apparent. The citizens of these two towns
are to send a protest to the Home Office asking that they may be
relieved of such intolerable nuisances. Fifteen of them have already
been imprisoned for theft.

The situation at Portsmouth was particularly difficult since many wounded
men and sick men had been invalided there from Spain for months before
the disbanding of the Legion in June 1837. They were accommodated in
Spartan conditions on board the *Swiftsure* hulk. The *Clonmel Advertiser* of
21 December 1836 refers to a report in an English paper of two hundred
invalids aboard the *Swiftsure*, 'made a receiving or hospital ship for those
sent home disabled, to remain until funds were obtained to pay the arrears
due to them, so as to enable them to return to their respective parishes'.
The question of supplies for the invalids and their cost figure frequently
in the Foreign Office and Admiralty despatches of the time. Arrangements
for paying arrears of pay and gratuities to the men at Portsmouth were
slow to be made. A Royal Navy purser was eventually deputed to help the
Spanish agent in discharging and paying them. The destitute condition of
the invalids on the *Swiftsure* led to repeated but vain petitions appealing
for help from the authorities. In January 1837 a Sergeant Wilkinson of the
Legion complained of impositions practised by the Jews of Portsmouth on
the invalids, who had been forced to sell any saleable items, including clothing. Admiral Maitland at Portsmouth wrote to the Admiralty in July 1837
about the expenses for rations issued to the invalids on the hulk, which
amounted to £40 18s. 6d.

With the arrival in July of more invalids on board the steamer *Isabel
the Second*, despatches refer to the crippled and diseased state of the men,
and their disposal. They were to be received into hospital and the expenses
charged to the Spanish government. Where to house them was a major
problem. In October sixty-five more invalids went on board the *Swiftsure*,
but in December orders were given that yet more sick and wounded men

brought home on board the *Isabel the Second*, lying off Gravesend, should be admitted to the naval hospital there and their costs charged to the Spanish government. Others were to be admitted to Chatham Hospital. In late December it was ordered that men of the Legion should be subsisted on board the *Swiftsure* 'until settled with by the Spanish government'. Settlement was very slow and petitions continued from groups of men and individuals waiting to be paid and discharged, and complaining of their destitute condition. The common reply to such pleas that they had no grounds for their complaints can have brought no comfort.

The anonymous author of *A Concise Account of the British Auxiliary Legion*, published at Scarborough in 1837, wrote that as soon as a man received 30s. he was immediately sent on shore about his business. Some of those who had received their pay and 'marching money' and who attempted to board the *Swiftsure* again were refused admission, being now expected to fend for themselves. The *Swiftsure* was still in use for the Legion's wounded in 1838.

The situation in ports and towns throughout Britain was similar. In August 1837 the *Dorset County Chronicle* reported the recent arrival at Poole of a small vessel of eighty tons burden, with 320 half-famished and ragged beings on board who had been sent from the Spanish shores with fourteen days' provisions, all of which had been expended before their arrival. Their reception was more generous than that of most of their mates; the report continues 'the poor fellows were put on shore at the mouth of the harbour without a shilling amongst them, and must have starved in the streets had it not been for the charity of several of the visitors and inhabitants'.

In London meanwhile, desperate veterans were besieging the house of the Spanish minister, Manuel de Aguilar, who complained and was promised immediate police protection against their importunities. Men of the Legion were begging on the streets and the press carried frequent police reports of prosecutions. A report in *The Times* of September 1837 under the heading 'General Evans and His Heroes' made political capital by drawing the attention of Lord Palmerston to the appearance at Marylebone Court before the magistrate of three wretched-looking men, dressed in tattered military jackets, all without shoes and stockings, who were charged with begging. They had been found by an inspector sitting on the pavement in the New Road, in a most deplorable condition. Round the neck of one hung a piece of pasteboard on which was written, 'Victims of Spanish ingratitude! – we are forced to appeal to the public to enable us to get to our homes, and are without food or clothing, or place of rest. We apply daily to the Spanish Ambassador, in the hope of getting our back pay and gratuity, but are always refused them. – Thus, without hopes of getting our money, we would leave London immediately, had we means of doing so.' They had served nearly two years under General Evans and had no shelter but that which yards and doorways afforded them. They said they had been several times to General Evans' house and had been ordered off. The magistrate, Lord Montford, was sympathetic, but could not help them and 'the poor fellows were discharged on promising not to solicit alms of the public again'.

CHAPTER SEVENTEEN

The new Legion

Back in the Spanish arena the chaotic process of recruiting for the new Legion resulted in a body of some 1,700 officers and men, most of whom would come to regret their decision to re-enlist. Major Duncan gave a useful review of the reorganisation of the Legion. He believed that General Maurice O'Connell, despite his undoubted bravery, had not the same influence over the men as Evans had had, and encountered great difficulties from the start. If Evans had accepted a poisoned chalice, O'Connell had inherited an even more deadly draught. It must be admitted that Wellington himself would have found the situation daunting. The men were receiving no pay for their new engagement, and the officers, though unpaid for *fifteen months*, were paying for their men's food out of their own slender purses.

Duncan lists the composition of the new Legion as 1,746 on 1 July 1837, made up of 122 officers, 121 sergeants and 1,503 rank and file, divided up as follows:

Corps	Officers	Sergeants	Rank and file
Rifles	26	32	341
Scotch	25	25	289
Irish	21	26	294
Lancers	22	26	267
Artillery	25	4	209
Sappers	2	4	52
Ambulance	1	4	51
Total	122	121	1503
GRAND TOTAL			1746

Within a few weeks of its formation, Colonel Wylde, the English Commissioner, described the state of the new Legion as 'one of disgraceful slackness and discontent'. He determined to appeal to General

Espartero, the only Spanish official who appeared to him trustworthy and determined, for redress of the Legion's grievances.

Indiscipline was rife among the Legion, but even more so in the Spanish Cristino army, among which mutiny soon broke out. The persisting non-payment of arrears and their resultant privations fuelled their sense of wrongs. The Spanish ministry of Calatrava was much resented by the army for its habit of transferring popular indignation from itself to the military by wholesale detraction of the officers and men, who were unable to defend themselves. Mendizabal, the minister of finance, was foremost with his calumnies, claiming that enough money had been sent to the army to fill their waist-belts with gold ounces, and that rations had always been supplied in abundance. The starving soldiers were easily persuaded that their officers had appropriated the pay which was said to have been so lavishly issued. Hence their generals came to be regarded as traitors, and junior officers dared not use their authority lest they should provoke a mutiny. The crisis developed first at Hernani and Santander in the division that had been commanded by General Evans, and was now under the Spanish Count Mirasol. Evans' efforts to obtain pay and rations for his men were well known, and the cry arose, when mutiny erupted, that only traitors were left to command them now that the English had left. Mirasol was attacked and his ADC killed while trying to pacify the troops. He was only saved from death by the intervention of Lieutenant Colonel F.C. Ebsworth of the 10th Regiment, who placed himself between the rifles of the mutineers and their target and was killed. Mirasol was bundled on board a British ship by Major Howe and Captain Hampton of the Legion's Artillery. Ebsworth was buried on Mount Orgull, where his tomb may still be seen (pl. 14). Mirasol handed over his command to the respected old General Jáuregui, *El Pastor*.

In August the Provincial Regiment of Segovia mutinied, and their commander, General Escalera, who had determined to make an example of the ringleaders, was brutally murdered. Similar atrocities by mutinous Cristino soldiers occurred elsewhere; in Pamplona General Sarsfield was murdered by men clamouring for their pay and claiming that he had stolen it. The British public were shocked by reports of these outrages. The *Morning Herald*, reporting Sarsfield's murder, wrote that even his horse was killed by the blind fury of the tiradores. Espartero, an honourable and patriotic officer, punished the guilty men.

The new Legion, though less rebellious than their Spanish colleagues, refused to obey General O'Connell unless they received their pay.

Meanwhile, some fifty officers of the old Legion remained in San Sebastian, refusing to accept a passage to England until paid their arrears. Morale among these men was at a low ebb and, as on previous similar occasions, duelling became popular. On 2 July 1837 the journal *Atlas* reported that Colonel Herman, formerly ADC to Evans, amused himself the other day by calling on Colonel McCabe of the Royal Irish to settle an old quarrel 'just by way of relief to the tedium incident to waiting for pay. Colonel Herman was shot in the mouth, lost a few teeth and a little warm blood, and the parties have been good friends ever since.'

THE MASSACRE AT ANDOAIN

It was in this unhappy situation and while General O'Connell was visiting Madrid in a vain attempt to persuade their Spanish paymasters to provide the financial and other support which they owed the new Legion, that one of the saddest chapters in the Legion's history unfolded.

General Leopoldo O'Donnell, who had the chief command in the queen's armies in the north, determined to advance from Hernani towards Andoain, some six miles to the south. On 9 September the army advanced with the Lancers, the Scotch battalion of the Legion and the Chapelgorris under General Jochmus skirmishing along the main road, while a Spanish brigade moved along the range of hills on either side. Somerville gives a detailed account of events based on eyewitness accounts of the catastrophe obtained later from survivors, officers and men of his former regiment, as it developed. The Artillery was very actively involved, but the Irish Regiment and the Rifles had refused to march until they had some assurance of pay; the Rifles were later persuaded to move after the main body, joining them at Andoain.

Howe and Skedd, with the Artillery 'wrought heavy and fearful work' on the enemy, whose dead and wounded were seen strewn at the points where they had made a stand. The Lancers greatly distinguished themselves again. Charging the Carlist cavalry, they came on a column of infantry which they mistook for their Spanish allies and after calling on the men to move out of the way, galloped through its openings to find themselves fired on from behind by the enemy. The Carlist cavalry, meanwhile, wheeled and retreated before the charging Lancers.

The troops reached Andoain early the same afternoon, having suffered very trifling loss, but having inflicted heavy casualties on the Carlists. As soon as he entered the town, which was surrounded by heights held by the enemy, O'Donnell set about fortifying it under fire from the hills. Reports began to circulate that Carlist reinforcements were arriving, but O'Donnell felt himself in as safe a situation as possible, with his right and left flanks protected by brigades of Spanish troops in the surrounding hills. Both wings commanded the fords of the river Oria in the front, and had thrown up breast-works for protection from the enemy's fire. The Cristinos' position was strengthened on 11 September by the belated arrival of the Rifle Corps under Colonel Wilson. An officer who survived the action later told Somerville how the Artillery, under Howe and Skedd, had completely cowed the enemy. Up to 12 September the Legion's losses in skirmishing and protecting their working parties were eleven officers and about two hundred men killed and wounded.

On the morning of the 14th, proof that the Carlists had been reinforced came with a heavy barrage from their guns, which had been brought up in the night and placed on the hills to the left of the town. Howe's artillery soon ended this bombardment, silencing the Carlist guns and wounding nearly every gunner who tried to work them. All was quiet again, and the garrison of Andoain piled arms and returned to their work of entrenching and fortifying.

The Carlist general had thrown his troops forward under the temporary cover of his guns, until they were silenced, so that they would be ready to advance. At this point a group of about three hundred Chapelchurries, the lightly armed, mobile Carlist soldiers equivalent to the Cristino Chapelgorris, was thrown across the river at the ford in front of the Infanta Cristino Regiment to probe the defences. The latter had piled arms, having just replaced a Spanish battalion that had gallantly repulsed their attackers, and were busy with their entrenching, but the moment they saw the enemy cross the river they ran, their colonel leading the way.

Somerville's account of the rout continues: 'This gave courage to the enemy, and column after column crossed the river at this point, while the Infanta regiment* was running away, and calling to the other Spanish regiments that the whole of the Carlists had crossed the river and they would all be murdered if they did not retire.' The Infanta regiment had left their arms piled, and some of the other Spanish regiments threw away arms,

---

* The same Cristino regiment which fled before Hernani the previous March.

ammunition and everything that would have impeded their progress in the race to Hernani.

Meanwhile in Andoain itself, the Artillery, the Scotch and Rifles of the Legion, not suspecting for a moment that their cowardly allies had deserted them, were at work fortifying their positions. Some of them remarked that 'there was a little skirmishing going on to the left', but the truth only dawned on them when they saw the enemy among the tents and piled arms of the Infanta Regiment, and heard and felt the bullets that came battering among them.

The order 'Stand to your arms' was given and two companies of the Scots were immediately ordered to ascend the hill. They drove the enemy, many times their number, before them, but to no avail. Surgeon Wilkinson's account makes special mention of Lieutenant Durkin, a mere boy, who distinguished himself at the head of a very few Scotsmen, dashing at the enemy on the hill, who fled in great confusion. (This must the same man, described as Ensign Darking, who operated on General Chichester's horse on 16 March as described by Somerville. Though listed as Hospital-Assistant in the Army List, he later served as Ensign. His diminutive height probably led Wilkinson to misjudge his age.)

On ascending and taking a higher position, the men of the Legion could see the Carlists thickly crowding in their rear, while the Cristino soldiers were flying in all directions from the fight. Their return was blocked and they were surrounded on every side. They were called on by the enemy to lay down their arms and told they would be given quarter. While this promise was being made they could see some of their comrades, who had been surrounded nearby and had surrendered, being murdered. They determined therefore to sell their lives dearly.

There were many and varied accounts, Somerville comments, of the manner and time of the deaths of the Legion. It would seem, from the evidence of the few who escaped, that many managed to fight their way into Andoain, but not before the village was beset on all sides. They were hemmed into the village square and there, without exception, put to death. A letter from an officer of the old Legion (*Cork Standard*, 13 October) reported that five officers and about thirty men defended themselves in the church of Andoain (pl. 17) until induced to surrender on promise of quarter, and were taken to Tolosa and murdered one by one.

Somerville commented bitterly, 'It is worthy of remark, that some of the Carlist officers most forward here, and most liberal of distributing mur-

derous death, were those whose lives had been saved by the English at
Irun, they having been exchanged for other prisoners a short while before.'

Somerville gives the exact numbers of those killed at Andoain by the
Carlists, with the names of the officers. Six officers and 60 NCOs and privates of the Scotch were killed; of the Rifles six officers and 59 other ranks.
Of the Lancers, Major MacKellar and two men were killed and three
wounded; five horses were killed and 14 wounded. The greater mobility
of the Lancers compared with the infantry must have helped more to survive. The Artillery had three officers wounded, two gunners killed and two
wounded. Somerville, but for his failure to get ashore to re-enlist, would
almost certainly have died with his comrades in the massacre. Their murder
affected him deeply and he devotes several pages to brief histories of the
thirteen officers killed and the manner of their deaths. Colonel F.R. Clarke
of the Scotch, who had been adjutant of the 12th British Regiment of the
Line for many years, was described as the most daring and reckless officer of the Legion. On 16 March, before Hernani he had been wounded in
one arm, which was still in a sling at Andoain. (The injury had been
adjudged equivalent to loss of a limb, and he had been awarded a pension
for life. Despite this, and the pleas of his friends, he had not resigned and
had reapplied for the new Legion.) Clarke had been trying unsuccessfully
to rally the fleeing Spaniards and was returning to where his men were
surrounded to die with them when he was killed by being torn from his
horse by the bayonets of the enemy.

Captain Dalrymple and Lieutenant Carnaby of the Scotch were killed
a short way from the village.

Captain Larkham, the nephew of a high-ranking British officer, had
gone to Spain to see active service before entering a British regiment.
Several times wounded in earlier actions, he was seen at Andoain wounded
and on his knees defending himself with his sword. Overpowered at last,
he was killed and his tartan plaid was held aloft as a trophy by his slayers.

Captain Courtney of the Rifles and his company defended themselves
nobly near the bridge, fighting to the last man. With him died
Lieutenant Siems.

Captain Forbes, a native and former merchant of Aberdeen, had
attracted critical comments in Somerville's Narrative of 1837, which he
later deeply regretted having made. 'His last act was one that covered a
multitude of former unsoldierlike sins,' for he fell in front of his company,
charging the enemy. Wilkinson reports that Forbes, who had a very pow-

erful horse, was encouraged to escape by a colleague, but refused. 'Forbes' reply was truly Roman in its character: "Colonel Clarke has not yet left the village. He is a British officer and in command, and it shall never be said that I deserted him.'"

Lieutenant O'Brian, formerly an ensign in the 7th Irish Regiment, was said by some to have once been a 'fancy-man' of the celebrated Mrs Clarke, the *natural* duchess of York. His brains were dashed out by the butt-ends of the Carlist muskets.

Lieutenant Haslam, also previously an ensign in the 7th Irish, fell a sacrifice to his own generosity in trying to save his fellow Rifleman, Lieutenant Townsend, who had been wounded. The last time they were seen he was carrying Townsend on his back.

Major MacKellar of the Lancers, a native of Port Glasgow, had served in Portugal and went out to Spain under Colonel Tupper of the 6th Scotch. On the retreat from Hernani he had saved the guns from capture, and it was a similar service on 14 September that cost him his life. He was at the head of the Lancers at Andoain and, seeing the Carlist cavalry about to cut off the retreat of the Artillery, he charged to save it and was killed in the charge by a ball in the heart. Wilkinson states that MacKellar's scarf and sword were secured by some of the Lancers, while young Lieutenant Cotter, by his side, whose horse had been killed under him at the same time, very coolly jumped into the vacant saddle and galloped off with the Lancers.

Somerville was deeply saddened by the deaths of the Shields brothers, whom he had known throughout his service. They were the only sons of a British officer who, with the elder son William, had fought in Portugal in support of the young Queen Maria. The father was killed and his son returned home, but then went out to Spain, he as captain and his younger brother Robert as ensign of the Grenadier Company of the 8th Regiment. Somerville had acted as their clerk in keeping the company accounts until promoted to colour-sergeant on their recommendations. Both had been dangerously ill with fever in Vitoria. The elder brother had been severely wounded on 5 May 1836, and again on the Venta hill, and was promoted brevet and later full major, while Robert was promoted to lieutenant and then captain. Their mother and sisters lived near Dublin, where they were born, and had often begged them to return home. When trying to force an entry into the village, after having led their two companies up the hill, Robert Shields fell wounded and his brother stood over his body defending it until he too fell and both were killed. Their comrade, Captain Larkham, was said by some witnesses to have been with the brothers when all were wounded and defending themselves in prostrate conflict at the same time. Surgeon Wilkinson relates that he, as Robert Shields' medical officer, had seen him on sick parade with an extensive boil over one knee, had considered him unfit for active service and ordered him to return to San Sebastian on 8 September, the eve of the advance to Andoain. This order had been countermanded by Colonel Clarke, persuaded by Robert's brother. Wilkinson regretted that as a result his life had not been spared to his family and friends.

Somerville lavished praise on the bravery and skill of the Lancers and Artillery during the retreat, exacting the highest price from the enemy for their almost Pyrrhic victory. The Lancers stuck close to the Artillery, charging the enemy in every direction. Lieutenant Baron Stutterheim and Captains Hogreve and Henderson were singled out for their conduct beyond all praise. Howe and Skedd of the Artillery gave the Carlists a volley of spherical case shot as the retreat to Hernani began. He wrote that many brave acts were done by others still living; General Jochmus and his ADC, Cotter, were often conspicuous. General O'Donnell himself had dismounted to try to rally his Spaniards, and became so exhausted that he would have been captured had not Colonel Arbuthnott dismounted and given him his horse; both officers escaped.

O'Donnell was said to have been in a state of partial distraction from the cowardly way in which he – and the Legion – were deserted by his troops, and the devastating effect of their flight. He knew that he owed his life only to the help of the Legion, when his own men refused him a helping hand. Some of the fleeing Spanish officers were cut down by O'Donnell himself for refusing to rally their troops and, Somerville adds, by two English officers, 'whom it may be as well now not to name'. O'Donnell could not rally the fugitives until he reached Hernani; he then found that nearly 800 stands of arms with ammunition in proportion had been thrown away, and that all the tents and provisions had fallen into the enemy's hands. The stores taken amounted, in all, to 800,000 rounds of ammunition and six weeks' provisions for five thousand men. The entire loss in killed and wounded was twenty officers and three hundred men. The Legion's dead were 13 officers and 123 other ranks.

THE ESCAPE OF SURGEONS WILKINSON AND BAYNE, CAPTAIN ALEXANDER BALL AND GENERAL O'DONNELL

Another member of the Legion who reported on the catastrophe was Staff-Surgeon Henry Wilkinson, who with his colleague Surgeon Bayne had remained as a medical officer to the new Legion. By a bizarre twist Wilkinson lived to relate the story of his own and his colleague's escapes from death. On 11 September a group of officers was sitting in the open on a low wall in front of the church when Lieutenant Elder of the Royal Artillery was hit in the face by a bullet, which fractured his jaw. In the absence of the medical officer of the RA, Wilkinson operated on Elder but could not find the ball. When the RA surgeon returned an argument arose between the two doctors, but the other surgeon had no greater success. Sitting outside again afterwards with fellow-officers who were rallying him about the disagreement, Wilkinson was explaining what had happened, and pointing to his own jaw, when another bullet struck him in a very similar situation, passing across his trachea to lodge superficially over the carotid artery, its force broken by 'a very large quantity of hair'. His fellow surgeon, Dr Bayne, extracted the ball. Wilkinson was sent back to Hernani and fortunately made a full recovery, his fine singing voice being unimpaired. Artistic as well as musical, he had made sketches of scenery in Spain throughout his service, and these were later worked up into coloured plates, lithographed by Thomas Shotter Boys and published in 1838 with a selection of Basque music. Although Wilkinson disclaimed any intention of writing a history of the Legion, his text contains valuable descriptions of his experiences, amplified by the account later given him by his colleague Dr Bayne, who escaped from the slaughter. This, together with the personal account of Ensign Ball, contributes to a dramatic record of these horrific events.

Alexander Ball, who had seen the flight of the Spaniards, was riding beside a ration wagon when his horse ran away with him along the road to Hernani. Dismounting, he ran along a narrow ravine, which was full of the abandoned impedimenta of the Infanta Regiment. The Legion's artillery continued to bombard the enemy and the Lancers repeatedly charged them. Ball eventually caught up with his commanding officer and the two men drank a bottle of 'champaign' which they found abandoned and, refreshed and remounted, rode on to the village of Urneite. Here the Lancers were extended in skirmishing order to prevent the further flight of the Infanta

Regiment. Colonel Parrera, their commanding officer, had his stripes torn off by Captain Hogreve of the Lancers, who also cut off the epaulettes of a Spanish captain. From Urneite, Ball and his companions returned to the safety of Hernani, which they had left six days before. General O'Donnell, who had narrowly escaped capture and death several times ordered Urneite to be set on fire; this may have partially relieved his feelings of shame and anguish, but his practice of burning Carlist villages would not have won over hearts and minds to the queen's cause.

Surgeon Bayne's escape from Andoain was reported by his colleague Wilkinson. Bayne, a very active man with great presence of mind and determination, was one of the last to leave Andoain. He quickly caught up with the rear of a Spanish battalion, huddled together like sheep in a deep lane (the same ravine, probably, which Ball had followed). Realising that his best chance was to put the Spaniards behind him as a buffer from the Carlists, he climbed up the steep banks and ran like a deer along the high ground, the Carlist bullets cutting up the ground around him and, by repeating this exercise two or three times he succeeded in placing four or five hundred men in his rear. His aim was to gain the high road to Hernani as he expected the Lancers sooner or later to attack the enemy, and he steered a course halfway between the mountains and the road, often almost falling from exhaustion. About two miles from Andoain he came up with the unfortunate General O'Donnell. 'The man who at daybreak had been in command of seven thousand men was now a fugitive on foot, without hat or sword.' He had twice been laid hold of by the enemy but succeeded in shaking them off. He was attempting to get up a steep mud-bank to reach the summit of the mountain, and asked a Spanish soldier who had made the ascent to give him his hand. The man continued his flight, paying no attention to his general's request. Bayne and a Scot by his side immediately offered help and hoisted him up the bank. O'Donnell later rewarded the Scotsman with a four-dollar piece. Bayne continued his flight and soon had the satisfaction of seeing the Lancers charge down the road to attack the Carlists. It was in this charge that Major MacKellar received his death wound; the ball pierced his heart, and he fell from his horse with an exclamation of 'O God!'

The disaster at Andoain and the murder of the officers and men of the Legion does not seem to have had as great an impact on public opinion as might have been expected.

The correspondent of the *Morning Chronicle* wrote a detailed account of the action on 16 September. Although apparently unaware of the murder of the Legion prisoners, he paid tribute to their bravery. 'Our defeat was complete. Never did a body of brave men act with more gallantry than the remnant of the devoted Legion did on this day. Their acts of personal prowess, devoted affection to each other, and heroism were brilliant, both as men and as soldiers.' He described the defence of the church 'from the steeple, from every loop hole and crevice which would permit the passage of a musket, keeping their enemies at bay, and playing dire and dreadful havoc amongst them below, the Carlists firing shells and round shot into the church.' A battery opened fire on them during the night, and a shell landing in the building caused an explosion in the ammunition stored there. 'It was now two o'clock in the morning; they were exhausted, and capitulation being offered, it was accepted.' O'Donnell sent a flag of truce to the Carlist general on the afternoon of the 16th, requesting an exchange of prisoners; this was agreed with respect to the Spaniards, but refused for the English. O'Donnell immediately returned a reply that if one Englishman should suffer after the capitulation, all the prisoners in the castle of San Sebastian would be shot, starting with the officers of the highest rank. No answer had yet been received, and the reason, in retrospect, is clear, all the prisoners having been killed while most were slaughtered and never even taken prisoner.

On 27 September the *Clonmel Herald* reported the disastrous defeat of the Legion; a Bayonne telegraphic despatch of 16 September had announced the complete defeat of O'Donnell and his utter rout from Andoain to Hernani. Accurate reports were slow to reach England. A Foreign Office despatch of 30 September referred to the enquiry by Mrs E. Haslam as to the fate of her son, Lieutenant Haslam, 'said to have been taken prisoner on the 16th inst. at Andoain'. The 4th of October brought the reply, 'Cannot inform her of the fate of her son'. No official account of the action had yet been received by the Foreign Office. It must have been several months before Somerville, with his network of contacts among past and present members of the Legion, was able to reconstruct the details of the débâcle; it would be good to think that Mrs Haslam did learn eventually of the heroic circumstances of the son's death.

William Bollaert in his later account (1870) recorded in a footnote almost precisely the members of the Legion who were put to death. The Annual Register for 1837 summarises the events at Andoain giving an account differing only slightly from Somerville's. Under the unexpected Carlist attack the Spanish troops were said to have shamefully fled and dispersed, without giving any indication of what was passing to the British regiments. These, supported only by two companies of Spaniards, defended themselves but at last, being driven into a church and surrounded by the Carlists, were compelled to surrender, when the greater number were said to have been put to the sword. The *Gentleman's Magazine* for October 1837 gave scanty coverage to the disaster, relating that twenty-five English officers were killed, with no mention of the dead among the other ranks or of the circumstances of their deaths.

The sadness and disillusionment of the Legion at this time were deepened with the return of General O'Connell from Madrid, almost empty-handed, having failed in his mission to obtain help from the Spanish government apart from enough money to pay the field allowance of his personal staff. The question must be asked whether, had he been present, the Irish Regiment would have advanced with the others to Andoain, and whether the outcome would have been any different if they had, apart from a greater roll-call of the dead. He could not have predicted the shameful desertion of the Spanish regiments. His indignation at the culpable neglect or wilful malevolence of those appointed by the Spanish government to deal with the Legion was vividly expressed in his final general order on 10 December, when the new Legion was dissolved.

CHAPTER EIGHTEEN

The end in sight

FINAL REORGANISATION OF THE LEGION INTO THE BRITISH AUXILIARY BRIGADE

It was not surprising that, after the tragedy of Andoain, the Legion continued to be dogged with problems related to low morale, arrears of pay and indiscipline, affecting officers and men alike. A paymaster of the Lancers was court-martialled for withholding the pay of an officer, and discharged the service.

Among the men discipline had degenerated still further, some being imprisoned in the castle for refusing to obey orders. Relations between Generals O'Donnell and O'Connell had soured irrevocably; it was said that O'Donnell, soon after the disaster at Andoain, had requested a court-martial on the latter, but this, if true, may have been a transient symptom of his tortured state of mind in the immediate wake of the defeat, and a search for a scapegoat.

The press in Britain devoted less space to the Legion after Andoain, but the *Atlas* of 15 October 1837 quoted in detail a letter from San Sebastian describing a recent expedition in which the Legion had taken part. It was a combined naval and military operation in which General O'Donnell on board the *Salamander* with four, and Brigadier Jochmus on board the *Phoenix* with seven companies of troops collaborated with Lord John Hay, Colonel Colquhoun and part of the artillery on the *Comet*. O'Donnell's division was to land at Ondorroa and seize all the boats used in the trade with France to supply the Carlist forces, and also, if possible, to free two hundred Cristino prisoners confined at Marquina, a village some two leagues inland. Jochmus' objective was to land at Deva and Motrico, take all the boats there and if possible capture the Carlist General Guidebalde, who was taking the waters at Cistona for the benefit of his health. Hay's part was to cover the re-embarkation of the troops. Although the landings were made successfully, the peasants raised the alarm by firing shots so that Guidebalde escaped and the prisoners were moved before O'Donnell's advance guard could reach them. O'Donnell could not pursue them, since the expedition had to re-embark with the tide. He did, however, succeed in capturing twenty-eight chassée-marées and other boats, which were brought back in triumph to San Sebastian laden with corn, oil, wine and flour, stores partly levied by the Carlists on the Cristino inhabitants, and partly landed recently from France. The correspondent wrote that the troops had pillaged the three small fishing villages 'besides committing great excesses in a convent of nuns near Motrico'. The next day the glacis at San Sebastian had the appearance of a fair, where the soldiers exposed their plunder for sale.

In December 1837 O'Connell decided to disband the new Legion. He issued his last general order from San Sebastian on 10 December, explaining his reasons, praising the courage and devotion of the men in battle and severe privation, and condemning the neglect or malevolence of the agents of the Spanish government to fulfil its obligations to the Legion. Three months had passed since he had sought redress for arrears of pay from the minister of war, and none had been offered. He spoke of threats which had been made to the corps of cavalry and artillery that they would forfeit their claim to gratuity if they should discontinue their service. This was not the case, and he promised to advocate their rights. O'Connell's concern for the new Legion at its dissolution prompted him to add a warning to officers and men alike to be guarded in their conduct until the means of conveying them to their own country should be provided for them 'in order to give no opportunity for persecution'. He no doubt had in mind the difficulties experienced in repatriating their comrades of the old Legion, many of whom still languished in Spain. If he had doubts as to the efficiency of the arrangements for getting the new Legion home, he was right, since the arrival and disposal of its officers and men were still exercising the Admiralty and other authorities in the summer of 1838.

This was a difficult period for the officers of the new Legion. Lieutenant L.C. Gregg of the 1st Regiment, a native of Cork, fell foul of O'Donnell, who had him arrested and deported to France the next morning. Gregg was accused of 'tampering with the men of the Artillery, advising them not to serve, whereas he had merely given them advice when they asked his opinion. He was owed at least £250 in arrears of pay and gratuity by the Spanish government, and had only £4 to his name.'

The Spanish government was anxious to retain the services of the lancers and artillery of the new Legion, arms which had proved of immense value in battle, the superiority of the gunners having been repeatedly demonstrated over the previous two years.

The Lancers, the 2nd or the Queen's Own Irish Lancers, had been under the command of Colonel W.H. Jacks from July 1835. A half-pay captain in the 20th Light Dragoons of the British army, he had commanded the Foreign Hussars in Sicily until the breaking up of that squadron in 1814. The Lancers had distinguished themselves in many actions in Spain but, as Somerville pointed out, they were not mentioned as often as the other regiments, nor as often as they deserved, because much of the corps had been detached from the Legion and attached to the Spanish army for much of their period of service. When the Legion left Vitoria for San Sebastian in early 1836 many of the Lancers were ordered to remain there by General Evans. At the time of release of the old Legion in June 1837, the Lancers in the interior had no orders to move to headquarters to receive their pay, and it was left to Colonel Jacks, finding his regiment neglected and apparently forgotten, to move them to San Sebastian, where he learned that there was no pay nor chance of it for the Lancers, though the other privates and NCOs of the Legion had nearly all been paid up to 10 June. Chidley Malony, Cornet in the Lancers, wrote in January 1838 to the editor of the *Globe* to refute Evans' claim that almost all the NCOs and men under his command had been paid. Malony had sailed for Cork in the *Columbia* with a large detachment of the Lancers, and saw the men landed, each having received four Spanish dollars, for which they could with difficulty get 15s. Each private was due from £10 to £15 arrears of pay.

The third reorganisation of the Legion took place in March 1838, with volunteers from the dissolved new Legion being invited to continue to serve the queen in Spain.

This was under the command of an officer named in the roll of officers in the Legion published in Somerville's History as Colonel R. de la Saussaye, appointed earlier to the quartermaster-general's department. He figured earlier in a duel in August 1836 with Major Richardson, in which three shots were exchanged without injury. He was commissioned in the queen's army, but his French-sounding name had been adapted from an earlier patronymic, according to Alexander Ball, who enlisted in the new corps and had little cause to respect or love him. According to Ball, he was in reality a Mr Sauce, formerly a butter merchant, a tall, powerful-looking Irishman with whom the queen dowager of Naples, grandmother of Queen Isabella, fell in love. He had been preferred under Ferdinand VII and was now promoted to the rank of brigadier-general.

Saussaye's first general order from San Sebastian, dated 21 March

1838, directed that the Auxiliary Corps, at present composed of the Reyna Isabella Lancers and the Artillery, should in future be known as the British Auxiliary Brigade. It numbered only 402 souls, almost equally divided between the two arms, with 30 officers (three staff), 31 sergeants and 341 rank and file. Clear conditions of service were laid down, the period of service being *until the termination of the war* (which would eventually be in August 1839). The pay was to be a fixed sum, exclusive of rations. Pensions were to be given to the wounded and to the widows of all killed in action or dying of infirmities contracted during the campaign. A gratuity of three months' pay and a free passage to England would be granted to every man at the end of the war. The discipline and interior economy were to be those of the *British regular forces*. The pay of the Artillery rank and file ranged from 3s. 10½d. per day for a staff sergeant to 1s. 3¼d. for a gunner, a fixed charge of 6d. per day being deducted for rations. How effective the prudent new conditions would prove to be in protecting the interests of the brigade time would show all too soon.

FURTHER ADVENTURES OF ALEXANDER BALL IN THE QUEEN'S SERVICE

Captain Alexander Ball was appointed quartermaster of the Artillery under Colonel Humfrey, who soon resigned the command, which then devolved on Major Edward Howe, noted for his skilful gunnery. The four hundred soldiers of the brigade numbered only four per cent of the muster of the original Legion of 1835, but they were picked men, tough and experienced in battle. Most of the information we have about the brigade derives from Ball's account.

From the start Saussaye behaved in a dictatorial way unacceptable to his officers and men, and inimical to the efficient functioning of the brigade. Major Howe, who had repeatedly saved the day in the actions of the previous two or three years, was dismissed with many of his officers. 'Thus did Spain,' Ball wrote, 'lose the services of a man, every hair of whose head (as Lord John Hay said) "was worth an ounce of gold to the Queen's cause."'

Ball accompanied Captain Frederick Hampton and Brevet-Lieutenant Colonel McIntosh to the battery of San Bartolomé in San Sebastian where the artillery were stationed. When the men learned that their officers were going home, they said they would also go, but some agreed to re-enlist if Captain Hampton were to remain. Saussaye then offered the command of the artillery to Hampton, who accepted it although, Ball believed, he was too young to have much experience in intrigue, which was entirely foreign to his nature.

It had been intended to raise an infantry battalion, but the attempt failed since only 150 men would re-enlist. These were placed under Hampton's command with about 50 old artillerymen, who volunteered only on condition that he remain and command them. After two months of drilling they formed a very respectable field battery, with about 120 men, 70 horses, four 6-pounders, two 12-pound howitzers and a dismounted rocket detachment. In a slight skirmish with the enemy at that time, Ball had never seen better field practice than shown by the brigade artillery.

Intrigue and jealousy were to be the enemies of the brigade. Saussaye had decided that Lieutenant-Colonel McIntosh, brigade-major, should replace Hampton in command of the artillery, and petty measures were taken to make him resign. McIntosh put Hampton and Lieutenant R. O'Connor under arrest on some pretext, and Saussaye told them that they were dismissed the service. Hampton then reminded him that the rules of the British service applied, and demanded a court-martial. A court of enquiry was assembled under Colonel Wakefield, commandant of the Lancers, at which all the charges were dismissed as not worthy of consideration. The ludicrous situation worsened when Saussaye sent the two officers a *polite note* to the effect that he did not require their services any further.

The position of Hampton and O'Connor was now intolerable, and both resigned. After the transport had sailed from Pasajes with the men who refused to volunteer, McIntosh who, according to Ball, knew as little about artillery as the man in the moon, was appointed commandant. So enraged was Ball at such intrigue practised on his friend that he resigned his commission. Another experienced captain had unfortunately resigned earlier and the entire officer cadre of the brigade's artillery now comprised two lieutenants and three second lieutenants. The men were understandably very upset by these developments. A Scottish gunner named MacDonald tried to desert, but was captured, court-martialled, found guilty and shot. The Cristino General Leon, who was asked to confirm the sentence, replied that he would never shoot an Englishman under any circumstances, 'but ere the answer arrived poor MacDonald was in eternity'. Ball wrote that he had heard this in Pamplona, but hoped it was not true.

The reduction of a fine, though small, fighting force to a state of near impotence was a sad contrast to the glory days of the Legion's artillery. It seems unlikely that the artillery can have contributed much to the queen's cause in the remaining year of the war. Indeed, as Ball later learned, Saussaye was forced to disband the artillery and convert them into lancers for want of a proper officer to organise them.

With the departure of Alexander Ball, who had served in the Legion since September 1835, we no longer have an historian of that period of decline. Ball's appetite for the military life however was still unsatisfied, and he remained in Spain as a soldier in the queen's cause until the end of the war in August 1839 and, as a civilian, for some time after, leaving a valuable account in his *Personal Narrative of Seven Years in Spain* (1846).

Ball at first considered joining the Chapelgorris, but later resolved to join the force raised by José Antonio de Muñagorri, 'an honest lawyer' who had raised the cry of *'Paz y fueros'* (Peace and privileges) in the Basque provinces in an attempt to persuade the Carlists to end hostilities. Under attack by the Infante Don Sebastian, he had taken refuge in France in the village of Sara, near the Spanish border. He was supported by the British and French governments. France gave asylum and funds to him and his followers and let him raise, equip, drill and pay his men in her territory, while Lord John Hay, still active in the Cristino cause, supplied him with muskets, ammunition etc. on behalf of the British government – to the annoyance of the British Tories. Muñagorri distributed circulars among the Basques, calling on them in the name of humanity to surrender their arms and to be 'no longer deceived by the pretensions of Don Carlos', assuring them that their treasured, ancient *fueros* would be respected. Over three thousand men had joined his standard. He wanted English officers to command his cavalry, and more men from the Legion, especially artillery officers. Ball's former colleague, O'Connor, from the Brigade, had joined his service and his artillery. Ball was happy to engage in the cavalry but was surprised, when he asked to see his troop, to learn that 'there were no horses'; he had heard, he wrote later, of the Horse-Marines, but never of the foot-cavalry. Money was abundant, however, and the lack of mounts would soon be remedied.

Sadly, the arrangement was terminated when, a little later, Lord John Hay and Colonel Colquhoun arrived from San Sebastian to review the troops. After they had a short interview with Muñagorri it was announced that the services of Ball and O'Connor were dispensed with. Colquhoun explained that the venture was an affair got up entirely by the Basques for their legitimate *fueros*, and that the Tories in England, especially Lord Londonderry, a constant critic and enemy of Evans and the Legion, 'would make a deal of clamour should Englishmen personally assist'. (The earlier permission for British subjects to fight for the queen's cause was no longer in operation.) It was with much pain and reluctance that Ball left the service, but with a full month's pay and allowances as Captain of Cavalry, without having ever mounted a horse or drawn a sword in the Cause.

His adventures in Spain, however, were far from over, and his narrative gives a useful picture of the last stages of the war. He travelled to Bayonne, which he found full of Carlist agents; some of them tried to get details from him of the Legion's casualties, and one man offered him an appointment in the Carlist service with the rank of major, an offer which Ball indignantly refused. Wearing the ribbons of the decorations from the 5th of May and the siege of Irun, he attracted much attention and some dislike. A Spanish Jesuit, to whom he admitted being a Protestant and a Freemason, was horrified, exclaiming, '*Un fra mason! pobre infelice! pobre infelice!*'

Continuing his travels, and commenting en route on the countryside and the life of the people, Ball came to Barcelona where he met a Captain Chinnery, another soldier of fortune with a chequered career. Leaving the British service, he had gone to Portugal to fight for Dom Pedro in the Miguelite war of succession, in which many Britons were involved, among them General Dodgin. When that war ended Dodgin set out to raise volunteers, English, French, German and Italian, to fight in Spain in the service of Queen Isabella. Chinnery had recruited a fine company of men, assuming command of them and taking them to Spain. As the senior captain in Dodgin's force, he had presumed that the first vacant majority would be his, but instead it was given to a Mr Richardson. Enmity and jealousy between the two officers led to Chinnery's arrest and to the consequent breakdown of discipline of his company in battle near Cervera. When he was restored to its command his company made a gallant and successful charge against the Carlists, to the admiration of General Dodgin and the whole army. It was at this crucial point that Dodgin received two musket wounds within ten minutes, and was about to resign his command to his second-in-command when the third and last bullet sent him to eternity.*

---

* From January 1838 Foreign Office records contain numerous letters from the widow and son of General Dodgin asking for the return of his effects and payment of arrears. The

His devotion to the queen's cause now led Ball to vow not to shave until victory was obtained. His appearance, he wrote, came to resemble that of a German Jew. To his disappointment there was no fighting in that part of Spain, near Valencia, and the game appeared like hide-and-seek. Many hours were spent on rural walks discussing botany and Genesis with Major Cusack of the Cacadores.

Blood continued to be shed, however, with the execution of deserters and of Carlist prisoners. General van Hallen had succeeded General Oráa as captain-general of Cristino forces with Colonel Borso as his second-in-command. Van Hallen was as ruthless as General Nogueras, notorious for having had Cabrera's mother shot, an act which had shocked the civilised world. The war in the central theatre of Spain became as inhuman as it had been in the Basque region before the Eliot Convention.

In a successful action in which Ball was involved, Borso took two or three hundred prisoners, and van Hallen ordered that they should all be shot, as a reaction to an order by Cabrera that no quarter should be given. Borso refused to allow the killing of his prisoners, whom he had promised quarter when they surrendered. He pointed out that many were wounded and unable to march, and would have been slain on the battlefield if quarter had not been promised them. Van Hallen was inexorable: 'Send them to hospital, cure them, and when they can walk they shall be shot' was his prescription. More than fifty men were marched to Murviedro and there shot, but many more were admitted to hospital, many of them with only slight wounds, and some with only scratches, in an attempt to save their lives. Borso was so disgusted by the shooting of the prisoners that he resigned his commission. Meanwhile Colonel Lacey, one of the British commissioners with the queen's army, exerted himself with Villiers, the British ambassador in Madrid. Ball believed that by the involvement of the British government the men in hospital were saved, being indebted for their lives to Colonel Lacey.

At this point Ball left Valencia and resolved finally to abandon the profession of arms. He remained in Spain, for which he felt a deep affection, and travelled to Madrid where he saw the queen-regent, Queen Isabella

British minister in Madrid was asked to secure his property and send his sword and medals to England. This had little effect, since in October 1840 Mrs Dodgin wrote yet again asking after the general's effects and the money due to him from the Portuguese government.

and the six-year-old Infanta Maria Luisa. He was unimpressed by Isabella, a girl of about eight, with a peevish face, pug-nose and surly countenance, and a cross and unpleasant temper like her father's. The young infanta, by contrast, was charming, and Queen Cristina altogether looked like a queen.

He attended a bullfight, but was disgusted by the sight. His criticisms of cruelty evoked Spanish comparisons with English bare-knuckle bouts and cockfighting, and accusations of hypocrisy.

THE PEACE OF VERGARA

The war continued in a desultory, but gory fashion. After five or more years of indecisive fighting the last months of 1838 saw a virtual stalemate on most fronts, apart from the theatre of Aragon, where Cabrera was still invincible. Many of the participants on both sides, and the suffering mass of the civilian population, had become heartily tired of war and longed for peace. The queen-regent was anxious to choose a suitable husband for Isabella, although she was only eight years old. Her suggestion to Villiers that Isabella might marry an English prince or a prince of the house of Coburg (Queen Victoria's mother being a princess of Saxe-Coburg) was firmly rejected by him, if only on grounds of the difference of religion and the Protestant succession.

The Carlist commander-in-chief, Rafael Maroto, a veteran of the Peninsular War, wars of independence in Chile and Peru, and the Portuguese war of succession, was as ruthless as any of his brothers-in-arms, or his enemies. He had five rival senior officers shot on the grounds of forestalling a conspiracy. The extremists had harboured some doubts as to Maroto's determination to fight to the bitter end, and had pressed Don Carlos to remove him from his post. The purge confirmed Maroto in his position, and in his power over Carlos. Espartero had resumed command of the Cristino army in the north, and was ostensibly the target for Maroto's attack. Maroto, however, was aware that an armistice would be welcomed by most of the people in the Basque provinces, whose demands for 'peace and the fueros' were increasingly heard.

Maroto sent emissaries to Espartero's headquarters to discuss peace terms, but the latter proved a hard negotiator. When Lord John Hay, still commanding the British naval squadron in the north, approached Espartero offering English mediation for an armistice, his hopes of a diplomatic victory were dashed; similar terms, he was told (guarantee of the *fueros*, a marriage between Don Carlos' son and Isabella, the expulsion of both Carlos and Queen Cristino from Spain and a pledge that Carlist officers could retain their rank if they joined the queen's army) had been offered earlier by Maroto. Espartero insisted that Maroto should declare openly for the queen and the Constitution. Colonel Wylde, senior English commissioner, also became involved in the discussions, and his contribution may have proved very important. In Britain the duke of Wellington, asked if he would raise the question of ending the Carlist war in the House of Lords, called down a plague on both their houses, saying that he would not give a toss-up for the choice between Don Carlos and Maroto, or the queen and Espartero, suggesting that they should all be hanged on the same tree to avoid the injury which might be done to a second, and that the Spaniards should be left to settle their own affairs – the policy which he had consistently, but unsuccessfully, advocated.

After Maroto's army suffered a further defeat, this is what happened. Maroto and his fellow general, Simon de la Torre, in command of eight battalions, agreed to accept an armistice on Espartero's terms. A last attempt by Carlos to reassert his authority failed when he insisted on reviewing Maroto's army, which refused to support him. With one faithful general, he rode off into Navarre.

At a meeting on 26 August Maroto and Espartero discussed and agreed to terms. Maroto secured the agreement of all his officers to these, and three days later the armistice was signed at Vergara. The two armies were drawn up in squares. Espartero appealed to Maroto's men, asking them if they wished to live as Spaniards under the same flag. 'These are your brothers who are looking at you!' he said. 'Run to embrace them as I embrace your general.' Espartero took Maroto in his arms and kissed him warmly, after which the opposing armies greeted each other as brothers and fellow-countrymen. The convention of Vergara thus became generally known as the *Abrazo*, or Embrace, of Vergara.

Carlos was powerless and left Spain on 14 September (just evading capture by Espartero's troops), followed by two thousand of his most ardent supporters. In France he was arrested and interned in a chateau at Bourges.

Continuing his travels through Spain as a civilian with a companion, Alexander Ball was still unaware of the peace of Vergara, and when they met a body of Carlist troops near Burgos soon afterwards the two men feared for their lives. Their former enemies gave them the good news of the armistice, and they rejoiced together that peace had finally come.

Up to the last moment, and beyond, draconian 'justice' continued on both sides. Ball was much affected by the case of an 18-year-old Carlist, the third and last surviving son of his mother, who was shot by the Cristinos as a reprisal, just after the peace had been signed, but before the official order to cease all military executions had arrived. He noted how often, when about to die, men on both sides had called on their mothers. The young Carlist's cry, *'O Dios, mi pobre infelice madre'* (Oh God, my poor unhappy mother) echoed the words of Captain Mould of the 10th Regiment after receiving his mortal wound on 5 May 1836: 'Lord, bless my poor mother.'

CHAPTER NINETEEN

Women and children last

In an age of total war casualties among civilians have become commonplace, but in earlier times British soldiers on a foreign campaign seldom had major concerns for the safety of their families at home. If their wives and children accompanied them to war, however, they became hostages to fortune.

During the eighteenth and nineteenth centuries, the other ranks of a regiment were allowed to take a specified number of wives with them, and in return these women carried out certain domestic tasks such as cooking and laundering for their husbands, and their comrades. They were said to be 'on the strength' of the regiment and were entitled to receive half-rations and to accompany the regiment when it went overseas. This was the situation in the Irish Brigade in the eighteenth century, and in the British army. When the 3rd Regiment was stationed in Jamaica in 1796 it carried with it typhus, the scourge of earlier armies, to add to the endemic yellow fever, and in eight months lost forty per cent of its strength from disease. Life for the surviving unsupported widows was hard, and many remarried to other men in the regiment. One woman remarried twice after losing successive husbands to disease. It seems that there was a tradition of supporting the widows and orphans of soldiers, and that their officers felt some obligation towards the dependants.

In the Peninsular War it was common practice for four to six women per company to accompany an army, that is, about sixty women to every thousand men.

Information on the numbers of wives, or partners, and children of the Legion is scanty. Charles Shaw records forty-three women and children as accompanying the two Scottish regiments to Spain. The dependants of the Irish regiments seem to have been far more numerous. Somerville in his History condemns 'a most reprehensible laxity' in raising the Irish regiments by permitting vast numbers of women to follow their husbands. 'Indeed to get men to fill up the regiments, whole families were taken over to Spain.'

No details are found in the published accounts as to what arrangements, if any, were made for the reception, housing and feeding of the regiment of women and children. No marriage or children's allowances were made to the men, and no rations were officially issued for their dependants. The chaotic situation which greeted the Legion on arrival in Spain and continued thereafter makes it likely that any arrangements were made on an ad hoc basis by commissaries overwhelmed by the demands of the situation, and almost certain that their accommodation was no better than that of the soldiers, and probably worse. Neither Evans in his short 'Memoranda of the Contest' nor Dr Alcock in his detailed account of the medical problems of the campaign, makes any reference to the care, morbidity and mortality of the hapless dependants, while other writers such as Somerville, Wilkinson and Ball quote only the odd dramatic anecdotal case, as when Ball records his horror at seeing the corpses of seventeen men and one woman in the dead house at Vitoria. The women and children were exposed to the same risks of infection as the men, and the wives of the officers, among whom mortality from typhus was high, probably fared no better. The Inspector-General of Hospitals, Dr Callender, lost his wife to what was called 'Walcheren fever' and she lies buried on the castle hill at San Sebastian. Her loss must have affected Callender, and this may perhaps explain why his deputy, Dr Alcock, seems to have been more active in the provision of medical care for the Legion. Despite the high mortality from typhus among the medical officers, deaths of their wives are not mentioned, and it seems likely that the married doctors wisely left their wives at home.

The miserable experiences of the march from the coast to Vitoria and the months in that city of death have been movingly described by some who survived them, but few references are found to the dependants. Somerville, however, typically helps to flesh out the bare bones, relating how, when the great march over the trackless mountains took place, these women were ordered to stay behind. 'Some insisted on following the main body of the Legion, and did follow; but a number amounting altogether to between four and five hundred, with about two hundred and fifty children, of all regiments, nearly three hundred of them belonging to the Irish brigade, were sent by sea to Santander, to come up by the main road with the baggage to Vitoria.' It was only possible to separate these women from their husbands by means of a subterfuge; they were sent to Santander, not to rejoin the Legion, but to be sent home to Britain. Many were persuaded to board the ships to be taken to Santander and thence back to England, but some, desperate to join their men, jumped overboard and tried to swim ashore. Most were picked up and returned to shipboard, but a few brave spirits reached the shore and followed the column on the long march, on which stragglers risked being picked off by the Carlists.

The case of one valiant 17-year-old woman is described by Surgeon Wilkinson of the 6th, who accompanied her husband and his regiment on the march to Vitoria. Though Wilkinson knew she was pregnant, he had not anticipated that she would go into labour for some weeks. She had marched nearly thirty miles the previous day with cheerfulness and apparent ease. To the doctor's annoyance, as the regiment was forming up in the morning, he found that she was very quickly to become a mother. He ordered his colleague, Assistant-Surgeon Jenner, to stay with her, and Colonel Tupper, commanding the regiment, ordered a guard of thirty men to remain. She was delivered of a fine girl who was later baptised by a priest in the village of Pomar as Donna Isabella Modena del Pomar Berry – although Mrs Berry was a Presbyterian.

A less happy story is told by Somerville in his Narrative of the deaths of an Irishwoman and her young child who, he says, were denied help by the colonel and the medical officer at Santander in December 1836. Another tragic tale in the Narrative is that of the group of desperate women who had reached the end of the first day's march to Vitoria. The night was spent on the banks of a river and next morning, when the troops were ferried over, sentinels were placed to prevent all but a favoured few from boarding the barges. One poor Irishwoman with an infant was loud in her prayers to be taken across. She managed to get into the barge, and was forced out, but continued to keep hold of it with one hand while it was pushed off, dragging her into the water. She was taken out and left there, with nearly fifty others, to find their way back to Corban, or remain and die where she was. Against all odds she managed to to cross the river and walked all day and night, catching up on 7 December with the straggling sick and worn-out men who formed the rear of the detachment. She had a fever and would have died by the roadside with her dying infant, had not some of the muleteers disobeyed orders and put her on a wagon, on which she continued her journey in pouring rain. It was ten o'clock before the regiment reached quarters, a cowshed knee-deep in water. Here the woman was laid in a bullock's stall where her delirious cries made the night tempest peculiarly wild and awful. Somerville and his comrades tried to soothe the infant, but it died in the arms of one of them, and at six next morning the mother was found to be dead also. Mother and child were buried by the Scots before they resumed their march at eight o'clock. The woman's husband was one of the many who died later in Vitoria.

The faithful women faced similar problems throughout the campaign. In May 1836 the Legion had returned to Santander and in appalling weather were embarking for the 16- or 18-hour journey to San Sebastian, to go into battle on 5 May. *The Times'* correspondent described the groups of soldiers' wives who were prevented from accompanying the troops, bewailing the day they ever saw Spain. 'One of these bereaved mourners, forgetting, in the extremity of her disappointment at being ordered out of one of the boats in which she had smuggled herself, that the temperature was still very low, threw herself into the sea, from which she was, however, speedily picked out and deposited on the shore, dripping like another Niobe.' The unhappy woman, who had survived the grim winter in Vitoria and the dangerous march from the coast and back again, probably spent the coming months in the discomfort of the Corban convent under the rule of its unsympathetic commanding officer.

Women of the Legion taken by the Carlists were not immune to ill-treatment. A Legion officer writing on 29 January 1836 described how, when a convoy was captured, not only were eleven soldiers and the officer in command, Captain Street, killed, but five English women were mal-treated. One was butchered for resisting and the other four were ill-used and then stripped naked. The word 'rape' was not used, but the words strongly suggest that it occurred (*Limerick Chronicle*, 5 March 1836).

The chances of war threw up some strange situations for accompany-ing wives. Alexander Ball describes how his servant, Private Stark of the 10th Regiment, was pounced on by Carlist lancers while watering his master's horse and taken to their headquarters at Salvatierra. He managed to persuade his captors that he had been about to desert, and his life was spared. Escaping about a year later, he rejoined the Legion at San Sebastian where he found that his wife, assuming him dead, had remarried to a Sergeant Charles. The two men agreed to settle the problem by tossing for the lady, the first three out of five, and the sergeant won. Stark was not unduly upset since his child had died shortly before, and he was there-fore a free man. The infant must have been one of many who died from disease and malnutrition in the difficult conditions of the war.

Ball's Narrative gives a further insight into the welfare of the children of the Legion. When the war ended he revisited Vitoria, where he found that the citizens had a very low opinion of the Legion, believing that they *sold their children* and ate raw beef. He discussed the first accusation frankly. 'The truth is that there were many children who lost their fathers and mothers and fell into the hands of the comrades of their parents, and God knows but the *promise* of one shilling per day, which was the pay of the soldiers of the British Legion in Vitoria, was little enough to support a man's own children, without being burdened with another's; and as people are much wanted in Spain, particularly males, in a few instances some farmers did purchase children, and no doubt believed that they were buying them from their parents. I am confident that General Evans never was aware of such occurrences, or he would not have allowed them. Still the children were much better provided for than if they had returned to England. They will never know the want of food in Spain.' These pragmatic comments seem sensible; under the Poor Law Amendment Act of 1834 in Britain the able-bodied could only receive assistance in workhouses, where it was the duty, and pleasure, of Dickensian Mr Bumbles and their ilk to discourage applicants by ensuring that the arrangements were unattractive. The orphans, if repatriated, would not have enjoyed a happy childhood. Nevertheless it is as well that Evans' political enemies did not learn of the situation since they would have been driven to yet fiercer denunciations, possibly blighting his future political and military career.

Arrangements were made for most of the Legion's widows and orphans to be evacuated to England. The *Waterford Mail* on 22 June 1836 reported the arrival of the *Royal Tar* at Portsmouth from Santander with wounded men, invalids and widows and orphans of those who had fallen in recent fighting. The ship was due to take out a further 150 recruits as reinforcements. There must have been further batches of dependants repatriated as the Legion's casualties increased.

Somerville's strong social conscience and interest in the human condition gave him deeper insights into the tragicomedy of life as enacted in the Legion. He became involved in helping his fellow-soldiers to obtain their rightful pay and gratuities, sometimes at considerable cost to himself, as in the case of Robert Miller, a sergeant in the 6th Regiment, who had died of wounds on 5 May 1836. His credit at death stood at £17-odd and he was also owed six months' gratuity. Somerville had no doubt as to Miller's next-of-kin, having travelled out to Spain from Glasgow on the same ship as Miller and Nancy Miller, who claimed to be his widow. Visiting Glasgow in 1840, Nancy Miller, who was then in extreme poverty, gave a legal authority to obtain payment of her late husband's arrears and gratuity. The Spanish office would only admit that she was owed £7 and Somerville agreed to buy her entire claim and to run all risks, giving her £5 on account and arranging to pay her fifty per cent on the amount recovered above £7 as soon as the certificate was issued by the Spanish agents. Within three weeks of her being paid the £5, another Mrs Miller came to see Somerville, claiming to be the rightful wife of Robert Miller, and 'calling Nancy many bad names, for having run off to Spain with Robert'. When her marriage certificate had proved her correct, legal proceedings were taken to prevent Somerville from obtaining a certificate on behalf of Nancy Miller. The trusting Somerville lost £5 in the affair. He was active in trying to obtain arrears of pay for many other men of the Legion, and in helping financially many of those awaiting pensions for their wounds who must have starved but for his help.

CHAPTER TWENTY

The aftermath of the war

'War has victims beyond the bands bonded to slaughter. War moves with armoured wheels across the quivering flesh and patient limbs of all life's labile fronds.'

Herbert Read, *The End of a War*

THE IMPACT ON RELATIVES OF THE LEGION

War casts long shadows, and the anguish of the bereaved families and friends of those who fell in the service of Spain was increased by the lack of accurate information. Newspaper reports in the British press of casualties in battle carried details of the officers killed and wounded, but seldom of the other ranks, while the heavy mortality of the Legion from disease was accorded little space. Occasional individual reports appeared, particularly in the Irish newspapers, of officers dying in battle or of fever. In May 1836 the *Clonmel Advertiser* recorded the death in Vitoria, of 'malignant fever', of Gerald Fitzgerald, in his 24th year, chief surgeon of the 7th Regiment. He was the third son of the late Gerald Fitzgerald, formerly a captain in the 11th Regiment of Foot, and grandson of Thomas Fitzgerald, the Knight of Glin. The death of Surgeon Newall of the 9th Regiment was reported in February the same year by the *Cork Evening Herald*, and Somerville's army list records that he was one of the many who 'died by fever'.

In December 1836 the *Cork Daily Advertiser* reported the death of Langworthy Garland Wills of the hospital staff at San Telmo. The mortality from typhus among the medical staff was particularly high. Eleven of the forty-five officers who died at Vitoria were medical men. According to Dr Alcock this represented a mortality of one in five among the doctors compared with one in ten of other officers, a statistic, he wrote, proving the zeal of the medical officers. In his 'Commonplace Book' Patrick Hayden, merchant of Carrickbeg, Co. Waterford, wrote in March 1836, 'My poor friend Nicholas White Esq, who joined the British Legion, died at Santerre (*sic*) in Spain of fever.' Somerville also mentioned the death of White, a captain in the Rifles.

Cork newspapers in August 1836 carried news of the promotion of Ensign Edward B. O'Hea of the 10th Regiment to lieutenant in the 4th Regiment, and a few months later in November of the death of O'Hea, 'our gallant young townsman', buried with military honours in San Sebastian.

The plight of the Legion quickly became known in Britain. Foreign Office records from 1836 onwards contain appeals from parents and relatives for the release of their sons and brothers; few succeeded. Between April and July 1836, Mr J. Doherty of Dublin wrote six times unsuccessfully to obtain the discharge of his son from the Legion. He was told, correctly, that the British government had no power to procure the discharge of men in the service of the queen of Spain. In November the Reverend Mr Heath wrote to the Spanish minister in London on behalf of Margaret Woolley, widow of a Legionary soldier, asking that her son, also serving in the Legion, should be sent home to England; but no reply was recorded.

Anxiety among family and friends of the men increased as news reached Britain of the losses caused by disease and battle, and the fate of those captured by the Carlists remained uncertain.

One case which attracted public attention was that of Mrs Sarah Howson of Chelsea, who wrote in April 1836 to ascertain the fate of her husband and two sons. Francis Howson and his sons, all musicians in the Legion, had been captured by the Carlists. Howson was a music teacher in London. His daughter Emma, married to an Italian musician named Albertazzi, was a renowned contralto who had sung leading parts at La Scala, Milan, and was most effective, according to the *Dictionary of National Biography*, in the florid music of Rossini. Mrs Howson's enquiry brought the usual responses; Colonel Carbonell of the staff was instructed to give information, and to send to HQ. Madame Albertazzi's fame led to General Evans himself being involved, but no further entries occur, and it seems likely that all three men were executed by the Carlists, although some of the Legion's musicians when captured were spared to serve in the military bands of the Pretender, who valued their skills highly.

It would have been difficult for ill-educated or illiterate relatives of the missing to write to the authorities, but even with the help of influential supporters such as clergymen and officers their enquiries produced no satisfactory answers. The Reverend Mr Heath and Captain Sandiland both wrote in 1836 from Edinburgh to ask if William Robertson were still alive, only to be told that his name was not in the returns of those killed or wounded, and that enquiries should be addressed to the hapless Spanish

Minister in London, who was unable to give an answer, though he must have suspected that Robertson was 'missing, believed killed'. The relatives of most of these men would never learn their fate, and this added to their difficulties in applying for pensions from the Spanish government.

THE STRUGGLE FOR PENSIONS

Medical boards. The first hurdle for a member of the Legion in pursuit of a pension was to obtain an appointment for examination by a medical board. Often a surgeon's certificate was needed for this. Composed of British army surgeons, the boards were held in various cities in mainland Britain, including the military hospitals in Chelsea and Woolwich, and later also the naval hospitals at Chatham, Plymouth and Gravesend. Others were held in Liverpool, Manchester (Salford Barracks), Hull and Stoke Military Hospital, while several invalids attended the Army Medical Department in St James' Place, London. In Ireland most were held in Dublin, at Beggar's Bush Barracks, but a few in Limerick, Cahirciveen, Athlone and Castlebar, suggesting that some effort was made to spare disabled men long and arduous journeys. Invalids from the Scottish regiments were examined in Glasgow and Edinburgh Castle. The Admiralty arranged for the Marine Joseph Gallagher, a blacksmith from Mayo who had served on the *Reyna Gobernadora* and *Isabella II* and two English invalids from the *Isabella*, to be examined in London.

In 1842 the expenses of £5 8s. 0d. of a surgeon to travel from Chatham to Chelsea to examine Legion invalids were approved by the Treasury. He probably examined twenty or thirty invalids since large batches were often scheduled for boards. Thus in August 1838 Thomas Kennedy and forty-nine others (unnamed) were scheduled for a board in Dublin. In September and October the same year six individuals, four of them officers, were listed for boards on specific dates. The much-wounded Colonel Atkyns of Cork was granted a board in Dublin in December 1838, and seems to have obtained a pension by January 1839; the multiplicity of his injuries may have contributed to this unusually speedy outcome.

Not all who applied for a medical board cleared this first hurdle. One who failed was Private M. Quinlan, who was denied a board by the Spanish minister and made five unsuccessful attempts in as many months to achieve one. Reapplying in June 1842, he was told 'cannot interfere in his behalf'.

In July he petitioned Lord Aberdeen, Foreign Minister at the time, with the same response. Producing a medical certificate gave no better results, and the correspondence lapsed in October, when Quinlan seems to have accepted defeat.

Assessing the price of an arm or a leg. The pensions awarded to private soldiers and NCOs varied from sixpence per day to an exceptionally generous two shillings, totalling from £9 2s. 6d. to £36 10s. 0d. per annum in old money.

Through the kindness of Professor Richard Holmes, I have studied 145 pension certificates in a 'British Legion List of Pensioners of Her Catholic Majesty's Government'. Details are given of the age, regiment, previous occupation, height, place of birth and proposed residence of the pensioners, with their injuries, sums awarded and in some cases dates of injury. Though the sample is small in relation to the total of the Legion, the social information provided is valuable. All but one of the medical boards took place in the British Isles; one was held in Santander.

All nine infantry regiments are represented in varying numbers, as well as the artillery, lancers and the hospital corps, with one Royal Marine and two seamen from the *Isabella II*.

The three Irish regiments, 7th, 9th and 10th, contributed 58 pensioners with 4 from the Lancers. Another 21 Irishmen serving in other regiments brought the Irish total to 83, over half of the group of 145 men. From the dates recorded most of the casualties occurred on 5 May 1836 and in March 1837, the two most costly battles of the campaign, when wounded officers and men totalled 382 and 640 respectively. On 5 May the 7th Irish suffered the heaviest casualties among the Irish regiments with 25 pensioners, compared to 19 in the 9th and 14 in the 10th. Casualties among the 7th had been particularly heavy according to contemporary accounts.

Most of the injuries were gunshot wounds, mainly of the leg, with some of the arm or shoulder, and few wounds of the chest or abdomen, which were more likely to have proved fatal. An exception was Private Peter O'Brien of the 10th, a servant from Kanturk, Co. Cork, who suffered a penetrating gunshot wound of the chest in September 1836, for which he received a pension of one shilling per day. The same pension was awarded to Patrick Leeson from Co. Clare, a labourer, for a gunshot wound through the right side of the chest. These men were fortunate; it was unusual for those with chest wounds at this time to survive.

Two men were amputees: Peter Purcell of the 9th, a shoemaker, suffered a gunshot wound of the right thigh, followed by amputation, while Edmund Cooney of the 10th, a labourer from Kanturk, Co. Cork, had had both legs amputated below the knees for gangrene complicating typhus. Both men were among the almost fifty per cent of the Irish pensioners unable to sign their names, and their pensions of a shilling a day would not have funded a high standard of living for those whose prospects of employment were poor, nor cushioned them in the Famine years to follow – if indeed the payments continued. The Scot, David Livingston of the 6th Regiment, was another who suffered the complications of typhus, losing parts of both feet from gangrene and undergoing amputation. He also received a shilling a day.

A compound fracture of the frontal bone from a sabre wound on 5 May 1836 brought Patrick Brophy of the 7th, a whitesmith by trade, a shilling a day which he elected to receive in London, where trade may have been brisker. Luck was on his side, since the mortality from head injuries, immediate and delayed, in the Peninsular War had been high.

Bayonet wounds were rare among the injuries recorded, perhaps because these were more likely to have proved fatal, either immediately or within weeks. All the more remarkable is the case of John Cheshire of the 1st Regiment, a labourer from Surrey whose certificate records '35 bayonet wounds in various parts of the body'. He retired to his home town with a pension of a paltry sixpence a day. The Glaswegian shoemaker George Ferguson of the hospital corps did better with ninepence a day for a bayonet wound of the left middle finger and loss of part of three toes of the right foot. No date is given for his injuries, but it seems likely to have been during the chaotic conditions of the retreat in March 1837.

The Dubliner Patrick Finegan, who served in the Rifles, received a pension of ninepence a day (£13 13s. 9d.) for 'injury to the cervical vertebrae causing partial paralysis of the left arm from a fall from a scaling ladder' at the siege of Irun on 16 May 1837, together with a gunshot wound to the right thigh (fig. 10). For a labourer these injuries must have represented a severe disability. It was in the same siege that Private May of the Rifles, a labourer from Liverpool, suffered gunshot wounds to the left hand and wrist for which he was granted the same pension. Private John Galvin of the 10th Regiment was awarded a pension of a shilling a day for chest wounds sustained on 1 October 1836 (fig. 11).

The highest pension of 2s. a day was awarded to Bugler David McKay of the 8th, an engineer who suffered loss of sight of the right eye and injury of the left, with a compound fracture of the right leg, caused by the explosion of a shell in the action of March 1837. He returned to Glasgow with his pension of £36 10s. a year. The fact that he made his mark rather than signing his name must reflect the severity of his visual loss, and casts doubts on his ability to earn a living in his peacetime profession.

William Harris of the 3rd received only 1s. a day for loss of sight of the left eye and impaired vision of the right caused by a gunshot wound. Such injuries would today raise the possibility of additional effects of the trauma, perhaps in the intellectual field. 'The partial blindness of both eyes' of Rifleman James Cryne, a labourer from Sligo, was probably the result of ophthalmia, a form of purulent conjunctivitis and a common condition, in the absence of a history of injury.* Cryne's pension was ninepence a day. An Admiralty board awarded the same sum to John Kirwin of the steamer *Isabella II* for 'injured vision from lightning'; no further details are given of this intriguing case.

The 2nd Lancers, who had been raised in Ireland and served longer than the rest of the Legion, contributed only four pensioners to the sample of 145. One of these had served as a lancer from the start, while the others had served in the infantry and/or artillery, before becoming cavalry in the new Legion and its successor, the British Auxiliary Brigade, their total service averaging five-and-a-half years. Two men disabled by gunshot wounds of foot and thigh were awarded sixpence a day, while a compound fracture of the face sustained in March 1837 brought the 40-year-old William Stinson, a silk cotton weaver from Co. Cavan, 9d. a day. The virtually blind Kerryman, Richard Manley, a victim of ophthalmia, was given 1s. a day. He had already been examined in Santander and he moved to London, where he may have been able to follow his trade as a weaver.

I have not seen any pension certificates relating to officers. Somerville's *History*, however, lists the names of 37 officers transferred to Invalid Establishment in consequence of wounds etc. received in the service. Not all of these received pensions, and many do not seem to have applied for a pension, while many officers who did apply, whether successful or not in their quest, do not appear among the thirty-seven listed.

Those officers placed on the Invalid List had been examined by medical boards in Spain. The Order Book of the Legion for the period June

---

* During the Egyptian campaign in 1801 ophthalmia caused partial or total blindness in thousands of British and French troops.

1836–January 1837 contains only one list of boards on officers. On 14 January 1837 fourteen officers were examined. They were drawn from all the infantry regiments and the Rifles. Only two cases involved wounds received in action, both sustained in the battle of the previous May. One lieutenant of the 10th Regiment was invalided for the effects of a severe wound not received in action (for which a duel seems the likely explanation), together with an attack of asthma. In ten other cases medical illnesses were diagnosed, with several cases of fever or ague, one of the chronic effects of the fever in Vitoria (presumed typhus), one of rheumatic arthritis and another of chronic liver disease. Two lieutenants suffered from venereal disease, one having been 'labouring under a severe attack of syphilis for the last six weeks and not likely to be fit for active duty for some time', a prognosis only too likely to have proved correct.

Venereal disease has for centuries been a major medical scourge of armies. It is inconceivable that these two young officers were the only men in the Legion's ten thousand to receive the 'wages of sin', especially since, as has recently been pointed out, officers were less vulnerable than other ranks as their wives could often accompany their regiments abroad without being subjected to a quota system. Large garrisons inevitably attracted prostitutes, leading often to a heavy drain on manpower, with up to a quarter of the British army's strength being infected in a given year. Syphilis and gonorrhoea affected 27 per cent of the soldiers of the 63rd Foot in 1844. Attempts were made in the British army to curb this running sore on the military body, with the establishment in the eighteenth century of 'hospitals for the reception of diseased women', or 'lock hospitals', where prostitutes were confined, but it is unlikely that any such control existed in the chaotic conditions surrounding the Legion, and the hard-pressed medical officers would have had little time to lecture men – or officers – on the perils of promiscuity. Dr Alcock's monograph is silent on the subject of VD, probably because he saw the problem as less important than other health hazards rather than from any sense of delicacy. Many men are likely to have fallen victim to these diseases but, like those injured in duelling, would not have been considered worthy of a pension for their pains, which would often have included the side-effects of treatment for syphilis, 'a night with Venus' leading to 'a lifetime with Mercury'.

Among the injured officers one of the most poignant cases is that of the unfortunate Irishman, Lieutenant P.A. Stack, a second lieutenant in the 3rd Regiment who was promoted to lieutenant in the 9th. Wounded in the battle of 5 May 1836, which produced a rich harvest of death and injury, he was invalided home. The sorry story starts in December 1837 when he wrote regarding his claim on the Spanish government for a pension. On 16 December he sought an interview, applying again three days later. In early January 1838 he was allotted a board at Chelsea Hospital on 12 January. He was now destitute. The board met but Stack was told on 30 January that he would receive his claim when the amount of pension awarded to other invalids was settled. He was eventually granted a pension, but in August 1840 he filed a complaint against the British Legion Commissioner for stopping it. His case dragged on, with a report on his claim in 1841, and his request from Letterkenny in 1842 for a re-examination or a pension. Three years later Stack wrote from Drogheda to request the return of papers relating to his claims, and was told 'cannot interfere further in his claim for services'. Three years of silence followed until 1848, when in July and August there were six more entries on his claim, with the same formulaic negative response. Stack again renewed his claim unsuccessfully in July and August 1850. More than fourteen years had passed since he had been wounded, and his dogged persistence had achieved almost nothing.

Another Irishman, Lieutenant F. Byrne, a relative of Colonel Charles Fitzgerald, had originally joined the Legion as a volunteer. He was dangerously wounded on 5 May 1836, and in May 1838 was examined by a medical board. A pension was awarded, but in 1840 this was in arrears and his mother wrote from Dublin asking that some money should be advanced to her son. In November 1842 Byrne applied to Lord Aberdeen for assistance.

It seems that pensions were often stopped, with no reason being given. Colonel John W. Wyatt of the 8th Regiment, described by Somerville as 'an officer much esteemed, but who had the misfortune to lose parts of both his feet by frost in Vitoria', wrote in 1845 to complain of delay in paying money awarded him by the medical board and also in payment of his pension for service in the Legion, but met a negative response. The next year his pension of £200 a year was stopped by the Spanish commissioner, who was then asked to restore it. An enquiry was instituted into the reasons for stopping the pension, and ruled that it would not have been stopped if he had served in the British army. Twenty-four entries appear between 1846 and 1848, the British authorities repeatedly urging settlement. The final entry, in October 1848, instructed the Spanish minister to continue payment of Wyatt's pension.

Bureaucratic delay often affected application for pensions. Colonel W.F. Campbell, initially a major in the 7th Regiment and promoted lieutenant colonel in the 4th, had been wounded in the Legion's two major battles, severely so in March 1837. In April 1838 arrangements were made for his examination by a medical board, but he was told that he must comply with the forms before he could assert his claim to a pension. Next he was told to produce documents to prove that he had received his wounds while serving in the Legion. In June a report of the medical board was produced; one hopes that it was favourable to him.

The widow of Captain Dalrymple of the 8th Regiment, one of those killed in the massacre at Andoain in September 1837, was told when she applied for a pension in July 1844, 'cannot interfere without she can shew that children of other deceased officers of the British Legion are in receipt of pensions'. Clearly a precedent was to be avoided at all costs.

Heroic conduct of a dead officer seems to have counted for nothing when his widow appealed for a pension. Captain J. Coyle of the 8th Regiment had died on 16 March 1837 before Hernani, leading his men against the Carlists, who greatly outnumbered them. In November 1838 Mrs Martha Coyle's claim for a pension drew the terse response, 'Sorry cannot afford her pecuniary aid'. She then appealed that part of her claim on Spain, as widow of an officer of the British Legion, should be advanced by the British government. Although the reply is not recorded it seems unlikely that her plea was granted.

In 1840 the widow of Major Robert Dundas, 7th Regiment, applied for a pension. Her claim was referred to General Alava, now Spanish minister in London. In ten days she had her reply, that it did not appear that Dundas had any credit or claim against the Spanish government, and also that he did not die in the service of Spain. He is known to have died of fever in Vitoria on 24 December 1835. Such specious reasoning from one of the major architects of the Legion's involvement in the queen's cause seems atypical of this honourable soldier.

Another bone of contention was the fact that the medical boards were composed of British army doctors who had no experience of the conditions in Spain, and were less likely to be sympathetic than surgeons who had served with the Legion. This explains the request in 1841 by Mr J. Cotter of Dublin that a 'Legionite' surgeon should attend at a medical board. His suggestion was referred to the Horse Guards, but it was decided that no addition could be made to the medical board at Dublin.

Officers were sometimes awarded a year or more's pay rather than a pension. There were advantages to the Spanish Treasury in paying a single lump sum rather than a continuing pension for an unpredictable period. Major Fitzgerald (one of six officers of that name in the Legion, and probably P. Fitzgerald of the 3rd Regiment, rather than one of General Charles Fitzgerald's two sons) had been wounded at Arlaban in January 1836. After a medical board at Chelsea in November 1840 he was awarded a year's pay in compensation. The same sum was awarded to Major Townley, severely wounded in May 1836. Captain R. de Burgh of the Rifles, dangerously wounded at Irun, was awarded eighteen months' pay of the rank he held when wounded. Cornet M. D'Aubley or D'Amblée, of the 2nd Lancers, who lost an arm in battle, put forward his claims in April 1838, but was told that the respondent had advanced him £6 from his own pocket, and that he had no right to complain. In 1840 Lieutenant Woods of the 9th was awarded eighteen months' pay in consideration of his wounds.

Medical boards were occasionally held outside Britain, when officers had moved to other parts of the Empire. In 1842 Major Beckham of the 7th Regiment, whose use of cylinder shot on the Carlists had been so effective, was in New South Wales, where orders were given for a medical board to be assembled on him relating to his injuries on 5 May 1836.

For private soldiers of the Legion the pursuit of a pension was more difficult than for their officers. Many may have lacked the will or the knowledge to apply. Press reports of ex-Legionaries charged with begging in the streets abounded, often couched in terms very critical of General Evans. The *Clonmel Herald* of 26 August 1837 carried a report headed 'The Reward of British Valour,' of a Private Hamilton of Durham, formerly of the 3rd Westminster Grenadiers, who was crippled in one arm and one leg and was charged with begging in the streets. He had been awarded, but never received, a medal for meritorious conduct and gallantry in two battles, and produced the citation signed by Evans and Considine, his military secretary. The kindly magistrate advised him to return to Durham and said he would defray his expenses and give him a trifle in addition.

Similar problems faced the widows and families of legionaries as early as January 1836, when Villiers was instructed to prevent the discontinuance of the pension of the widow Evans. In August 1837 Thomas Carthy of Cove wrote to ask about arrears of pay due to his son, who was killed in the queen's service; he was told to present an affidavit. Another case concerned Private Patrick Murphy of the 7th Regiment, whose father Thomas wrote from Dublin in 1840 with a claim for arrears of pay for his son, who died of wounds in 'St Elin's' Hospital, San Sebastian. He was told that his son's name did not appear in the list of debts and credits of deceased men of the 7th Regiment, or in the list of those whose heirs had a claim to gratuity. Thomas Murphy produced an affidavit that his son was wounded and died at San Sebastian, but the outcome is unknown.

Repeated requests for arrears of pay due to other ranks of the Legion were made from 1836 onwards. Men wrote, sometimes repeatedly, to request an interview with the Spanish minister in London. None seem to have been granted. Often a sergeant would write on his own behalf and that of his fellow-Legionaries; they were almost always told to apply to the Spanish minister in London. Many of these letters came from Portsmouth, Portsea, Gosport or Plymouth, where groups of men were held awaiting pay and disposal. The invalids housed on the *Swiftsure* hulk at Portsmouth were destitute. Lieutenant-Colonel Wetherall, attached to the department of the Spanish Colonel Carbonell, was now a 'Commissioner for the settlement of claims'. In July 1837 he delayed the departure of the steamer *Messenger*, about to convey five hundred invalids to Cork, so that he could pay them their gratuities. Ten days later he was 'in difficulties in settling their affairs' and threatened to resign his invidious situation. The men at Portsmouth refused to go to Ireland until they were clothed. At the same time Sergeant-Major Hughes wrote from Portsmouth directly to General Evans on the claims of the NCOs and men of the Legion. Evans received many similar pleas, but could not respond positively to them. Requests from Portsmouth continued for the next few months. In October a visit by a Spanish agent to discuss the disposal of the men there was promised as soon as the Spanish minister had funds. In November Colonel Jacks of the lancers proposed that the sanction of the British Parliament should be obtained to guarantee a loan to Spain for liquidating the Legion's claims. In December applicants were being told that these claims should be forwarded through General Evans.

The chaotic situation was still unresolved by the next year. By April 1838 many Irishmen of the Legion had been repatriated and were housed in barracks on Spike Island in Cork harbour, but arguments raged as to whether they should still be fed from government stores or be discharged, and how many had received their pay and marching money so that they could be sent home.

For many officers, safely repatriated, the situation was little better, even though they were more likely to have friends in high places. A committee of officers was appointed under Colonel Claudius Shaw, late of the artillery, to effect a settlement of their claims. Its proceedings were noted in Foreign Office records and in correspondence in *The Times* from 1837 onwards. Shaw had written earlier to Palmerston, who had agreed to write to Villiers in Madrid to make representations to the Spanish government. In January 1838 no satisfactory answer had been obtained, although Villiers was still pressing the Spanish ministry.

In May 1838 a meeting of officers was held in the Imperial Clarence Hotel, Cork, to read and consider replies to various letters and to petition Parliament for help over the Legion's unsettled claims.

Charles Gallwey, formerly major in the 10th Regiment, who had been severely wounded on 16 March 1837, took the chair. The secretary, Mr C.J. Keays, read out the reply of General Evans to his earlier appeal for help. Evans pointed out that he himself was owed more arrears than any other man of the Legion (£5,000) and that he had done his best to achieve settlement of their claims, though as yet without effect. He would continue his efforts in what seemed to him the most appropriate way. The extreme deficiency of money and embarrassment of the Spanish government was the main cause of failure. He believed the best hope of success depended on the exertion of the influence of the British ministry on their behalf. He warned against relying on the pretended sympathy or advocacy of their political opponents, or making accusations against British ministers to whose assistance he looked for redress. Evans was again sitting as MP for Westminster, and his necessarily diplomatic reply clearly disappointed the meeting.

The secretary also read out letters he had written to Lords Melbourne and Palmerston and the Spanish ambassador, receiving an acknowledgment only from Melbourne. A petition to the House of Commons from the officers, NCOs, privates and others of the Legion was drawn up and signed by the officers present, and by the chairman and secretary on behalf of over seven hundred NCOs and privates in the city and county of Cork. Three cheers were given for the chairman and three cheers for the press, since twenty-three Irish and seventeen English provincial papers had noticed their previous meeting, and were zealously co-operating with them. There was much sympathy for the plight of the many Irish members of the Legion, whose circumstances were probably worse than those of their comrades in Britain, and were to become unimaginably more grievous a few years later with the onset of the Great Famine in 1845.

Intermittent correspondence on the problem appeared in the columns of *The Times* over the next few years, in which their political affiliations often coloured the writers' opinions. In April 1840 the Association of Officers of the British Legion met at the Sun Tavern, where a letter from Lord Londonderry was read out expressing his appreciation for a vote of thanks for his efforts on their behalf. While equally critical of the Spanish and British governments, and feeling deeply the hard case of the officers, he believed that the position of the men under their wounds and sufferings was equally deplorable. He could not believe that the queen-regent could not scrape together £300,000.

Letters to *The Times* continued. A correspondent in November 1841, who had served in the Legion, argued like Londonderry; a sum of money had reached Paris to be used for paying the claims of the French Legion, so that the unfairness of the Spanish government towards the British Legion had become more obvious. 'The fate of those whose bones lie bleaching on the Spanish soil,' he wrote, 'seems preferable to that of others who returned to England maimed in health and limb, physically disabled from acquiring a livelihood by their honest exertions, and neglected by those who should watch over their welfare.'

In October 1844 Miguel Castaneda, agent for the payment of the late British Legion, felt impelled to write to the Editor about a recent report in its columns of two Legionaries who claimed not to have been paid. Wellington himself had been involved in correspondence about one of these men. Castaneda insisted that both men had been fully paid. Frequent press reports appeared of ex-Legionaries begging in the streets, claiming not to have been paid, and the truth of their complaints was impossible for the public to gauge.

Castaneda's unenviable task made him the target of much abuse from men who had been denied their just pay and gratuities. On 3 March 1845 *The Times* published its last word on the subject, a lengthy advertisement from Castaneda, stating that

> the compensation promised by the Spanish government in the arrangement made in 1840 for carrying the payment of the British Legion Certificates into effect having been settled by the British and Spanish governments at five per cent on the total amount of

these certificates, the same will be PAID on the 3rd March next, and on every succeeding Monday, Tuesday and Thursday, from 10 to 3 o'clock, to those persons only who served in or were connected with the above corps, and who did not transfer their certificates.

How many of the men owed money would have had access to copies of *The Times* is an interesting speculation.

The year 1845 saw many references in official records to claims by former members of the Legion for arrears of pay, gratuities and pensions. These concerned 43 individuals, 37 NCOs and privates and six officers from all parts of the United Kingdom except Wales. Many were writing for the first time, asking where to apply, while others had campaigned fruitlessly for several years. Some had lost their certificates. Some widows or relatives of the dead complained about their discontinued pensions. Many were promptly told that they had no claim, and that a previous decision could not be changed. One Irish soldier had some initial support from one of his officers, Lieutenant Colonel Wright, who wrote from Bengal but later decided not to interfere on behalf of Private E. Moriarty. Captain Cannan, who had been seriously wounded on 5 May 1836, wrote to ask if he should go to Madrid to urge his claim; directions were later issued that the British minister should assist him in prosecuting his claims, and it does not seem that he went to Madrid. Cannan, who had served in the 6th Regiment and was promoted colonel in the 10th, was described by Somerville as a skilful and clever officer, but capricious in temper. After leaving the Legion he had served in India, and in 1838 had written from Hurryhur, Madras, to request the honour of knighthood for his services in Spain, a request that was not granted. Another dissatisfied officer was Colonel Wetherall, who had been involved in the difficult arrangements for the lodging and feeding of men of the Legion and their transport to Ireland. He was now in Canada, engaged in the war against the 'habitants', the French-Canadians who were in revolt against British rule, a campaign in which many ex-Legionaries were involved. He wrote in February asking the British government to urge his own claim on Spain. This claim was partially met; he wrote later that he had received his arrears of pay for his service in Spain, but not for the time spent as Commissioner for the liquidation of Spanish claims.

The duke of Sotomayor replaced Castaneda as Spanish minister in London in 1846, a year with only a slight reduction in the Legion's claims to twenty-nine (including one officer), with the familiar problems of lost certificates, pensions denied or discontinued and negative responses. Sotomayor proved no more generous than his predecessor. If a certificate were presented late no leeway was allowed, and he was deaf to a personal appeal from General Evans on behalf of one man's claim.

An entry in the 'Domestic Various' records dated 19 May from Buckingham Palace, the Queen's Warrant to the Treasury for the grant of a pension of £700 per annum to Sir Arthur Aston, late minister in Madrid, stands out in contrast to its neighbour, a repeat request for an answer to the application of Mr T. McDonald regarding the stopping of his pension.

Eighteen forty-seven saw only three items related to the Legion's claims, all from officers. The fourteen claims in 1848 included four from officers. The claims of seven men and two officers were discussed in 1849. Colonel Wetherall was told that the government could not urge his further claim until diplomatic relations with Spain, which had recently been broken off, were renewed. Mr Castaneda, again in post, wished to know how a British pensioner would be dealt with if guilty of theft. The case was that of J. Costello, whose pension he perhaps hoped might be forfeited. He was told that a pensioner of the British government would be deprived of his pension during imprisonment for a misdemeanour and, if convicted of felony, would lose it altogether. Castaneda was also exercised by the case of an officer who had been convicted of uttering false coin, and had since died. He wanted to know if the widow of a British officer in a similar situation would continue to receive her pension. He was told that there was no precedent of a British officer being convicted of felony, so it seems likely that the widow retained her pension. At this late date, fourteen years after the disbanding of the Legion, an enquiry came from a man about his brother, who had been in the Legion; the predictable reply was that he must obtain information on his brother's fate from Mr Castaneda.

CHAPTER TWENTY-ONE

Spain's later history

'History books begin and end, but the events they describe do not.'
R.G. Collingwood, *Portraits in Miniature*, 1931

After the signing of the peace treaty, Cristina tried to persuade Espartero to form a new ministry and to support a municipal reform bill, which would have deprived the municipalities of most of their independence, centralising political and administrative power in Madrid. This move was intensely unpopular with the progressives, who regarded the bill as unconstitutional, yet against Espartero's advice Cristina signed the controversial law. Remaining firmly opposed to it, Espartero offered his resignation as commander-in-chief, which she refused to accept. There followed uprisings in Madrid and the provinces against the bill, and in 1840 Cristina, unable to gain the support of Espartero or another minister to form a stable government, decided to abdicate as regent and sailed to Marseilles, leaving her two daughters under the guardianship of Espartero, who became regent in her place. She was accompanied into exile by several Spanish officers and politicians, including Leopoldo O'Donnell, who had survived the defeat and massacre at Andoain in 1837, and reached the rank of captain-general in 1839, not yet aged thirty. Cristina lived comfortably in France, with a town house in Paris, and also owning Malmaison, the Empress Josephine's old home.

Espartero's regency lasted three years, and it was in this period that Isabella's marriage became the topic of anxious European discussion. In fact, Isabella's heart was already being treated as a pawn in the great game of statecraft when she was a child of six. The project of her marriage to her cousin, Don Carlos' eldest son, the Infante Carlos Luis, was now reconsidered. Other candidates were Francisco, duke of Cadiz, son of Don Carlos' younger brother and Carlota; the duke of Aumale, son of Louis-Philippe of France; and Prince Leopold of Saxe-Coburg, cousin to both Queen Victoria and Prince Albert, and future king of the Belgians. Espartero fell from power in 1843 as a result of a military revolt, and was received as a welcome guest in England. His successor, General Narvaez, formed a coalition government. It was decided to declare Isabella queen a year before the official age of fourteen in order to avoid a struggle for the regency.

The thirteen-year-old queen was not blessed with beauty; both Alexander Ball shortly before, and Washington Irving, the American minister to Spain, who watched the ceremony when she swore to observe the constitution, contrasted her very unfavourably with her younger sister in looks and carriage. To add to her problems Isabella suffered from the disfiguring skin disease, ichthyosis, with a dry, scaly, flaking, fish-like skin, which thermal and seabaths had alleviated only temporarily. In character, Isabella was described as precocious, irresponsible and ignorant. Though advanced in some ways, she was immature in others, both in her behaviour and physically, with delayed onset of puberty and an eating disorder, leading her to eat and drink to excess and to become increasingly obese, a problem which would follow her into adult life. Cristina's return to Spain in 1844 to a rapturous welcome, while not resulting in a reform of her daughter's uncontrolled behaviour, allowed her own marriage to her lover, Muñoz, to be at last openly acknowledged with his ennoblement as duke of Rianzares. She could now become more involved in the matter of her daughter's marriage. She did not favour Carlos Luis, nor did Isabella herself who, on seeing his portrait, declared that she would not marry a man with a squint. In 1845 Don Carlos abdicated his claim to the throne in favour of Carlos Luis. The new pretender took the title of Count of Montemolin and was proclaimed by the Carlists of the Basque provinces and Navarre as Carlos VI.

Eventually Francisco of Assisi, duke of Cadiz and son of Carlota, was selected as husband for Isabella despite rumours that he was impotent, while the duke of Montpensier, fourth son of King Louis-Philippe, was espoused to the Infanta Luisa. Isabella was now aged sixteen. The marriages took place simultaneously.*

Fears that Isabella might be childless, so that Luisa would remain next in line of succession, and the possibility of a link between the royal families of Spain and France, were allayed when Isabella bore a son, the

---

* Since the French government under Louis-Philippe had promised the British that the queen's sister should not marry a French prince until Isabella was married and had children, Palmerston was very angry at the duplicity of the double marriage, and the Entente Cordiale was ruined.

future Alfonso XII, and Louis-Philippe lost his throne. The child's paternity was suspect; only six months after their marriage Isabella and Francisco had separated. Years later she noted, 'What shall I say of a man who on his wedding night wore more lace than I did?' Indeed 'Paquita', as Francisco was known, put it about that the boy was not his own, and accused the queen of infidelity. Nonetheless the child's birth was the occasion of great rejoicing.

Carlist operations resumed in 1846 in Catalonia, first with guerrilla campaigns and later, when Cabrera returned from exile, on a larger scale, but the young pretender Montemolin failed to enter Spain, and with Cabrera's departure in 1849 the war ended. Cabrera returned to England to marry a young Englishwoman and settle down on her Surrey estate near Virginia Water as a country gentleman, never to fight again.

Juan, the second son of Don Carlos, had married the sister of the duke of Modena, who in 1848 gave birth to a son, Carlos, and later to a second son, Alfonso, who was to maintain the claims of Don Carlos' line until the next century.

Isabella's reign could scarcely have been more different from that of her young contemporary, Victoria, the dutiful queen of England. Nature and nurture were equally deficient. Gribble [1913] wrote that Isabella's tragedy could be stated in a sentence: 'She danced away her throne. Not only was her love of dancing excessive, but her choice of partners was unfortunate.' Two previous generations gave her examples of queens of Spain taking commoner lovers. Her education was so bad that it could hardly have been worse. Initially very popular with the people and generous to a fault in matters of charity, she was under the influence of her confessor and the supposedly stigmatic 'Bleeding Nun,' Sor Patrocinio.

Despite the birth of an heir to Isabella, the Carlists refused to accept defeat. Don Carlos having died in Trieste in 1855, his son Montemolin issued a call to arms to the Carlists in Spain the following year. This came to nothing. In 1860 a more ambitious, but ill-planned and bungled attempt was made, ending in fiasco. Reprisals were few: Isabella and her ministers were lenient, a general amnesty was announced, and Montemolin was pardoned and freed to leave Spain after renouncing his claim to the throne. The Infante Juan, however, now claimed that in view of his brother's 'abdication' the right to the throne had passed to him and his family. When Montemolin repudiated his renunciation, claiming that it had been obtained under duress, there were now two Carlist pretenders contending in a hopeless cause until in 1861 cholera killed Montemolin, his wife and his brother Fernando, leaving Juan as the sole pretender.

Isabella's reign was drawing to a close, less as a result of any efforts of her rivals for the throne, than the chaotic state of the realm. To its Portuguese neighbours Isabella's Spain was known as 'the madhouse over the border'. Age had not brought maturity and she persisted in middle age in follies that might have been excusable in her youth. Her undiminished sexual ardour produced a steady series of scandals, and the public's tolerance of her private life was becoming exhausted. Her latest lover, the son of an Italian cook, was one of the last straws to break the loyalty of the army. Leopoldo O'Donnell, faithful to Isabella since the war, found he could not rely on her word. She was viewed generally by Spaniards as unbearable: *'esa señora es insoportable'*.

Don Carlos, elder son of Juan and grandson of the pretender Carlos V, now became the choice and the hope of the Carlists. In 1868 a coup d'état took place. In September, while Isabella was on holiday in San Sebastian, General Juan Prim arrived at Cadiz helping to organise a revolt among the Spanish fleet, landing and establishing a revolutionary junta and being joined by conspirators from the Canary Islands. The fleet sailed along the coast to Barcelona, proclaiming the revolution. Battle was joined in late September between the revolutionary army and loyal government troops, who were decisively beaten. The victors marched on Madrid. Isabella left San Sebastian on 30 September for voluntary exile in France after thirty-five years on the throne.

The 20-year-old Carlos could now press his claim, but would meet many obstacles. The results of elections in the Cortes gave hope to the Carlist cause but at the same time an organised republican party was presented as an electoral option and won many seats while the progressives formed a majority. Isabella, who did not formally abdicate until 1870, named her son Alfonso as her successor despite a decree of the Cortes excluding all Bourbons from the throne. A new monarchist party hailed the 12-year-old prince as King Alfonso XII.

General Prim, faced with the need to find a democratic king in Europe, excluding the Bourbons, reviewed the possible candidates, who included General Espartero, the king of Portugal, a Coburg and a Hohenzollern prince favoured by Bismarck, and Montpensier, Isabella's brother-in-law. Eventually Amadeo, duke of Aosta, second son of King Victor Emmanuel of Italy, was chosen, and agreed to let his name go forward for election by the Cortes. An elected monarchy has its problems: though Amadeo topped the poll, the republicans performed well, and the assassination of Prim shortly before Amadeo's arrival in Madrid in January 1871, and the protests of both Isabella and Carlos, made for uneasy prospects for a peaceful reign for the man whom the people nicknamed 'King Macaroni'. He held the throne, striving to rule as a constitutional monarch, only until 1873.

The second Carlist war had started in May 1872 with the heavy defeat of the Carlist army at Oroquieta, and the narrow escape of Don Carlos himself from capture. When Amadeo abdicated in February 1873 the republican party acted quickly; the Cortes voted overwhelmingly for a republic, and a general election gave the republicans a mandate to establish a federal democratic republic of Spain. This in turn acted as a spur to the Carlists fighting for the monarchy and for their prince-in-waiting. Volunteers flocked to his standard, arms were smuggled in, and in May 1873 the Carlists heavily defeated the republican forces. Carlos himself returned to Spain in July to a popular welcome.

As before, the Carlists were predominant in the Basque provinces in the countryside while the republicans, like the Cristinos before them, kept control of San Sebastian and Bilbao. Yet again Bilbao was besieged by the Carlists but was eventually relieved by government forces. Losses were heavy on both sides, with Carlist victories often suggesting their cause would ultimately triumph.

An indirect English involvement in the conflict began when Isabella's son Alfonso, who had been educated in Paris and Vienna, enrolled in 1874 at the age of sixteen as a cadet at the Royal Military College, Sandhurst. Isabella had renounced her right to the throne in his favour in 1870, and the Alfonsist party had gained much support. The minister Cánovas del Castillo was in close touch with Alfonso and his mother, and in 1874 drafted a manifesto, which the prince signed at Sandhurst. The Sandhurst manifesto was widely published in Spain and Europe. In it Alfonso thanked his supporters for their loyalty and assured Spain that he would establish a constitutional and hereditary monarchy and would be a good Catholic and truly liberal. He was proclaimed king of Spain amid great enthusiasm, and arrived in Madrid in January 1875, when Spain once more became a monarchy.

Carlos would not accept defeat; the war continued and his army defeated the government forces at Lacar, where Alfonso narrowly escaped capture. The defection of Ramon Cabrera, the former Carlist general in exile in England, and of other allies in Spain, reduced the pretender's chances of success. Though savage fighting continued until early in 1876, Carlos' cause was now lost and the territory he controlled was dwindling. On the last day of February 1876 Carlos crossed into exile in France with a small body of loyal troops and senior officers. He never entered Spain again, and died in 1909, his only son Jaime succeeding him as pretender.

Alfonso XII died of tuberculosis in 1885 and was succeeded by his posthumously born son, Alfonso XIII. Spain was tranquil for a time, but the collapse of General Primo de Rivera's military dictatorship, which had replaced parliamentary democracy between 1923 and 1930, strengthened the renewed and growing demand for a republic. Republican gains in the municipal elections of 1931 impelled Alfonso to hand over his royal prerogatives and to leave Spain, since it seemed that civil war was otherwise inevitable. His departure ushered in the Second Republic. This had enemies both on the right among Catholics and monarchists, whether Carlist or Alfonsist, and on the left in the powerful and militant trade union movement with its anarchist leaders and anticlerical attitudes. Churches and convents were burned and looted. A republican constitution drawn up by the Cortes, dividing church and state and declaring that Spain had no religion, united Catholics and monarchists to oppose the march of secularism. On the death of his 80-year-old uncle, Jaime, the Infante Alfonso succeeded as the Carlist pretender under the name of Alfonso Carlos. The Carlists became known as the Traditionalists, and were conspiring to overthrow the republic by force.

The Spanish Civil War of 1936–9 was waged on both sides with no less ferocity than earlier civil wars involving what Richard Ford in his *Gatherings from Spain* described as 'this volcanic people'. Its complex story has been recounted by many writers, including Gerald Brenan and Anthony Beevor, and will not be detailed here. General Francisco Franco, with Spanish troops and help from Nazi Germany and Fascist Italy, eventually overthrew the Socialist government and established himself as *caudillo* (head) of an authoritarian régime, afterwards skilfully maintaining Spanish neutrality during the Second World War. His centralising policies were deeply unpopular with the Basque people, whose hopes of their *fueros* and autonomy were suppressed. He expressed his intention that the monarchy would be restored after his death as early as 1947, and in 1954 he and the pretender Don Juan de Borbon agreed that Juan Carlos, son of Don Juan and grandson of Alfonso XIII, should take precedence as Pretender to the throne. Formally named by Franco as the future king in 1969, Juan Carlos ascended the throne in 1975 on the death of the *caudillo*. Less *'Franquista'* and more liberal in his attitudes than the dictator had anticipated, he determined to disprove the prediction that he would only be remembered as 'Juan the Brief', and has presided over a gradual return to democracy in Spain despite internal political difficulties and two attempted coups.

What of Carlism and Basque separatism in the twenty-first century? Conditions for most Spaniards today are far better than in the past, and a third Carlist war seems as unlikely as a campaign for the restoration of the Stuart line of the monarchy in Britain, yet, as with many other movements for the independence of smaller regions, such as Catalonia, from their big brothers and historic masters, the desire of many of the Basque people of Spain for self-government has not diminished. ETA (*Euzkadi Ta Askatasuna*: Basque Homeland and Liberty), the military wing of Basque separatism, is active and claims lives in acts of terrorism in cities such as San Sebastian and Madrid and holiday resorts in southern Spain. Despite some concessions by the government, including the institution of a Basque Parliament in Vitoria, the demands for greater independence continue. Peaceful demonstrations occur regularly as well as episodes of violence. Visitors to San Sebastian are greeted by posters in English reading 'Tourists, you are welcome. But please remember, you are not in Spain, you are in the Basque region' – a milder message than that with which the Basque people would have greeted the bemused men of the British Legion in 1835, but one in which the same principle is explicit.

On the steep and rocky hillside of Mount Orgull, below the restored castle of San Sebastian, scene of savage fighting in many wars, the tourist of today can visit the 'cemetery of the English' (pl. 13; figs. 13, 15). The tombstones are in a far worse condition today than they were as depicted 165 years ago. A large and once impressive monument to the men of Wellington's army who fought to free the peoples of Spain from the yoke of Napoleon has suffered severe damage by vandals over the years, while in very recent times the massive monument on the sheer rock-face has been defaced. On the arms of Great Britain and of Spain, placed side by side, the escutcheon of Spain has been covered by graffiti, while the huge iron eagle which until recently surmounted it has been displaced and in September 2001 could be seen lying far below on the hillside, the work of hotheads whose determination matched their ingenuity and acrobatic skills.

The further careers of General Evans and others who served in the Legion

Some of the principal players who served in the Legion and survived the war without serious injury had remarkable and successful careers in later life in the profession of arms, in politics, diplomacy, engineering, medicine and other fields. Five were later knighted for their services; these included Evans, three of his officers and Dr Rutherford Alcock.

General Evans Evans' own military career had begun as a volunteer in India in 1806. He then served in the Peninsular War in 1812 and in America in 1814 and 1815 before returning to Europe in time to join Wellington's army in Belgium to face the resurgent Bonaparte at Waterloo. In 1812 he had two horses shot under him, and again two years later in America at the battle of Bladensbury. He had captured the Congress House (White House) at Washington with only two hundred light infantry, and was later severely wounded before New Orleans. At Waterloo two more horses fell dead beneath him, and he is said to have been the staff officer who gave the word for the Union brigade of cavalry to charge.

When the British army of occupation left France in 1816 Evans, who in 1815 had gained three steps in rank in only six months, from captain to lieutenant colonel by brevet, reverted to the substantive rank of captain and went on half-pay.

After some years in retirement Evans entered politics as a radical and in 1831 was elected MP for Rye. He lost that seat and failed in his first attempt to win Westminster in 1832, but in 1833 defeated Sir John Cam Hobhouse to gain the seat. He was sitting as MP when he was given command of the Legion.

Returning to Westminster in 1837 Evans met a tirade of hostile criticism from his Tory opponents, who had sniped at him continually throughout the campaign. His promotion to full colonel in the British army and appointment as Knight Commander of the Bath in August 1837, in addition to Queen Cristina's award of Spanish decorations, roused his enemies to new heights of vituperation, with uproar in the House of Commons. The press reacted according to their political allegiances. The Tory *Essex Standard* wrote of Evans sitting in the British senate 'with all his blushing disgrace thick upon him', and even suggested he should be put on trial to clear himself of the guilt of the slaughter by sword and sickness of thousands upon thousands of British subjects. Palmerston, whose agents Evans and the Legion had been, supported him, believing that his award was well earned and properly bestowed. Wellington's approval had not been sought, and his response, had he been consulted, was predictable. George Villiers, appointed a Grand Commander of the Bath, had often been at loggerheads with Evans while Minister in Madrid. He was outspoken in writing to his brother: 'he absolutely constrains me to vomit ... His seat in Parliament was his idol, and his coming here – staying, fighting and going – all had reference to what he thought would be his constituents' opinions.'

Earlier, the liberal *Oxford City & County Chronicle*, publishing in full the letter written to Don Carlos by General Soroa after the Legion's capture of Irun under the heading 'Carlist Testimony to the Humanity of the British Legion', had written 'We do not delude ourselves that the Carlists of the British Parliament and press will be affected as these Carlist officers have been; their love of despotism, which is allied to the cause of Toryism, is too strong to yield, even were Don Carlos himself to eulogise the British Legion.' In February 1838 Evans was chairman at a large public dinner in London for Daniel O'Connell, who had supported the Irish involvement in the Legion and shared his liberal views. Evans praised the Liberator as the object of the attention of the whole empire, and the admiration of the best and most enlightened men not only of England, but of the world. Both men were the targets of vicious attack by their enemies in Westminster.

Evans' parliamentary career waxed and waned. He lost his seat in 1840, regained it five years later, and was re-elected in 1852. Promoted major general in 1846, lieutenant general in 1854 (his rank in the Legion), he went out to the war in the Crimea. At the battle of Alma he was severely wounded in the shoulder, but remained with his men and repulsed the Russian sortie from Sebastopol on June 26th, winning praise from Lord Raglan. Invalided on board ship in Balaclava harbour, he left his bed on hearing the firing on 5 November which heralded the battle of Inkerman, assisting his brigadier, the Irishman General Pennefather, with advice throughout the battle.* On returning home to Westminster he received the thanks of Parliament and was appointed GCB and a Grand Officer of the Legion of Honour. He was promoted general in 1861. Re-elected for Westminster again in 1857 and 1859, he retired from political life in 1865 and died in London in January 1870 aged 82, being buried in a family tomb in Kensal Green Cemetery.

Evans' military career spanned nearly half a century, and his period in Parliament thirty-four years, alternating between war and politics in a way that would soon become impossible. Regarding his service in Spain, there is no doubt as to his bravery. Of his military activities, conflicting views were expressed by many, including some who served under him. Some of his own officers were critical of his failure to pursue the enemy further when the tide of war ran in favour of the Legion. The comments of Alexander Somerville seem fairer to Evans than those of some of his officers, acknowledging the difficulties facing him, with an army on paper of some ten thousand men, but in practice no more than five thousand effective soldiers, and often fewer than this, opposed to an almost limitless force, and fighting a 'scrambling kind of war' in inhospitable terrain amidst a hostile populace where orthodox campaigning was very difficult.

Perhaps the comments of a professional soldier, written forty years later, give a more accurate assessment of Evans and the Legion's achievements. Major Francis Duncan of the Royal Artillery wrote in 1877 of the unprecedented difficulties under which Evans laboured and of the complete trust his men had in him despite his failure to get justice for them. Duncan believed that Evans was not merely brave as a soldier, fairly good as a strategist, unselfish as a man and sensitive to the honour of England, but was so sympathetic with those serving under him that his health repeatedly broke down under disappointment at being unable to secure for them the rewards and rights to which he considered them entitled. His later success in the Crimea argues against the charges of incompetence made by Villiers and other critics.

The accusations of tyranny and undue use of flogging levelled against Evans by the Tory press and by officers such as Richardson were probably motivated by political bias or personal rancour. The Order Book of the Legion, kept at its headquarters in San Sebastian, contains entries showing Evans' care for his men. On 29 June 1836 a court of enquiry was held into two incidents. The first was the case of Captain Middleton of the 9th Regiment, who had struck Private Patrick Kilary in the ranks on the face with his drawn sword, draw-

---

* Evans' role and that of Ireland in general in the Crimean War are reviewed by Murphy (2002).

ing blood. The court had excused the officer for his action in view of the man's insubordination, but Evans overruled their verdict. 'It is impossible the Lieutenant General can continue this officer in the Legion. His name accordingly will be struck from the strength this
day. The duty the Lieutenant General performed was a painful one, but he owes a protection equally to all ranks.' The second case concerned a major who had struck his servant
when the latter was drunk, and had him flogged. In this case also the court was lenient, but
Evans criticised their verdict. The officer, he wrote, should not have struck his servant, but
the provost should have flogged him. When courts martial sentenced a sergeant and four
privates of the 10th Regiment to be shot to death for their part in the mutiny of August
1836, Evans commuted the sentences to transportation with hard labour. Commenting on
Evans' return to London in June 1837, the *Limerick Chronicle* gave a harsh verdict on his
involvement in Spain: 'It is a pity that a generous, fine-hearted fellow as he is, should ever
volunteer his life and fortune for a worthless nation such as the Spaniards are.'

Charles Chichester (1795–1847)   The son of Charles Chichester, a Devonshire landowner,
and Honoria French of Rahasane, Co. Galway, he was brought up as a Catholic and educated at Stonyhurst, entering the army in 1811. He served in Malta, Sicily, Genoa and
Marseilles, and later in India and America.

Promoted lieutenant colonel, unattached, in 1831, Chichester was appointed brigadier-
general in the Legion in 1835, serving throughout the war. He was appointed lieutenant
colonel in the 81st Foot in 1839 and knighted in 1840. He commanded his regiment for
several years in the West Indies and America. He married his cousin, Mary Constable, in
1826, and they had a numerous family. He died in Toronto in 1847 after an illness of a
few days, at the age of fifty-two. Probably the best senior officer in the Legion, he was also
considered one of the best regimental commanding officers in the British army, and was
described as a fine soldier, a genial, large-hearted man, ever ready and unselfish in encouraging merit in any grade, and with ideas of tactical instruction far in advance of the practice of his day.

William Reid (1791–1858)   Another talented officer, Reid was a polymath Scot whose
career occupies three pages in the *Dictionary of National Biography*. He entered the army
at Woolwich in 1806 and studied practical surveying before being commissioned in the
Royal Engineers in 1809, joining Wellington's army in Lisbon in 1810.

In the Peninsular War Reid was involved in many actions including the three sieges
of Badajoz and that of Ciudad Rodrigo, being wounded several times. In Spain he fought
at Vitoria and at the siege of San Sebastian in 1813, where he blew in the counterscarp and
was again wounded in the neck. Battles in France followed and in 1814 he was involved in
the unsuccessful attack on New Orleans. 1815 saw him in the Netherlands, and he then
took part in the march to Paris and the capture and occupation of the city after Waterloo.

In 1816 Reid was on board the *Queen Charlotte* during the bombardment of Algiers,
working the guns with his sappers. Promoted to brevet-major in 1817, he was placed on
half-pay in 1819 when the Corps of Royal Engineers was reduced, but returned to full pay
in 1824 and was posted to Ireland, where he was appointed to the Ordnance Survey. Next
he was involved in quelling the Reform riots in the west of England, and in 1831 went to
Barbados, where he rebuilt the government buildings which had been blown down in a
hurricane. This led him to the scientific study of storms and to the later publication of *The
Law of Storms*, a valuable work for the guidance of seamen, and to his election as a Fellow
of the Royal Society.

His interlude in the Legion, when he was again on half-pay, gave Reid, already a veteran of twenty-five years, further experience of shot and shell and further awards for valour.

In 1839 Reid was appointed governor of Bermuda, where he worked to improve the lot of the coloured population, who had been recently freed from slavery. He established parochial schools and improved the backward agriculture of the islands, training the people in improved methods of cultivation and starting a public library. Appointed governor-in-chief of the Windward West India Islands in 1846, Reid devoted himself to improving the condition of the people and to developing the colonies' resources. A monument to his memory was erected in Hamilton by the people of the Bermudas.

Returning to England in 1848, he resumed military duty as Commanding Royal Engineer at Woolwich in 1849 and in 1850 became chairman of the executive committee of the Great Exhibition to be held the following year in Hyde Park.

In 1851 he was appointed governor and commander-in-chief at Malta at a difficult time, when the war in the Crimea was straining the island's resources to the uttermost, and succeeded in meeting all demands. For the benefit of the Maltese people he founded an agricultural school, introduced new species of the cotton plant and seeds adapted to the climate, established barometers to warn fishermen and sailors of impending gales, and developed the old library of the Knights of Malta into a public library for the community.

Back in England in the summer of 1858, Reid died after a short illness, with remarkable achievements in war and peace to his credit. His wife predeceased him by nine months and they were survived by five daughters.

Maurice O'Connell (1812–1879)   O'Connell, who fought in the Legion between 1835 and 1837 and commanded the new Legion briefly in 1837, had close links with Australia. He was born in Sydney where his father, of the same name, was lieutenant-governor of New South Wales. His mother was the daughter of Admiral Bligh of the *Bounty*. Educated in England, Scotland, Dublin and Paris, where he was a military student, the young O'Connell entered the army as an ensign in the 73rd Regiment of Foot in 1828. In 1835 he was placed on half-pay, and raised the 10th Regiment of the Legion, the Munster Light Infantry, in Cork, in which he was gazetted lieutenant colonel.

On returning to England O'Connell was attached to the 51st Regiment and in 1838 was appointed captain in the 28th, which he accompanied to New South Wales under his father's command, serving as military secretary. When the regiment returned to England he sold out and settled in New South Wales, devoting himself to country pursuits and especially to the breeding of horses, becoming one of the leading authorities in Australia.

He entered the legislative council for Port Phillip in 1845, but soon became involved in the settlement of Port Curtis and later in the legislative assembly for the colony of Queensland, becoming President of the Council in 1861, a post he held until his death in 1879. He was awarded a public funeral. His bust, presented to him by the council in 1878, stands in the council chamber.

Duncan MacDougall (1793–1862)   As the only officer of the Legion to have a memorial in St Paul's Cathedral, MacDougall's military exploits are listed on his monument (fig. 15).

MacDougall, like Evans, had served in the American war and taken part in the capture of Washington and other battles. In the Peninsular War he was at the sieges of Badajoz, Burgos and San Sebastian, and saved the regimental colours at Salamanca despite being wounded. He commanded the 79th Highlanders until he retired from the British army to join the Legion in Spain.

During his year with the Legion MacDougall did everything possible to improve the conditions of the men, and his early resignation robbed them of a powerful protector who was prepared to exert himself on their behalf. When the war was over he strove, with Evans and Dr Alcock, to obtain just pay and pensions for the neglected veterans. The high regard in which his colleagues held him is shown by the sword presented to him by the senior officers of the Legion on his retirement, with the names of the donors engraved on its steel blade. It is preserved in the National Army Museum, Chelsea.

In 1859 MacDougall was involved in the Volunteer Movement, forerunner of the Territorial Army, raising the Lancashire Artillery Militia. He was knighted for his services and died, aged 69, in 1862.

Charles Fitzgerald (c.1785–1855) Fitzgerald, whose gallantry in battle at the head of the Irish Brigade was noted by Somerville, was distinguished by panache as well as bravery in a family noted for its fighting spirit. His nephew, Lionel Charles Fitzgerald, had served in Portugal in the Miguelite war between 1832 and 1834, and his brother Edward had fought at Waterloo. An uncle, George Robert Fitzgerald, is described in *Burke's Irish Family Records* as a famous duellist, known as 'Fighting Fitzgerald', an eccentric, quarrelsome and reckless, 'an undutiful son, a bad brother and a worse husband'.* It is arguable that Charles Fitzgerald inherited some of the abrasive temperament of his bellicose uncle, and was more fitted for the profession of arms than a successful career in peacetime. This seems consistent with his unhappy later history.

On leaving the Legion Fitzgerald's financial situation was critical. As the father of eight children, and a litigant in a long and costly lawsuit, he needed an adequate and regular income. Too old to continue a military career, he hoped to find that income in the British Consular Service. Courageous and hot-headed, he lacked the temperament for a diplomatic career, as time soon proved.

In January 1838 he was appointed consul at Mahon in the Balearic Islands at a salary of £300 a year, with permission to trade but no entitlement to a pension. He had little time to deal with his affairs in Ireland before taking up his post, having stayed in Spain after most of his comrades had left. Reaching Mahon in early April he at once busied himself with his consular duties, which were largely concerned with the movements of foreign and British shipping, reporting these to the Foreign Office and corresponding with Villiers in Madrid and the commander of British naval forces in the Mediterranean. He reported a rumour, which proved false, that the United States were about to declare war on England, and that its squadron had been put on a full war establishment. Suspicion of French intervention was reflected in his report of the arrival in the port of Mahon of a French man-of-war, with much bustle and secrecy, and the news that the duke of Nemours, one of the sons of the ex-King Louis-Philippe, was on board in strict incognito.

---

* According to Burke, and to Somerville-Large (1975), he kept a private company of *banditti* which he called his 'volunteers', which he merely used to bully his neighbours; fortified an old rath on his estate with guns stolen from a Dutch ship; hunted at night in order to avoid his enemies, the meets being held by torchlight; incarcerated his father and tied him to a pet bear – for which, with other acts of cruelty, he was imprisoned, escaped but was recaptured by six companies of foot, two troops of cavalry and a park of artillery; was eventually released owing to illness; and had his rival for the colonelcy of the Mayo Volunteers, a Mr McDonnell, murdered, for which he was tried and condemned to death. He was hanged at Castlebar on 12 June 1786. (It is said that the hangman's rope broke twice and it was only at the third attempt that the execution succeeded.) He had been educated at Eton, as Burke relates laconically.

Fitzgerald's family concerns led him to apply to Palmerston in March 1839 for six months' leave from August, when the long-running lawsuit over his mother's estate required his presence in Dublin. His son Hervey had been on the commander-in-chief's list for a commission in the army by purchase for three years. Another son was due to enter the Royal Military College at Sandhurst, and financial arrangements had to be made.

Palmerston sympathised with Fitzgerald's difficulties and he was not only granted leave of absence but was also given the more lucrative consulship at Cartagena at a salary of £400 a year and permission to trade, but no pension. Though his commission at Cartagena was dated January 1840, he only took up his post a year later. His bad relations with his previous vice-consul in Mahon were later to involve him in greater troubles.

Fitzgerald approached Palmerston in June to request an extension of his leave until October, since his lawsuit, on which the financial future of his children depended, would come to a head in late September*. His creditors were getting clamorous and he could not silence them. Meanwhile he was alert to other chances and was disappointed to learn that the post at Genoa had already been filled. Later he offered his services to the government in 'Syria, or any part of the world', where his recent knowledge of guerrilla warfare might be of advantage, but his offer was refused.

On 8 January 1841 the new consul was finally in post in Cartagena, writing to the patient Palmerston that a violent attack of gout had prevented him from arriving earlier, or from writing.

Fitzgerald's activities in Cartagena produced a steady stream of despatches to and from London, reflecting not only his own anxieties, but also those of the Spanish government and of Arthur Aston, Villiers' successor as British Minister in Madrid. In April and May 1841 he was reproved for irregularity in his despatches. Worse followed in May when the Gibraltar-based British vessel *Dolphin* was seized at sea by a Spanish coastguard ship and confined by the customs authorities in the port of Cartagena on a charge of smuggling. Soon afterwards, HMS *Jaseur*, commanded by Captain Boultbec, RN, arrived and, on Fitzgerald's orders, forcibly carried off the *Dolphin*. Next, another British ship, the *Triumph*, was taken at sea by the Spanish coastguards, who Fitzgerald believed resembled pirates rather than protectors of the Revenue. Complaints were made by the Spanish government and questions asked in the Cortes. Aston investigated the case and on 25 May suspended Fitzgerald from his post. He returned to England to explain his conduct, taking depositions from the crew of the *Triumph*. He was replaced in September 1841 by Consul Turner, who was explicitly forbidden to trade.

No consular post in Europe was available, and Fitzgerald's next appointment was to Mobile, Alabama. This was his last post and a miserable one, the penultimate chapter in his life. The consular archives were very deficient, as he reported to Lord Aberdeen, Palmerston's successor as Foreign Secretary in Sir Robert Peel's ministry, who was far less sympathetic to his plight. Fitzgerald's temperament clashed with that of his American hosts, leading to a flood of despatches between Mobile and London, with complaints from both sides of the divide. An altercation with a magistrate in Mobile led to complaints to the United States government and to reports from the British minister at Washington to the Foreign Office. Lord Aberdeen expressed his strong disapproval of the consul's demeanour and language, threatening removal from his post unless he restrained his temper.

---

* His request was supported by influential friends, Mr Dillon Browne, Sir William Brabazon and Lord Clanricarde in Ireland, and his elder brother, Lieutenant Colonel Thomas Fitzgerald, in Wincanton.

Fitzgerald's health was suffering from the unhealthy climate of Alabama and several severe attacks of fever. His work was made difficult by the twenty-five miles separating the town of Mobile from the bay where he had to deal with British merchantmen. He felt that the British captains had become affected by the freer attitudes of the Americans towards authority, and were lacking in respect to him and inclined to favour American interests. He also believed that drunkenness was rife among the British captains and that British trade would suffer unless the situation improved.

Deteriorating health and finances led him to ask about the consulship at Leghorn, but this post had been filled. He was granted permission to leave Mobile during the unhealthy summer months to escape the yellow fever, and moved to the healthier climate of Quebec for some months.

Eighteen-forty-four was an *annus horribilis* for Fitzgerald. Pressing financial demands compounded his physical problems. The Foreign Office ruled that he must pay the £10 owing for a painting of the queen's arms for the consular office. Much more serious was a Foreign Office despatch received in March regarding an outlawry judgement taken out against him in Spain by his former vice-consul in Cartagena, who claimed he was owed £500. Since the salary of an outlawed government officer became forfeited to the crown while the outlawry continued, he must obtain reversal of the outlawry or prove that it was obtained under circumstances that reflected no discredit on himself.

His need to return home was now urgent and he was granted leave of absence until 1 January 1845 (which was to be the day of his death). His explanations about the debt were considered unsatisfactory. He returned to London and in July 1844 was living at 217 Piccadilly, where his correspondence with the Foreign Office continued over what he saw as Fayzan's extortionate demands. He claimed, corroborated by his solicitor, that he had offered him £200, which was all that he owed, and that this had been refused.

Writing in October to Lord Aberdeen, Fitzgerald told him of his continuing ill-health caused by the sickly climate of Mobile, enclosing a certificate from his physician. Dr Waddington wrote that he was under his care on account of general debility and glandular swellings of the neck, the result of functional disorder of the liver and bowels (induced by the unhealthy climate of Mobile) and that a protracted residence in England was essential for his recovery.

Fitzgerald was now very ill indeed. His last letter to Aberdeen was dated 9 December 1844. Sir Duncan MacDougall, who had served with him in the Legion, had interceded with Aberdeen that he should not have to return to Mobile, and listed his debts, with five sons in the army, a wife and three children at home, and only his half-pay and consular salary to support them. Fitzgerald assured Aberdeen that he wanted to pay all he owed, begging for another consulship where he could support his family and begin to liquidate his debts.

It is as well that Fitzgerald was neither made to return to Mobile nor appointed to another post, since he now had only three weeks to live. He died on 1 January 1845, aged fifty-eight, in Margate, Kent. His death certificate gave the cause of death as 'scrofulous inflammation of the glands'.*

---

* This term has no precise significance in modern medicine; the reference to glandular swellings in the neck and general debility, while not specific, would be compatible with tuberculous lymph nodes in the neck, associated perhaps with more widespread tuberculous infection, or with some form of leukaemia or lymphoma. The attribution of his illness to the unhealthy climate of Alabama is uncertain, though he could well have acquired an infection there, and the conditions may have aggravated a pre-existing disease.

Though he had escaped death on the battlefields of Portugal and Spain, Fitzgerald may at times have wished that his life had ended heroically under enemy fire on 5 May 1836. He had striven hard to provide for the needs of his large family, but it does not seem that they were with him at the time of his death.

Charles Shaw (1795–1871)   Shaw had entered the British army by purchase as an ensign in 1813 and served in the 52nd Light Infantry in Holland in 1814. At the time of Waterloo he was on baggage-guard duty at Brussels, but took part in the march to Paris and its occupation. When his regiment was disbanded he went on half-pay, but soon returned to full-pay status in the 90th Regiment, and also enrolled as a military student in Brunswick to improve his qualifications for a military career, and to see something of the Prussian army. In 1818 Shaw was again placed on half-pay and became partner in a wine business in Leith, but also took command of the volunteer corps of sharpshooters and established the first military club in Edinburgh. On the outbreak of the Miguelite war in Portugal in 1831 he was appointed captain of a light company of marines in the service of Dom Pedro, joining the fleet of Admiral Sartorius, and later saw much action in the Miguelite siege of Oporto. When the war ended in 1834 Shaw was active in seeking a financial settlement between the officers and men of the British contingent and their Portuguese paymasters, with only limited success. The Spanish war now offered more opportunities for a soldier of fortune and he became involved in recruiting for the British Legion in Scotland. The two Peninsular campaigns form the basis of what the *Dictionary of National Biography* described (with some justice) as Shaw's rambling and egotistical 'Personal Memoirs' of 1837.

In 1839 he became chief commissioner of police in Manchester, holding the post until 1842, and was later knighted for his services. He married in 1841 and had one son. Later he lived in Germany, where he died in 1871 and was buried with military honours.

Dr Rutherford Alcock (1809–1897)   The son of a doctor, John Rutherford Alcock, who abandoned his first name early, began his medical education at fifteen. Apprenticed to his father, he entered the Westminster and the Westminster Ophthalmic Hospitals as a student under the distinguished surgeon G.J. Guthrie.* and studied also in Paris, where he combined his medical programme with courses in art and literature and also mastered French and Italian.

Medically qualified in 1832 at the age of twenty-two, Alcock was recommended by Guthrie as a surgeon for the Anglo-Portuguese force being raised for the dynastic war in Portugal in the service of Dom Pedro and his daughter against the pretender, Dom Miguel. The prospect of gaining experience in military surgery and medicine was attractive, and the day after accepting the offer he set out for Portsmouth and the Azores, soon transferring to the British marine battalion under Colonel Hodges. In the two years of the chaotic and bloody civil war Alcock made his mark and gained golden opinions for his skill, devotion to duty and disregard of danger in action. Charles Shaw wrote later of seeing the twenty-three-year-old Alcock in the most exposed situations, dressing officers and men with the same coolness as if he were in a London hospital. He quickly learned practical surgical

---

* George Guthrie had joined the 29th Regiment as assistant-surgeon when just sixteen years old, had gained unrivalled experience of military surgery in the field in the Napoleonic wars and made important contributions, particularly stressing the need for early rather than delayed amputation in gunshot wounds of the limbs, a view shared by the great French military surgeon, Dominique Larrey (Howard, 2002, p. 44).

lessons from treating hundreds of injured men, and recognised the importance of early amputation of limbs severely injured by ball and bullet as a life-saving measure to avoid, as far as possible, the complications of gangrene and infection, a lesson taught him by Guthrie. Shaw quotes the grimly pragmatic criticism of this policy by Dom Pedro: 'You British are fond of amputations because your men are to have pensions, and that is expensive.'

When the Portuguese war ended with victory for Dom Pedro, many of the British Pedroite officers and men enlisted in the British Legion in 1835 to support the Cristino cause in the Carlist war that followed. Alcock served as Deputy-Inspector of Hospitals in Spain from 1835 to 1837 and returned to civilian life with a wide experience of military surgery, a towering reputation and decorations from Portugal and Spain. Shaw praised Alcock's humane attitude to his patients in another letter, commenting on the fate of the disabled men of the Legion: 'Alcock has had a difficult card to play. He knows well that there are many disabled poor fellows who, if they were in the British service, would be sent to England, certain of receiving their pensions; but he is also aware that a poor fellow sent to England from the service of Queen Christina instead of receiving his pension, is generally left to starve. It is therefore from a praiseworthy charity that he keeps many in hospital, under his own eye, in order that they may in this manner get as much as will keep body and soul together.'

Back in England, Alcock published a small volume in 1838, *Notes on the Medical History and Statistics of the British Legion in Spain,* presenting the lessons of his experience and giving vivid descriptions of typhus with discussion of the impact of the adverse living conditions of the Legion on the morbidity and mortality of disease. Some of these lessons had still not been learned sixty years later at the time of the Anglo-Boer war, experience in which led to the establishment of the Royal Army Medical College.

Alcock had great sympathy for the sufferings of the men of the Legion after their return to Britain and was active on their behalf in trying to achieve settlement of the many claims for arrears of pay and pensions, and also of those relating to the Portuguese war. He later wrote that the six years of his Peninsular experiences had been 'the most stirring and attractive of his life'.

Professional success in civilian life followed for several years, with prizes from the Royal College of Surgeons.*

His marriage in 1841 brought Alcock domestic happiness, and a glittering career in surgery lay ahead with a chair in military surgery at King's College, London when, at the age of thirty-five, he was struck by a cruel illness which caused paralysis of his hands and arms and made his career in surgery quite impossible. Partial recovery occurred spontaneously, but seven years later he still suffered from what he called the 'mysterious' afflic-

---

* While in Spain Alcock built up a collection of pathological material to illustrate the effects of musketball and other injuries. He and his team of surgeons prepared ten volumes of clinical case notes relating to most of these macerated specimens, often accompanied by his own drawings of high artistic quality. Most of the specimens were from limbs amputated for battle wounds, while some came from postmortem examinations in cases considered not amenable to surgery, such as injuries to the pelvic bones, abdominal or thoracic cavities.

In 1843, when illness had ended his surgical career, Alcock sold his collection to Sir George Ballingall, Regius Professor of Military Surgery in the University of Edinburgh, who incorporated it with material of his own in a museum which he established. The related manuscript material is in the Special Collections Section of Edinburgh University Library, together with a volume of clinical case notes of sick and wounded soldiers during the earlier Miguelite war, in which Alcock had cut his surgical teeth (Kaufman et al., 1996, Kaufman, 2003).

tion, which was attributed to rheumatic fever, and never recovered the full use of his hands, so that the legibility of his writing was marred to the end of his life. In retrospect the diagnosis seems likely to be one of the Guillain-Barré syndrome or acute infectious polyneuritis, a paralytic disorder only recognised many years later in France and Britain.

Though his brilliant and promising career in surgery was so dramatically cut short, Alcock was enabled to embark on a completely different and honourable vocation when he was appointed to the office of a consul in China under the Treaty of Nanking, concluded in 1842. His career as consul and minister in China and Japan was documented by Alexander Michie in his two-volume book, *The Englishman in China during the Victorian Era* (1900). During a very difficult period in Anglo-Chinese relations his fearless and resolute conduct over many years won Alcock further renown. The terrible ravages of the the Taiping rebellion reached the southern capital, Nanking, in March 1853, when the city surrendered and its Tartar garrison of twenty thousand were put to the sword. Relations between the Chinese government troops invading Nanking and the foreign officials and community were extremely poor, and eventually the British and Americans took reprisals for the aggression of the Chinese soldiers on their settlements. Their forces were composed of British and American sailors and marines, some sailors from merchant-ships in port, and some two hundred residents as infantry volunteers. Consul Alcock accompanied the English force, and the American vice-consul the United States group. The attack was completely successful, with very little resistance. Alcock's views on the need for vigorous efforts to protect British subjects abroad coincided with the strongly held views of 'Lord Pumicestone'.

After the end of the Opium Wars in China Alcock was made a Knight Commander of the British Empire, and was for six years the British Minister Plenipotentiary in Peking. The expansion of the influence of the European powers and the United States in China and Japan, in the missionary field and in trade, with recurrent attacks on the hated foreigners, including the Boxer Rising, tested Alcock's powers of diplomacy to the full during his twenty-seven years' service in the Far East.

His obituarist (*British Medical Journal*, 1897) pointed out that it was not only in the art of bellicose diplomacy that Alcock distinguished himself. He persuaded the Japanese to take part in the International Exhibition of 1862, which introduced many in Europe to the graceful arts of the Far East.

The last twenty-seven years of his life were spent in England, where he returned to his first love, medicine, resuming contact with the Westminster Hospital and its medical school after a lapse of forty years, and becoming one of the vice-presidents to the board. Unsatisfactory accommodation needed major structural changes and heavy expenditure. Reform of the nursing situation was needed, since the pay of the nurses had for many years been held at a low level, so that the best nurses were enticed away by the lure of better pay elsewhere. Against some medical opposition the change was made, the cost of nursing was doubled at a bound and the standard markedly improved. Acutely aware, from his military experience, of the effects of overcrowded and insanitary living conditions on infectious disease and on public health, Alcock was assiduous in his efforts to improve the situation. His efforts contributed to the statutory notification of cases of infectious disease required by the act of Parliament of 1889.

Alcock died in November 1897 after a short illness, his intellect unimpaired until within a few days of the end. To a friend who had suggested a biography he wrote: 'In worldly things I have been exceptionally favoured by opportunities, many of them unanticipated, and rather fortuitous than by any efforts or merits. My early life was marked by a great rashness, and a readiness to accept responsibilities which savoured much of presumption and confidence from conceit in my powers to deal with whatever fell in my way – very different from my retrospect in old age and the sobered estimate my judgement is now disposed to form of all I undertook and accomplished, and the risks I accepted, through my fifty years of active life.'

To a reader more than a hundred years later there seems no justification for self-reproach over a life well spent.

Alexander Somerville (1811–1885) When reading Somerville's account of the British Legion it is difficult not to feel respect, tinged with affection, for the writer. The *Dictionary of National Biography* refers to his chivalric temperament, which was as notable as his impractibility. These words conjure up the term quixotic, but the giants against which Somerville tilted were no mere windmills.

His compassion for the sufferings of his comrades and their unhappy dependants shines through his writing, while his sense of humour and his sharp eye for the foibles of some of his officers, his descriptive powers and his philosophical musings in the midst of carnage, make his narrative an unusual product of its time and his class. The bullet, which at Irun lodged among the books he carried strapped to his greatcoat, would have found no such billet among the impedimenta of his fellow legionaries.

Somerville had hoped to find in Spain the material for a book of travels. His fertile pen later found many other subjects when he directed his attention to social, economic and political topics.

The Chartist movement was active in Britain, with firebrands such as Feargus O'Connor supporting violent protest, when in 1839 Somerville was invited to join an insurrectionary movement in Wales. This he opposed, arguing against the use of violence in his publication, *Warnings to the People on Street Warfare*, drawing on his own experience in Spain and the tragic effects of revolution in that unhappy land. Like Daniel O'Connell, he preached the merits of the ballot over the bullet. 'Britain has her warlike politicians, who cry for revolution by force of arms. Heaven help them and her,' he wrote, 'if she had a revolution, such as they desire her to have!' He addressed the young, unfitted to judge of what is right and what is wrong by reason of their youth, who outnumbered all others who form street mobs, with arms in their hands: 'Youths of Nottingham, from fourteen to twenty! Beware of the monkey who would make cats'-paws of you!'

Letters that Somerville wrote to the *Morning Chronicle* on the Corn Laws attracted the attention of Richard Cobden, who sent him on a tour of rural England to gather information for the Anti-Corn Law League. His enquiring and analytical mind was put to good use in this project, and later as a correspondent for the *Manchester Examiner* in 1845–6, and again in 1847, when he was sent to Ireland to report on the state of agriculture and the horrific effects of the potato blight and famine that followed. When warned of the risks of armed robbery by starving peasants on the Irish roads he replied that he would not take a weapon with him, but would instead fill a carpet bag with loaves and bread and cheese, 'ready, if any hungry Tipperarian or dweller on the Waterford mountains should present a blunderbuss at me, to put my hand into the bag, pull out, present, and throw him a bullet of bread; not fearing but that this style of defence would be more effective than a defence by powder and lead'. He was deeply sympathetic to the starving people and his writings, *Letters from Ireland during the Famine of 1847*, give detailed accounts of the wretched conditions of the rural poor throughout Ireland and an analysis of the political economy of the country. He describes the hovels in which most of the people lived. Some of their owners had previously had a few perches of haggard, or garden, on which to grow food, but since the failure of the potatoes in 1845 and '46, the rent of 30s. each was not paid and the hag-gards had been taken from them. A tenant and his wife in Co. Limerick, both sick with fever in their wretched hut, were without fire or food, without air or light but what came through the roof, which was nearly touching their fevered heads. Their wretched bed was on the wet puddle of the floor. The farm on which they lived, Somerville tells us, belonged to Captain Bateson, MP, who had voted the other day against the out-door relief clause of the New Poor Law. The men usually employed on this and neighbouring farms at that season of the year were on the public works. 'The farmers say, that none of the men are worth their "keep", at present, "keep is so dear".'

Somerville's *Autobiography of a Working Man*, by 'One Who Has Whistled at the Plough,' appeared anonymously in 1848, incorporating accounts of the British Legion and his experiences in Britain and Ireland as a journalist. Unfortunately his impressive literary output did not bring the financial rewards it deserved, and in 1858 he fell victim to the mismanagement or fraud of certain literary agents or publishers.

In that year some of his friends arranged for him and his family a passage to Canada, but the New World brought him no greater monetary success than the Old. His wife died soon after they arrived in Montreal, and he settled down to a career in journalism, editing for a time the *Canadian Illustrated News* and publishing in 1866 *A Narrative of the Fenian Invasion of Canada*. Refusing to accept any financial help, he sank into poverty and on 17 June 1885 he died in a shed in York Street, Toronto.

Despite his humble and unpromising beginnings, Somerville's achievements were remarkable. Had he been born with more advantages he might have achieved much more as a social reformer in a career he himself described as 'persistently devoted to public well-being and to the removal of antagonism between extremes of society'.

Morgan David O'Connell (1810–1887)   In August 1835, at the age of twenty-five, the newly qualified Dr O'Connell set out from his father's home in Kilmallock to Cork to enlist as assistant-surgeon in the 10th Munster Light Infantry, then recruiting officers and men for the Spanish war under their colonel, Maurice O'Connell.

Having gained his surgical qualification the same year, he could have had little prac-tical experience of medicine or surgery. The same was true of the two other surgeons of the 10th, Doctors M. Grove of Cork and Thomas Maybury from Tralee, but in the next two years they were to learn in the hard school of experience. Most of their colleagues were young and no more experienced than they, although some, like Rutherford Alcock, had served in the earlier campaign in Portugal, or in other little wars in Greece or South America.

O'Connell was present throughout his regiment's service in Spain, and survived both the epidemics of typhus and other diseases which killed so many of his medical colleagues, including Grove, and the fighting, including the bitter battles of 5 May 1836 and March 1837, without a wound. He received the medals conferred for these two actions (pls. 18, 19; fig. 12). His portrait in the uniform of the 10th Regiment (pl. 1) was painted after March 1837, since he wears the yellow facings of the Irish Brigade, formed in February of that year, and both decorations.

Returning to civilian life in Kilmallock in 1837, he took his MD from Glasgow University in 1838 and became a Fellow of the Royal College of Surgeons In Ireland in 1845. Private practice would have provided part of his income, but events soon led to his becoming preoccupied with caring for the poor of Kilmallock and its neighbourhood, who became mired in the misery of famine and disease as the potato crop failed in the summer of 1846, attacked by the fungus which had unknowingly been brought into Ireland by ships from America. So dependent were the people on the potato that its dearth proved a death sentence for many thousands of men, women and children. The famine was accompanied by diseases of starvation and poverty, particularly typhus and dysentery, and by the associated disruption of society. Scurvy, previously rare in the Irish peasantry, in contrast to their European counterparts, soon became common, adding its burden of spontaneous bleeding to the other disorders.

A 'welfare state' of sorts already existed in Ireland and Britain. In 1833 provision had been made 'for the most effectual relief of the destitute poor of Ireland' by an Act of Parliament which divided the country into administrative areas called Unions, adminstered by local Boards of Guardians, some members being ex officio and others elected. Limerick had four Unions; that of Bruff, shortly to become the Kilmallock Union, was declared in January 1839. Its Board of Guardians had thirty-seven members. A workhouse was built in Kilmallock, and a master and matron were appointed at salaries of £45 and £30, with a male and a female teacher. In March 1841 it opened its doors to thirty destitute people, and six months later housed 258, male and female, adults and children. With accommodation for 800 souls, it proved adequate until November 1846, when the total failure of the potato crop and the onset of winter led to a rapid rise in the number of inmates, reaching 1,036 on 26 December.

O'Connell had been appointed medical officer to the workhouse, and was deeply concerned by the deteriorating situation. From his experience of the dreadful conditions in Vitoria eleven years earlier, and of the effects of overcrowding on the morbidity and mortality of typhus and other epidemic disease, he knew the inevitable consequences if conditions were not remedied. He wrote in December 1846 to the Board of Guardians with the firm opinion that the workhouse could not accommodate more than 800 people without engendering disease. The infirmary should be properly furnished to provide for the fever cases occurring daily.

Feeding the inmates was also a huge problem. By February 1847 they numbered 1,207, and the average weekly deaths had risen to six. O'Connell drew up a dietary for children of various ages from two to fifteen (presumably on the basis that younger children – if not orphaned – would be breast-fed). The Minute Books of the Union show that the main provisions were Indian meal bread, gruel and soup. Children from two to nine were to get eight ounces of white bread for dinner and four ounces for lunch at midday, and on two days a week half a pint of soup, with 'the usual substitute' on the other days. Older children were to get ten ounces of Indian meal bread for dinner, with one pint of gruel, and on Sundays and Thursdays one pint of soup each in lieu of the gruel. O'Connell reported that the Indian meal supplied was far too coarse and hence injurious to the health of the paupers,* and that it should be ground finer or sifted. On such a diet it is not surprising that hungry workhouse boys should climb out to steal turnips, and appear before the magistrate when caught.

O'Connell's strong social conscience did not spare the Board of Guardians in his appeals for the wretched inmates of the workhouse. Early in 1848 the Board had unwisely decided to close the auxiliary fever hospital at Garryvoe, opened only the previous year. He wrote, 'begging most respectfully but fearlessly' to decline acting on this recommendation. He referred to 'the fearfully increasing sickness for the last two years, and the vast influx of wretched beings who flock hither to our workhouse, and come here rather to die

---

* A universal complaint with this unfamiliar food, which was supplied from America.

than to live, and who, whether living or dying, diffuse the seeds of pestilence around them.'
As he wrote these words O'Connell must have been reliving his experiences in Vitoria, the
city of death.

In a letter to the Board of Guardians published in the *Limerick Chronicle* in May 1847
he wrote of the unfortunate victims of hunger and famine fever who, in the spring of 1847,
unable to find accommodation in the workhouse, had gone to the town's ruined Dominican
priory, and had there lain down to die, just as other fever victims had done thirty years
before. Nine poor souls were now lying there. 'It would,' he wrote, 'bring heart-sickness
to an Ethiopian to behold one of those poor souls, the widow Galwey, within the last week,
swollen with dropsy herself, sitting on a cold stone over her daughter raging with fever,
and endeavouring to soothe her troubled thoughts and quench, with river water, her parched
tongue. This poor girl is since removed to a more generous and peaceful world, and her
poor aunt, too, who made some struggle to attend on her, died in the undertaking.'

His account continues: 'The widowed mother is still in the ruins, with the cold wind
blowing in on her, and on the night of her daughter's burial, the cows of the Abbey farm
came in on the helpless creature, and ate the small wisp of straw from under her.' Little
seems to have been done, and in another letter to the Guardians on the invalids in the ruins
O'Connell, in righteous anger, told them: 'This is ... particularly the poor man's question:
you are his guardians. His health is his property – and, health gone, house and land, income
and credit, tools, furniture, clothing and independence and, too often, honesty, all follow
and go with it. The wealthier can always take care of themselves.'

The wealthier and the middling sort, however, were not immune from the toll of
typhus. The columns of the *Limerick Chronicle* at this time regularly recorded the deaths
from typhus among the upper and middle classes. The lord lieutenant of Ireland, Baron
Lurgan, himself had died of typhus at Lurgan Castle in his fifty-second year, as reported
on 1 May that year. Many of those involved in the care of the poor and sick fell victim,
accounts often referring to the fever caught in the discharge of their duties – a coroner at
an inquest, apothecaries at workhouses, poor law guardians, bank managers, collectors of
customs, inspectors of constabulary, surgeons to infirmaries and clergymen of the rival faiths
ministering to their respective flocks, so that the Protestant minister at Ballymena and a
Roman Catholic curate in Co. Leitrim rubbed shoulders in the lists of dead on 22 May.

Hope that the Famine was over was dispelled by the reappearance of the potato blight
in 1848, and further partial failures of the crop in 1849 and 1850 prolonged the agony for
several years.

During 1848 the numbers in the Kilmallock workhouse continued to grow, until no
more bodies could be crammed in. Auxiliary workhouses and fever hospitals were then
opened in other centres in the Union area. The threatened hospital at Garryvoe had survived, thanks to O'Connell, and there was another nearby; the number of destitute poor
and sick in the various institutions in the Kilmallock Union peaked at about 3,500 by the
end of December 1848, with up to fifty deaths a week.

Horrific though the statistics in Kilmallock were, Co. Limerick was far from being the
worst affected area. The 1851 Irish census showed that the population had fallen from over
eight million in 1841 to 6,574,278 over ten years. In Limerick the average annual excess
mortality from 1846 to 1851 was 10–20 per thousand, while in neighbouring Tipperary it
was 20–30, in Cork 30–40 and in Mayo and Sligo 40–50 (Irish census 1851).

Public works provided only very limited relief for men still able to work on road-build-
ing and other schemes, the wages paid being kept below the 'normal' rates for each dis-
trict, while food prices spiralled. On 5 May 1847 the *Limerick Chronicle* recorded that 'the

number of labourers suffered to remain on the public works in Ireland since May 1st was 280,000'.

Evictions of those who could not pay their rents and the fear of starvation and disease fuelled an unprecedented exodus of about 1,800,000 people between 1846 and 1855. Britain, America, Canada and Australia received the refugees, whose passage to the New World killed off many of the sick in the crowded 'coffin-ships' conveying them. From the start of the spring season of 1847 to 8 May, a total of 5,537 passengers were carried from Limerick to North America in thirty-six ships. Although the price of a berth had risen to £5, which at any other time would have been prohibitive, the applicants were so eager to embark that tickets were held at a premium. The larger landlords would often pay for the passages of their 'surplus tenantry'; among these was Lord Palmerston.

Dedicated as he was to helping his patients, O'Connell was fortunate to survive the typhus which, during the Famine years, killed so many of those caring for the sick. As in Spain, he was spared to serve his patients and to found a family.

In 1850 he married Maria, daughter of Dr William Barry of Park House, Kanturk, Co. Cork. They had six children. One daughter died aged fourteen, and their eldest son, William, died aged nineteen while a medical student in Dublin. Two sons became doctors, one of whom followed a career in army medicine, serving in two wars and four continents. Of their two surviving daughters, one became a nun and the other married.

O'Connell continued his medical work into old age. He was exposed again to scenes of gunfire after an interval of thirty years during the abortive Fenian rising in Kilmallock on Ash Wednesday, 6 March 1867, when the police barracks were attacked, and he treated a wounded man who had been injured in the shooting and lay in the street, being later rewarded by his grateful patient with the gift of a silver salver. A Celtic cross in the town commemorates the rising, in which three men died, including a young medical student, Michael Clery, hit by a police bullet.

The even tenor of O'Connell's life was disturbed again in 1882 when one of Charles Stewart Parnell's sisters visited Kilmallock. With the 'uncrowned King of Ireland' still in Kilmainham jail, passions ran high. O'Connell's refusal to illuminate his house to mark the visit resulted in his windows being broken.

In 1885 he registered in Kilmallock the birth of his first grandson, my father, and two years later died, aged 77, in Charleville, Co. Cork. He was buried in the family burial ground at Ballingaddy, witnessed, it was said, by a couple of thousand people. The Latin inscription on his memorial records his two years' service with the Legion in Spain, and his forty arduous years as Medical Officer to the Dispensary and Workhouse of Kilmallock.

Some notes on the uniforms, weapons and medals of the British Legion

Less is known of the Legion's uniforms than of those of the regular British army, on which, like their weapons and equipment, they were modelled. The subject was reviewed by Cairns (1998) who drew on various sources, including the volume, *Twelve Views in the Basque Provinces*, published in 1837 by Thomas Lyde Hornbrook, assistant-surgeon in the First Lancers. His twelve lithographs, based on drawings done on the spot, give detailed views of the infantry coatee, a long-tailed, single-breasted garment with facing colours on collar and cuffs, and with a kind of white epaulette. Crescent 'wings' seem to have replaced the epaulettes, according to Charles Shaw's memoirs (ii, 423), in the case of the three light infantry regiments, 5th, 7th and 10th, and this is borne out by the portrait of Assistant-Surgeon O'Connell of the Irish Brigade (pl. 1). The red shell-jacket, single-breasted with plain collar and cuffs in the facing colour was the alternative to the coatee. Hornbrook's depiction of the attack on the gate of Irun shows the light company of the 1st Regiment wearing shell-jackets, with the Royal Irish in coatees and forage-caps, but led by their officers, including the doughty Brigadier Fitzgerald, in shells. Trousers were shown as dark grey or blue, but in May and June 1836 the Legion wore white trousers, a better target for the enemy and also harder to keep clean. Among the Scottish regiments full Highland dress seems only to have been worn by the piper of the 6th, although Somerville mentions 'tartan plaid' and tartan scarves' worn by the 4th and 6th. The impractical nature of the kilt in the Peninsular War, in freezing nights in the Pyrenees and in mosquito-ridden areas, had led to several Highland regiments adopting trews or trousers instead (Holmes, 2001).

As to headgear, the Legion's shako was very similar to the 1828 pattern of the regular army, with ball tufts, but later forage-caps, wide-topped and without peaks, as shown in the caricature illustration of the Legion by Giles (fig. oo) were introduced.

Officers' uniforms were illustrated more often than those of other ranks. A dark blue frock coat was often worn in action, with a red sash and a shako. Augustus Losack, an officer of the 4th Regiment, complained that the elaborate uniform decreed by its colonel made it the costliest of the infantry regiments (Ellison, 1970).

Carswell (1999) mentions two items of Legion uniform that survive. A long-tailed coatee, possibly of Capt. R. Paget of the 6th Scotch Grenadiers, is in the collection of the Scottish United Services Museum in Edinburgh Castle, while a shako in a museum collection in the Channel Islands is said to have belonged to Colonel Tupper, commanding officer of the 6th, who was mortally wounded on 5 May 1836. It is possible that other items of Legion material survive unrecognised as such elsewhere in the British Isles.

The officers' uniforms of the Legion's Lancers were discussed in detail by Carman (1985) who illustrated the magnificent lance-cap on schapska belonging to Major James Rait of the 1st, or Reina Isabella Lancers. It has a gilt-rayed plate with silver mounts of the Spanish arms above the regimental devices and a five-hooped crown. The shield bears the quartered arms of Castile and Leon with the pomegranate for Granada below, and the inescutcheon has the three fleur-de-lys of 'Old France'. Below is a skull on two crossed bones with a scroll bearing the inscription '*O Gloria*'. The lower part of the cap has a wide band of gold lace with a pattern of oak-leaves and acorns symbolising the regiment's English origin. Rait's red coatee or jacket repeats the pattern of contemporary British lancers, with shoulder scales and yellow facing colours on the collars, cuffs, plastron front and turn-backs of the skirts.

Although the officers of the 2nd, or Queen's Own Irish, Lancers were envied by some First Lancers for the glitter and brilliancy of their uniform, very little of this seems to survive. Carman mentions a sabretache in Madrid, an undress jacket in Newport, Rhode Island, and a badge with 'Queen's Own Irish Lancers', a large '2', the royal monogram and a shamrock.

The colours and facings of the various regiments, based mainly on the data in the British Legion lists of June and October 1836 (Cairns, 1998), were as follows:

1st Lancers (Reina Isabella)	Red, faced yellow
2nd Lancers (Queen's Own Irish)	Red, faced yellow (or white)
Rifle Corps	Green, faced red
Artillery	Blue, faced red
Engineers	Red
Medical Department (staff)	Faced scarlet
Commissariat	Faced black velvet
3rd Regt (Westminster Grenadiers)	Red, faced white
4th Regt (Queen's Own Fusiliers)	Red, faced blue
5th Regt (Highland Light Infantry) (disbanded 28/2/36)	Red, facings unknown
6th Regt (Scotch Grenadiers)	Red, faced blue
7th Regt (Irish Light Infantry) (incorporated into Rifle Corps 19/3/37)	Red, faced buff (or yellow)
8th Regt (Highlanders)	Red, faced red
9th Regt (Irish Grenadiers)	Red, faced yellow
10th Regt (Munster Light Infantry), (consolidated with the 9th Regt into the 'Royal Irish', 19/3/37 –	Red, faced (deep) green Red, faced yellow after 19/3/37

MEDALS AWARDED TO THE LEGION

The two main medals were for the actions of 5 May 1836 and March 1837 (pls. 18, 19).

A detailed description of the former is given by Irwin (1910, p. 56). The obverse shows a lion *statant et guardant*, surrounded by the collar of the Golden Fleece. Above is the word *Espana* and below *Agradecida* ('grateful'). On the reverse is a Maltese cross with crowns in the angles and, in the centre, within a wreath, 'S. Sebastian, 5 de Mayo 1836'. The ribbon is blue with two yellow stripes near the edges (not purple, as stated by Irwin). The medal was issued without names. Another medal for the same action is a large double silver cross, inscribed on the obverse, surrounded by a laurel wreath, with the name of the recipient on the reverse.

The Order of San Fernando, awarded for the actions of March 1837, was one established earlier. The gold Maltese cross, enamelled in white, carries a gold ball at each of its eight points, and is suspended from the top by a laurel wreath, enamelled green (worn off in my example). The obverse shows an enamelled figure of St Ferdinand and, within a blue enamelled circle, the words *Al Merito Militar*. On the reverse are two gloves under a crown, surrounded by a blue enamelled circle, inscribed *El Rey y La Patria* ('King and Country'). The ribbon is crimson with orange edges.

The National Army Museum in London has a sword of the Legion, of the 1822 British infantry officers' pattern, with the arms of Spain replacing the royal monogram on the guard. Its ownership is not known, but it carries the figure 2, suggesting that its owner was in the 2nd Regiment, which was disbanded in February 1836 due to severe mortality in its ranks. The Museum also preserves the colours of the short-lived 5th Regiment, which probably never saw action, since this unit was also disbanded at the same time as the 2nd.

Bibliography & references

Alcock, Rutherford, *Notes on the medical history and statistics of the British Legion in Spain* (London, 1838).

Anderson, R.C., *Devils, not men: the history of the French Foreign Legion* (n.p., 1987).

Annual Register, 1836 and 1837

Ball, Alexander, *Personal narrative of seven years in Spain* (1846).

Beevor, Anthony, *The Spanish Civil War* (London, 1992).

Bollaert, William, *The wars of succession in Portugal and Spain from 1826 to 1840*, vol. 2, *Spain* (London, 1870).

Borrow, George, *The Bible in Spain* (London, 1843).

Bowen, Elizabeth, *Bowen's Court* (London, 1942).

British Auxiliary Legion of Spain – Army List, August 1835–March 1837

Butler-Clarke, H., *Modern Spain, 1815–1898* (Cambridge, 1906).

Cairns, Conrad, 'The uniforms of British forces in Spain, 1835–7', *Journal of the Society of Army Historical Research* 76 (1998), 11–20.

Carman, William Y, 'The British Auxiliary Legion, 1835–7', *Journal of the Society of Army Historical Research* 79 (2001), 1–2.

——, 'The Lancers of the British Auxiliary Legion in Spain', *Journal of the Society for Army Historical Research*, 63 (1985), 63–7.

Carswell, A.L., 'The British Auxiliary Legion', *Journal of the Society for Army Historical Research*, 77 (1999), 219.

Casselman, A.C., *Richardson's War of 1812, with notes and a life of the author* (Toronto, 1902).

Chaloner, E.J., Flora, H.S., Hart, R.J., 'Amputations at the London Hospital 1852–1857', *Journal of the Royal Society of Medicine*, 94 (2001), 409–12.

Costello, Edward 'Memoirs, containing Recollections of the Peninsular War, and Present Civil Strife in Spain', *United Service Journal* (1839–41).

Duncan, Major Francis *The English in Spain; or The story of the war of succession between 1834 and 1840* (London, 1877).

Ellison, David (ed.), 'The Losack Letters', *Journal of the Society of Army Historical Research* 48 (1970), 242–8.

Evans, Sir George de Lacy, *Memoranda of the contest in Spain* (London, 1840).

Farr, Reverend Thomas, *A traveller's rambling reminiscences of the Spanish war* (London, 1838).

Ford, Richard, *Gatherings from Spain* (London, 1970).

Gribble, F., *The tragedy of Isabella II* (London, 1913).

Hackett, General Sir John, *The profession of arms* (London, 1983).

Hayens, H., *The British Legion: a tale of the Carlist war* (London, n.d.).

Henderson, R., *The soldier of three queens: a narrative of personal adventure*, 2 vols. (London, 1866).

Henningsen, C.F., *A twelve months' campaign with Zumalacárregui* (London, 1836).

Henty, G.A., *With the British Legion: a story of the Carlist wars* (London, 1903).

Hogg, Colonel Gilbert, 'Diary kept in the British Legion and the previous Portuguese War', unpublished, 1834–37 (in the estate of R. John Corbett).

Holmes, Richard, *Redcoat: The British soldier in the age of horse and musket* (London, 2001).

Holt, Edgar, *The Carlist wars in Spain* (London, 1967).

Humfrey, Lieut. Col. J.H., *A concise account of the campaigns of the British Legion in Spain* (London, 1838).

Irish Census, 1851.

Irwin, D.H., *War medals and decorations issued to the British military and naval forces and allies, from 1588 to 1910*, 4th ed. (London, 1910).

Kaufman, M.H., Purdue, B.N., Carswell, A.L., 'Old wounds and distant battles: the Alcock-Ballingall collection of military surgery at the University of Edinburgh', *Journal of the Royal College of Surgeons of Edinburgh* 41 (1996), 339–50.

Kaufman, M.H., 'Clinical case histories and sketches of gun-shot injuries from the Carlist War', Historical Review, *Journal of the Royal College of Surgeons of Edinburgh* 46 (2001) 279–89.

Kaufman, M.H., *Musket-ball and sabre injuries from the first half of the nineteenth century* (Edinburgh, 2003).

Keegan, J., *The face of battle* (London, 1976).

Meller, Captain H., 'Recollections of the campaign in Spain by a captain of the late British Auxiliary Legion', *United Service Journal* (1838–9).

Memoranda on medical diseases in the tropical and sub-tropical war areas, HMSO, both London 1919 and 1942 editions.

Michie, Alexander, *The Englishman in China during the Victorian era, as illustrated in the career of Sir Rutherford Alcock, KCB, DCL* (Edinburgh and London, 1900).

Murphy, David, *Ireland and the Crimean War* (Dublin, 2002).

Read, D., Glasgow, E., *Feargus O'Connor, Irishman and Chartist* (London, 1961).

Richardson, Joanna, *Fanny Brawne: a biography* (London, 1952).

——, *Keats and his circle: an album of portraits* (London, 1980).

Richardson, Major J., *Journal of the movements of the British Legion by an officer, late of the quartermaster-general's staff* (London, 1837).

——, *Personal Memoirs* (Montreal, 1838).

Robertson, I.C., *Wellington at war in the Peninsula, 1808–1814: an overview and guide* (Barnsley, 2000).

Schull, C.R., *Common medical problems in the Tropics* (2nd ed., London and Basingstoke, 1999).

Somerville, Alexander, *A narrative of the British Auxiliary Legion* (Glasgow, 1838)

——, *History of the British Legion and war in Spain* (London, 1839).

——, *Autobiography of a working man by 'One who has whistled at the plough'* (London, 1848).

Shaw, Colonel Charles, *Personal memoirs and correspondences, comprising a narrative of the war for constitutional liberty in Portugal and Spain*, 2 vols (London, 1837).

Somerville-Large, P., *Irish eccentrics: a selection* (London, 1975).

Sudley, Lord (trans. and ed.), *The Lieven–Palmerston correspondence, 1828–1856* (London, 1943).

Thompson, C.W. (under the pseudonym of 'An Officer of the Ninth Regiment'), *Twelve months in the British Legion* (London, 1836).

A volunteer in the queen's cause: a concise account of the British Auxiliary Legion, commanded by General Evans in the expedition against Don Carlos (Scarborough, 1837).

Wellard, J., *The French Foreign Legion* (London, 1974).

Wilkinson, Henry, *Sketches of scenery in the Basque provinces, with a selection of national music, arranged for pianoforte and guitar; illustrated by notes and reminiscences connected with the war in Biscay and Castile* (London, 1838).

Woodward, Llewellyn, *The age of reason*, 2nd ed. (Oxford, 1962).

REFERENCES

pages 15, 22, 23   'C.F. Henningsen': see Henningsen, 1836.

page 27   'Lady Palmerston wrote': see Sudley, 1943.

page 29   'link with the poet John Keats': see Richardson 1952 and 1980.

page 30   'fragging': see Holmes, 2001.

page 31   'Woodward': see Woodward, 1962.

page 37   'Ensign H. Meller': see Meller 1838-9.

page 46   'true and ready-made soldiers': see Henderson, 1866.

page 51   'unlimited liability': see Hackett, 1983.

page 57   'march to Vitoria': see Costello, 1839-41.

page 63   'General Bernelle': see Wellard, 1874.

page 65   'on the part of the Tories': see Richardson, 1838.

page 72   'lower limb amputations': see Chaloner et al., 2001.

page 87   'Wellington himself ...': see Keegan, 1988.

page 155   'Duncan gives ...': see Duncan, 1877.

page 195   'as has recently been pointed out': see Holmes, 2001.

page 207   '... Isabella's heart ...': see Gribble, 1913

Index

When surnames appear with varied spelling in different sources, such as the Army List of the Legion, newspapers, books, articles and Foreign office records, the alternative spellings are listed in brackets, e.g. Shields (Sheilds). Variations in place names are treated similarly, e.g. Breviesca (Briviesca).

In some cases when the same surname appears in different texts or lists without Christian name, initial or contextual clue, it is impossible to be sure if the names refer to the same or different people. (The records of the Legion were far less detailed than those of the contemporary British Army.)

k.   = killed or mortally wounded in action (where known, the place or date
                 is given in brackets)
'died of fever' = died of epidemic typhus in Vitoria, Santander or elsewhere.

Aberdeen, Lord, foreign minister, 192, 196, 216
Aguilar, Manuel de, Spanish minister in London, 158
Aitken, Pte., 8th Regt., k. by friendly fire (June 1836), 92–3
Alava, Miguel de, Spanish minister in London, 22, 25, 197
Albertazzi, Emma, 190
Alcock, Dr Rutherford, deputy inspector of hospitals, 3, 67, 69–73 pass., 88; his further career, 218–21
Alfonso X, king of Castille and Leon, 5
Alfonso XII, king of Spain, birth, 205–6; education, 208; proclaimed king, 208; Sandhurst Manifesto, 208; death, 209
Alfonso XIII, king of Spain, 209
Almaden mercury mines, 116n
Allez, J.W., Capt. and Adjutant, 4th Regt., k. in action (Ayete), May 1836, 84
Allez, Peter, Brevet-Major, 9th Regt., brother of above, 84
Allez, D., Lt., later Capt., 4th Regt., brother of above, 84
Amadeo, duke of Aosta, elected king, 207–9
Ametzagana (Ametza) hill, 91, 102–5 pass., 121
amputation for gunshot wounds, Dr Alcock's comments and practice, 71, 218
Andoain, defeat and massacre of the Legion, 162–7
Apostolic party, 8, 9, 13

Apthorpe, J., Col., 8th Regt., 101, 110
Arbuthnot, Alexander, Brig.-Gen., 28, 144, 167
Arlaban, battle of, January 1836, 74–8
Army List of the British Auxiliary Legion of Spain, 3
Artillery, Legion's, 29; recruitment 45–6; success of, 102
Asgill, Capt., 4th Regt., 106
Astigarraga, 141
Aston, Sir Arthur, later British ambassador in Madrid, 203
Atkyns (Atkins), R., Lt.-Col., Rifles, 106, 191
Atlas, 162, 172
atrocities, Carlist, 21, 23, 94; by Chapelgorris, 93
Ayete, battle of, 5 May 1836, 79–90

Backhouse, H.G., Capt., Artillery, k. (Oct. 1836), 104, 106
Backhouse, John, under-secretary, foreign office, 20
Ball, Alexander, Ensign, 10th Regt, 37, 51, 63, 122–3, 168, 175–82 pass.
Basque, fueros, 15; language, 15; people, 15–16; provinces, Biscay, Alava and Guipuzcoa, 15
Bayne (Bain), J., Asst-Surgeon, 6th Regt., 168–9
Bayonne, 6, 20
Beatson, W.F., Col., 10th Regt., 95
Beckham, H., Col., 7th Regt., 136, 198

Bernelle, General Joseph-Nicolas, Commander of French Foreign Legion, 46, 55, 63

Bilbao, Legion's billets in, 56; first siege of, 23; second siege, 113–15

Blackburn Standard, 156

Bollaert, William, 170

Bonaparte, Joseph, brother of Napoleon, king of Spain 1808, 6

Bonaparte, Napoleon, emperor, 6

Borrow, George, 106n

Breviesca (Briviesca), 57, 59–60, outbreak of typhus, fever hospitals

British Auxiliary Brigade, formed March 1838, after dissolution of New Legion 174–7

British Legion (British Auxillary Legion), birth of, 25–30; commander-in-chief, 26; disbandment and repatriation, 150–9; recruitment of, 31–46; regiments of, 32; new Legion, 150–2, 160–70, 173; uniforms, weapons and medals, 226–8

Briton, dog of 6th Regt., wounded, 103–4

Brophy, Patrick, Pte., 7th Regt., pension, 193

burial of the Legion's dead, in Breviesca, 59; in Vitoria, 68–9; in San Sebastian, 87, 106, 210

Butler, W., Lt., 8th Regt., 130

Byrne D., Capt., Paymaster, 7th Regt., 67

Byrne, F., Lt., 9th Regt., pension, 196

Cabrera, Rámon, Carlist Gen., 21, 180, 206

Callender, John, MD, inspector general of hospitals, 62, 184

Calomarde, Francisco, Spanish minister of Justice, 9, 11–12

Cannan (Cannon), R., Major, 6th Regt., Col., 9th Regt., 99, 110, 202

Campbell, W.F., Lt.-Col., 4th Regt., 197

Carlism, the rise of, 8–12

Carlos, Don (Carlos V.) pretender to Spanish throne, 6–14; exiled to England, 19–20; returns to Spain, 20; finally leaves Spain after Peace of Vergara, 181; abdicates his claim to throne in 1845, 205

Carlos IV, king of Spain, father of Don Carlos and Ferdinand VII

Carlota, elder sister of Cristina, 9–14, 18

Carbonell, A. de Rámon, Col., 4th Regt., staff, 190; later commissioner for settlement of Legion's claims, 199

Carnaby, W.H.C., Lt., 6th Regt., k. (Andoain), 165

Carthy, Thomas, father of dead Legionary (k. unknown), claims arrears of pay 198

Casa Eguia, count of, at 2nd siege of Bilbao, 114

cavalry, limitations of their use in Spain, 101

Chadwick, Courtney, Lt., 3rd Regt., mortally wounded (Oriamendi), 87

Chapelchurris, 53; at Andoain, 163

Chapelgorris, 53; cruelty of, 93, 132, 144

Charles, Sgt., 186

Cheshire, John, Pte., 1st Regt., pension 193

Chichester, Charles, Col., and Brig.-Gen., 27, 49, 51, 52, 54, 77, 91, 97, 105, 108–9, 130, 145, 150; further career, 213

Chinnery, Capt., 178

Clarke, F.R., Col., 8th Regt., k. in action (Andoain), 165

Clarke, W.A., Lt.-Col., 6th Regt., and staff, 28

Clonmel, Royal Artillery battery at, 29

Clonmel Advertiser, 99, 100, 157, 189

Clonmel Herald, 34, 36, 170, 198

Colquhoun, James N., Col., Royal Artillery, 29, 91, 93, 102, 106, 120, 127, 140, 177

commissariat of the Legion: its deficiencies, 63–5

Considine, W., Col., Military secretary, 50, 87

Constitution of 1812, 7–8, 18

Cook, Capt., Rifle Brigade, believed lost at sea, 155

Cooney, Edmund, Pte., 10th Regt., amputation, pension, 193

Corban convent, Santander, 51, 58, 186

Córdova, General Luis Fernandez de, Cristino commander, 13, 56, 57, 61, 67, 74–5, 89

Cork Chronicle, 36

Cork Constitutional, 38

Cork Daily Advertiser, 189

Cork Evening Herald, 35, 37, 54, 89, 136, 189

Cork Evening Standard, 99, 103, 133, 136, 137, 147, 155, 156, 164

Cork, recruitment of 10th Regt., 33–7

Cortes (Spanish Parliament), 6–12

Costello, Edward, Capt., Rifle Brigade, 30, 57

Costello, J., 203

Cotoner, F., Lt.-Col., ADC to Gen. Evans, 87, 142

Cotter, Lt., afterwards Capt., 2nd Lancers, 166, 167

Cotter J., Brevet-Capt., Major and Col., 9th Regt., 121, k. (Oriamendi), 126–8

Courier, 77, 95

Courtney, J., Capt., Rifles, k. (Andoain), 165

Cove [of Cork] (Cobh), 39

Coyle, J., Capt., 8th Regt., k. (Oriamendi), 124, 130

Coyle, Mrs Martha, his widow, 197

Cristina, Maria, queen, queen-regent, 4th wife and widow of Ferdinand VII, mother of Isabella II, 6, 9–24 pass.; 204–5

Cristinos, 6–24 pass.

Cruise, Alexander, Col., 38

Cryne, James, Rifle Brigade, pension, 194

Cunningham, Neil, Pte., 6th Regt., shot by Carlists, 118

Dade, Asst. Surgeon, 1st Regt., 54

Dalrymple, H., Capt., 8th Regt., k. (Andoain), 165, 197

Darking (Durkin, Durkan), Ensign, 8th Regt., 130–1, 164

Dash, Royal Marines' dog, wounded and decorated, 138

d'Aubley (d'Amblée), M., Cornet, 2nd Lancers, pension claim, 198

de Burgh, E., Capt., Rifle Brigade, pension, 198

de Lancey, Oliver, Col., 8th Regt., mortally wounded (Oriamendi), 138

Deans, Sgt., 6th Regt., k. (June 1836), 94

decorations of the Legions: battle of Arlaban, 76; battle of Ayete, 90, 227–8; battle of Oriamendi, 227–8

deserters, from British Army to Legion, 38–40; from Legion to Carlists, 100; from French Foreign Legion to Carlists, 66

Dickson (Dixon) Lothian, Col., 7th Regt., 37, 53

Dickson, Capt., suspected traitor, 146

discipline in the Legion, 51–2, 98

Dodgin, Gen., 178

Doherty, J., 190

Dorset County Chronicle, 158

Dublin Mercantile Advertiser, 34n

Dublin, recruiting in, 33

duelling in the Legion, 100, 162

Duncan, Francis, Major, Royal Artillery, his 'The English in Spain' quoted, 3, 115, 119–20, 134, 155, 160, 212

Dundas, Robert, Major, 7th Regt., 66, 197

Durango Decree, 24, 34, 54, 92, 118

East India Company, officers serving in the Legion, 27, 101

Ebsworth F.C., Lt.-Col., 10th Regt., murdered by mutinous Spanish troops at Santander, 161

Eliot, Lord, and the Eliot Convention, 22–4

Ellis, W.F., Lt. Col., 1st Regt., 85

Elosegui, José de, baker suspected of poisoning the Legion's bread, encourages desertion, executed, 67–8

Espartero, General Baldomero, Cristino commander, 50, 109n, 114, 161, 180–1, 204

Essex Standard, 211

ETA (Euzkadi Ta Askatasuna, or Basque Homeland and Liberty), 210

Evans, George de Lacy, Lt. Gen., commander-in-chief of British Legion, accepts command, 26; arrival in Spain, 50; publishes his 'Memoranda', 72; at battle of Arlaban, 75–6; at battle of Ayete, 5 May 1836, 84–9; unsuccessful attack on Fuenterrabia, criticised by his senior officers, 95–6; coolness in battle, slightly wounded Oct. 1836, 104; Oriamendi, his unsuccessful attack on Hernani, 121–37; successfully attacks Hernani, Iran and Fuenterrabia, May 1837, 139–44; praised, 149; the Legion's unsettled claims, 200; his further career, 211–13

Evans, R.L., Brig.-Gen., brother of above

Famine, Irish, 222–3

Farr, Revd Thomas, 143–8

Ferdinand and Isabella, and the Basque fueros, 15

Ferdinand VII, king of Spain, 6–13

Ferguson, George, Pte., Hospital Corps, pension, 193

Fielding, W., Capt., Rifle Brigade, k. (Oriamendi), 138

Finegan, Patrick, Rifle Brigade, injuries and pension 193

Fitzgerald, Charles Lionel, 9th Regt., Col., later Brig.-Gen., 5, 77, 83, 110; further career 215–18

Fitzgerald, Gerald, Surgeon, 7th Regt., died by fever 189

Fitzgerald, Harvey, Major 9th Regt., son of Charles Fitzgerald, 110

Fitzgerald, H., Lt. 9th Regt., another son of Charles Fitzgerald, 110

Fitzgerald, P., Major, 3rd Regt., pension, 198

Flinter, Brig.-Gen., Cristino general, 116

Forbes, A., Capt., 8th Regt., 145, k. (Andoain), 165–6

Foreign Enlistment Act, suspended to allow Legion to be enlisted, 25

Foreman (Firman), Lt., and Adjutant, 4th Regt., 102

'forlorn hope' at siege of Irun, 142

Fortescue, M., Major, later Col., Rifle Brigade, 83, 110

Francis I, king of Naples, father of Cristino and Carlota, 9

Francisco de Paula, Infante, husband of Carlota, 9

Francisco, duke of Cadiz, marries Isabella II, 205

Franco, General Francisco, 209–10

Franks, M. Capt., 10th Regt., died by fever 36

French Foreign Legion, 46–7, 63, 66

Fuenterrabia (Hondaribia) unsuccessfully attacked, 95–6; captured by the Legion, 147–9

fueros (Basque privileges), 15

Gallagher, Joseph, Marine, pension, 191

Galvin, John, Pte., 10th Regt., pension, 193

Gallwey, Charles H., Capt., 10th Regt., 37

Gartland, Dr, 106n

Gartland, Lt., 10th Regt., k. (Oct. 1836), 106

Gentleman's Magazine, 171

Godfrey, Edward Lee 8th Regt., Col., promoted Brig. Gen., 44, 58, 61, 75, 90, 96–8, 100–1, 111, 137

Gómez, Miguel, Carlist Gen., 8, 54

Globe, 174

grave-robbers in Dublin, discharged to join the Legion, 65n

Greenock, arrival of Scots Legionaries at, 153–6

Greenwood, Surgeon, 4th Regt., 59

Gribble, Francis, quoted 206

Grove, M., Asst. Surgeon, 10th Regt., died by fever 37, 62

Guernica, 52

Guidebalde, Carlist general, 172

Gurrea, Ignacio, Capt., ADC to Gen. Evans, 149

Gurrea, Miguel, Field Marshal, 146; k. at siege of Tolosa, May 1837, 149

Gurwood, Col., mission to Spain with Lord Eliot, 22

Guthrie, George J., Military surgeon, his influence on Dr Alcock's practice, 218

half-pay British officers in the Legion, 28

Hall, G.B., Capt., 9th Regt., and Major on staff, 50

Hallen van, Capt.-Gen., of Cristino forces, 1838, 179

Hamilton, J.H., Capt., Artillery, 146

Hamilton, Pte., 3rd Regt., charged with begging, 198

Hampton, Frederick, Capt., Artillery, 175–176

Harding, Sir Henry, MP, hostile to formation of the Legion, 136

Harispe, Count de, French general, congratulates Evans, 90

Harley, Lt.-Col., 4th Regt., 137

Harris, William, Pte., 3rd Regt., pension, 194

Haslam, T., Lt., Rifle Brigade, k. (Andoain), 166, 170

Haslam, Mrs E., 166, 170

Havelock, J., Capt., 5th Regt., died by fever 66

Hay, Lord John, Commodore, RN, 84, 90, 95, 111, 114, 133, 172, 177, 180

Hayens, Herbert, author of historical novel on 1st Carlist war, 4

Henderson, R., Capt., 1st Lancers, 54, 167

Henningsen, C.F., Capt., British officer with Carlist army, 15, 22, 23

Henty, G.H., historical novelist, 4

Herman, G.F., Capt., Rifle Brigade, promoted Lt.-Col., and Military secretary, 50; duelling, 162

Hernani, attacked unsuccessfully, Oriamendi, 95–6; captured by Evans, 139–41

Hill, Lord, commander-in-chief, British Army, 28

Hogg, Gilbert, Lt., later Major and Lt.-Col., 8th Regt., his unpublished diary, 3; 29, 57, 101, 111, 123–38 pass., 140, 145; in New Legion, 151–2

Hogreve, F., Capt., and Riding-Master, 1st Lancers, in New Legion, 167, 169

Holy Alliance (Austria, Prussia, Russia, Sardinia), 13

Holmes, Professor Richard, pension certificates of the Legion, vii, 192

Holt, Edgar, quoted, 2, 134

Honan, Michael Burke, correspondent of *Morning Herald*, 92, 118

hospitals of the Legion, 69–70, 106

Howe (How), Edward, Col., Artillery, 140, 162–3, 175

Howson, Francis and his sons, musicians in the Legion, captured by Carlists, 190

Hughes, Sgt.-Major, claims of NCOs and men of the Legion, 199

Humfrey, J.H., Lt.-Col., 175

Infante Cristino Regiment at Andoain, 163–4

Inman, Lt., 1st Lancers, 73

Irish Brigade, 77, 79–89, 92, 148–9

Irun, captured by the Legion, 141–7

Irving, Washington, quoted, 205

Isabella II, queen of Spain, 2, 6, 10; succeeds her father under regency of her mother, 13; declared queen, 205; her character, 205–7; her lovers and suitors, 204–7; marriage to duke of Cadiz, 205; gives birth to Alfonso XII, 205–6; leaves Spain for exile in France, 207

Isabella of Braganza, queen, 2nd wife of Ferdinand VII, 9

Ituralde, Carlist general, 17

Jacks, W.H., Col., 2nd Lancers, 39, 174, 199

Jackson, Lt., 3rd Regt., k. (Oct. 1836), 106

Jackson, J., Capt., 6th Regt., father of above

Jáuregui, Cristino general (El Pastor), 17, 91, 111, 136, 161

Jenner, Asst. Surgeon, 4th Regt., 185

Jochmus, A., Col., 8th Regt., 111, 167, 172

Juan (Infante, Juan III), Carlist pretender, 206

Juan, Don, father of King Juan-Carlos, 209

Juan-Carlos, king of Spain, 209–10

Kean, Peter, Sgt., 9th Regt., 138n

Keays, C.J., 200

Keegan, John, quoted, 32, 81

Kennedy, Thomas, Pte., medical board in Dublin, 191

Keogh, John., Capt., 9th Regt., 28

Kilary, Pte., 9th Regt., 212

Kinloch, John, Col., 1st Lancers, 97

Kirby, W.R., Major and Lt.-Col., 1st Regt., 106

Kirwin, John, pension for visual loss caused by lightning, 194

Knight, Lt. and Capt., 1st Regt., ADC to Gen. Chichester, k. (Ayete), 54, 85

La Saussaye (de la Saussaye), R., Lt.-Col., 10th Regt., 99–100; commands reorganised Legion March 1838, 174–177

Lacey, Col., British Commissioner with the queen's army, 179

Lancers, 1st, Queen Isabella's, 46, 58, 97, 102–3

Lancers 2nd, Royal Irish, 46, 92

Larkham, Capt., 8th Regt., k. (Andoain) 165, 167

Le Marchant, J.C., Adjutant-general, 50, 130, 137

Leeson, Patrick, Pte., pension, 192

Leon, bishop of, prominent Carlist sympathiser, 12

Liberals, Spanish, 8–7

Limerick Chronicle, 36, 37, 39, 90, 130n, 186, 213, 224

Lindo (Lindon), Louis, Paymaster, 2nd Lancers, husband of Fanny Brawne, 29–30

Livingston, David, Sgt., 6th Regt., amputation, pension, 193

London Gazette, 26

Londonderry, marquis of, 35, 76, 178, 201

Losack, Augustus, Capt., 4th Regt., 44–5

Louis XVIII, king of France, 8

Louis-Philippe, king of the French, 13, 19, 46, 150

Loyola, 123

Lugariz, fort of, 84

Louisa Fernanda, Infanta, sister of Queen Isabella, 10, 180

McCabe, J., Major and Col., 7th Regt., 162

McDonald, T., pension query, 203

McDougall, Duncan, Brig.-Gen., 51, 65, 76–7, 89, 214–15, 217

McKay, David, Bugler, 8th Regt., pension, 193–4

McKellar, P., Major, 6th Regt., k. (Andoain), 165, 166, 169

McIntosh, J., Lt., 10th Regt., 99

McIntosh, —, Brevet-Lt.-Col. in British Auxiliary Brigade 1838, 175–6

Madrid, entry of Cristina, 10

Mahon, Lord, critical of Evans' appointment, 27

Malony, Chidley, Cornet, 2nd Lancers, 174

Manchester Examiner, 221

Manley, Richard, Lancers, pension for ophthalmia, 194
Maria II, queen of Portugal, 13, 29, 218
Maria Amelia of Saxony, 3rd wife of Ferdinand VII, 9
Maria Antonia of Naples, 1st wife of Ferdinand VII, 9
Maroto, Rafael, Carlist general, at Peace of Vergara, 180–1
Martin, W., Major, 8th Regt., later 2nd Lancers, Lt.-Col., 92; paymaster in the New Legion, 151–2
May Pte., Rifle Brigade, pension, 193
Maybury, Thomas, D., Surgeon, 10th Regt., 36
medical boards, 191–203
medical officers, high mortality among, 69–70, 189
medical services of the Legion, 69–72, 87–8, French support in care of Legion's wounded at Irun, 147, 218–19
Melbourne, Lord, 34, 200
Meller, H.J., Ensign, 10th Regt., 37, 75, 79
Mendijaz, attacked by Cristino forces with Legion, 74–5
Menzidábal, Juan Alvarez, Spanish minister of Finance, 76–7, 161
Merino, Jerónimo, Carlist guerrilla leader, 8, 16
Middleton, Lt., 1st Lancers, 106
Middleton, Capt., 9th Regt., 212
Miller, Robert, Sgt., 8th Regt 187–8
Miller, Mrs Nancy, his alleged widow, 187–8
Mina, General, Cristino commander, 21
Mirasol, Count, attacked by his mutinous troops, 161
Mitchell, Bruce, Major, 8th Regt., 29, 86
Montemolin, Carlos Luis, count of, pretender, son of Don Carlos, 206–7
Montpensier, duke of, 4th son of King Louis-Philippe, marries the Infanta Luisa, 205
Morning Chronicle, 92, 133, 169, 221
Morning Herald, 92, 118, 136, 161
Morning Post, 147
mortality of the Legion, 69–73
Moriarty, E. Pte., 9th Regt., 202
Mostyn, —, Capt., 4th Regt., k. (Oriamendi), 138
Mould, P.R. Capt., 10th Regt., 86, k. (Oriamendi), 182
Muñagorri, José Antonio, de, 177

Muñoz, Fernando, lover and later husband of Cristina, 18; created duke of Rienzares, 205
Murphy, Patrick, Pte., died of wounds; father claims arrears of pay 199
Murphy, T., Cornet and Riding Master, 2nd Lancers kills Capt. Smith in duel; later killed Carlist peasants and captured soldiers, 100
Murray, Col., Irish officer on Carlist staff 138n
mutiny in the Legion, 96–9

Nangles, Sgt., 7th Regt., 67
Navarre, province of, 15, 17
Newall, Surgeon, 9th Regt., died by fever, 189

Oarzun (Oyarzun), 141
O'Brien (O'Brian) J., 7th Regt., k. (Andoain), 166
O'Connell, Daniel, M.P., 32n, 212
O'Connell, Sir Maurice Charles, 28
O'Connell, Maurice Charles, son of above, Lt.-Col., commanding 10th Regt., 28, 51, 99, 128; becomes Adjutant-Gen., 137; commands New Legion, 150; further career, 214
O'Connell, Morgan David, Asst. Surgeon, 10th Regt., 37, 62, 130n, further career, 222–5
O'Connor, Capt., 3rd Regt., 101, 106
O'Connor, Feargus, Chartist, rumoured to be about to join the Legion, 34
O'Connor, R., Lt., 9th Regt., 85, 176–7
O'Dell, Thomas, Capt., 10th Regt., 99
O'Donnell, Hugh, Ensign, 10th Regt., 37
O'Donnell, José, Col., Cristino officer, 17
O'Driscoll, R., Capt., and Adjutant, 8th Regt., k. (Oriamendi), 130
O'Hea, Edward B., Ensign, 10th Regt., died by fever, 190
Old Castile, Legion's march to Victoria, 57
Old England, 37
O'Leary, John, Major and Lt.-Col., 10th Regt., 28
Oñate, Don Carlos' court at, 72
Ophthalmia, 194
Oráa, General, chief of staff to Espartero, 120
order book of the legion, 3, 106, 194–5, 212
Orgull (Urgull), 83; cemetery of the English; tombs of the Legion's officers, 210

Oriamendi, battle of (before Hernani), 119–38
Oxford City and County Chronicle, 211

Paget, Lord William, Col., 2nd Lancers, 87
Palmerston, Lord, foreign secretary in Whig government, 13, 16; Quadruple Alliance, 19; 216
Parkes (Parke), E., Capt., 10th Regt., duelling, 100
Pasajes, attacked by Carlists, 1 Oct. 1836, 93
Pearce, W.G., Lt., 4th Regt., 38
Pedro, Dom, father of Maria II of Portugal, brother of Dom Miguel, Portuguese pretender, 13, 29, 218
Pedroite officers in the Legion, 29, 30
P. & O. line, 45
Penisular War, 7
pensions, the struggle for, 191–9
pension certificates, 192–4
Phoenix, HMS, in action 5 May 1836, 84, 91
Pierce, Capt., 1st Regt., 144
Polden, Major, recruiting in Dublin for 7th Regt., 37
Portsmouth, destitute Legionaries at, 156–158
Portugal, Quadruple Alliance, 19; Miguelite war of succession, 13, 19, 29, 218; Don Carlos exiled to, 12
Portugalete, 55, 114
Polish lancers in the Legion, 103
poisoning of Legion's bread suspected, 67–8
Pragmatic Sanction, 6, 11
Prim, General Juan, 207
Primo de Rivera, José Antonio, 209
Purcell, Peter, Pte., 4th Regt., amputation, pension, 193

Quadruple Alliance, 1834, 19, 46
Quinlan, Pte., M., refused a medical board, 191–2

Ramsey, Percival, Capt. 4th, Col. 5th Regt., 146
Richardson, John, Major, 6th Regt., 65–6
Richardson, Quartermaster Sgt., 7th Regt., deserter to Carlists, 67
Riego, Rafael de, Col., Liberal rising, 8; Riego's hymn, 100
Reid, —, Lt.-Col., 153
Reid, William, Brig.-Gen., 77, 87, 95; further career, 213

Roberts, P.H., Capt., 8th Regt., 144, 145
Robertson, A.C., Capt., 8th Regt., 106
Robertson, William, 190
Rodil, José Ramon, Cristino general, 13, 18, 21, 105
Ross, Malcolm, Col., 6th Regt., 28, 95, 117, 140, 148
Rothschild family, 116n
Royal Artillery, British, in action of 5 May 1836, 84
Royal Engineers, British, in action of 5 May 1836, 84
Royal Marines, British, supporting the Legion, 84–5, 91, 95, 132–4
Royal Tar, steamship, 39, 45, 48, 51, 187

Salamander, HMS, at battle of Ayete, 5 May 1836, 84, 91
Salic Law, 5–6, 10
San Bartolomé, convent, 50
San Francisco, convent, 50
San Sebastian (Donestia), 5, 31, 48, 108–12
San Telmo, convent, Legion's hospital, 87–8, 106
Sandhurst Manifesto, 208
Santa Barbara hill, 126, 140
Santander, Legion at, 49, 58–9
Saracen, HMS, at siege of Bilbao, 1836, 114
Sarsfield, Pedro, Cristino general, 119–22, 161
Sarsfield, Patrick, and the Wild Geese, 14
Scilly Isles, Legionaries shipwrecked, 155
Scott Charles, Pte., 8th Regt., 124
Sebastian, Don, Infante, son of Don Carlos, 121, 127
Segastibelza, Carlist general, 80, 87
sergeants' mutiny, 100
Shaw, Claudius, Lt.-Col., Artillery, 75, 148, 200
Shaw, Charles, Lt.-Col., 6th Regt., 29, 40–2, 74–7, 81–90, 95–6; further career, 218
Shaw, S., Major, Lt.-Col., 10th Regt., 75
Shields (Sheilds), Robert, Capt., 8th Regt., 98, 124, 125, 132, 145, k. (Andoain), 166–7
Shields (Sheilds), William, Major, 8th Regt., 125, k. (Andoain), 166–7
shrapnel shell, 131n
Siete Partidas (Seven Laws), 5
Sims (Siems), G.S., Lt. 4th Regt., k. (Andoain), 165
Skedd (Skidd), R., Lt., Artillery 109, 162

Smith, W.A., Capt., 2nd Lancers, killed in duel, 100

Somerville, Alexander, Sergeant, 8th Regt., 30, 42–4, 58–60, 79–90 pass., 98, 101, 121–38 pass., 151–9 pass., 165–7; further career, 221–2

Soroa, General, Carlist governor of Irun, 149, 211

Spectator, 89, 105, 136

spherical case shot, see shrapnel shell, 131n

Spike Island, Cork Harbour, depôt of 10th Regt., repatriated Irish soldiers housed in barracks, 199

Stack P.A., Lt. 3rd Regt., Capt., 9th Regt., pension, 195–6

Standard, 26, 99, 149

Stark, —, Pte., 10th Regt., 186

Stinson, William, Lancers, pension, 194

Steele, Richard, officer in Royal Marine Artillery, quoted, 134

Street, J.B., Capt., 9th Regt., shot by Carlists when captured, 186

Stutterheim, Baron G., Lt. 1st Lancers, 167

Swan, G.C., Lt.-Col., 5th and 7th Regt., 99

Sweenie, Sgt., seduces deserters from British army, 39

Swiftsure, hulk, Legion invalids accommodated at Portsmouth, 157–8, 199

Talbot, W., Major, 9th Regt., 38

Thompson, Charles W., Lt. 1st Regt., later 9th Regt., 48–56 pass., 58–60, 74–5, 77, 80–8 pass.

Times, The, 2, 20, 52, 88, 102, 104, 105, 115, 137–8, 149, 156, 186, 200, 201, 202

Tipperary Free Press, 28

Townley, Charles, Lt., later Major, 1st Regt., pension, 198

Townsend, R.T., Lt., Rifle Brigade, 166

Tupper, William, Col., 6th Regt., k. in action (Ayete), May 1836, 5, 87, 185

Tweed, sloop of war, supports the Legion, 91

Typhus epidemic, in Vitoria, 61–73; mortality and morbidity, 64, 69, 70; amputation, 71–2; in the Irish famine, 70

Urumea, river, 80, 91, 123

United Service Journal, 2

Valdes, General Cayetano, Cristino Commander-in-chief, 23

Vergara, the Peace or Embrace of, 180–2

veneral disease in the Legion, 195

Venta hill, 53, 124, 126, 135

Victoria, heir-presumptive, queen of England, 13

Villiers, Sir George, British minister in Madrid, 21, 22, 200, 211

Vitoria (Gasteiz), 57, 61–73

volunteer officers in the Legion, 41n

Wakefield, W. Lt.-Col., 1st Lancers, 102

Waterford Mail, 187

Waterloo men, in the Legion, 94

Wellington, duke of, 6, 16, 22, 32, 89, 181

Westminster Grenadiers, 3rd Regt., 32, 45, 49, 55, 101

Wetherall, Lt.-Col., commissioner for settlement of claims, 199, 202

Wheat, P.J., Lt., Rifle Brigade, k. (Irun), 143

White, Nicholas, Capt., Rifle Brigade, died by fever, 189

Wilkinson, Sgt., invalid at Portsmouth, 157

Wilkinson, Henry, Surgeon, 5th Regt., 39, 87, 164, 167–9, 189

William IV, 13, 20, 25, 84

Wills, Langworthy Garland, hospital staff, died by fever, 189

Wilson, General Sir Robert, earlier British expeditionary force in Spain, 8

Wilson, Col., Rifle Corps in New Legion, 163

Wilson, —, deserter from Legion, directs Carlist Artillery until killed, 114–15

Wood, C., Major, 4th Regt., 129

Woods, J., Lt. 9th Regt., pension for wounds, 198

Woolley, Margaret, widow and mother of Legionaries, 190

women and children of the Legion, 183–8

Wright, Capt., 10th Regt., 99

Wright, Lt.-Col., 10th Regt., 202

Wyatt, John W., Col., 8th Regt., pension, 196

Wylde, William, Col., senior English commissioner with the queen's army, 68, 120, 150–1

Zumalacárregui, Tomás, successful Carlist general, 8, 16–17, 20–23; mortally wounded at siege of Bilbao, 113